Y0-BEL-834

HOLT SOCIAL STUDIES

OUR OREGON

JoAnn Cangemi General Editor

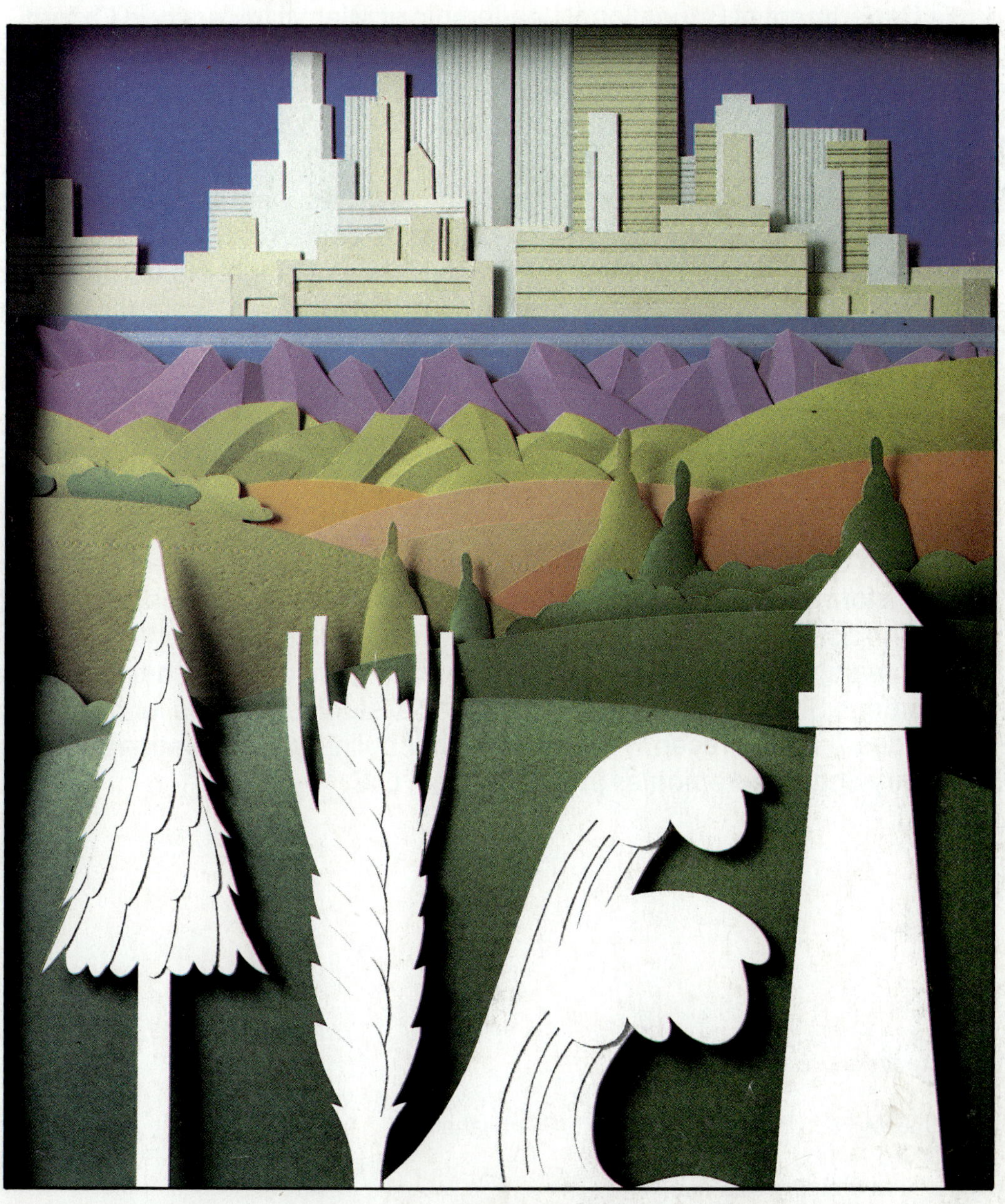

Holt, Rinehart and Winston, Publishers
New York · Toronto · Mexico City · London · Sydney · Tokyo

GENERAL EDITOR FOR *HOLT SOCIAL STUDIES*

JoAnn Cangemi is Professor of Education and Director of Graduate Studies in Education at Nicholls State University, Thibodaux, Louisiana. She received her Ph.D. in Elementary Education from Louisiana State University. Prior to her university work, Dr. Cangemi taught in the public elementary schools for ten years. She was the 1981 recipient of the Merit Teacher Awards given by the National Council for Geographic Education.

CONTRIBUTING WRITERS

Lucille Beisner is Curriculum Supervisor, K–12, and Director of Gifted Programs for the Richmond, Indiana Community Schools. She also teaches Curriculum Development in the Graduate Department of Educational Leadership at Miami University in Oxford, Ohio. Dr. Beisner earned her doctorate in Curriculum at Ball State University and her M.Ed. in Supervision at Miami University. She taught in the public elementary schools for several years and has served as a state evaluator of textbooks.

Jayne Freeman is a classroom teacher at the Seth Lewelling Elementary School, North Clackamas School District, in Milwaukie, Oregon. Ms. Freeman received her B.S. in Elementary Education from the University of Illinois. She has taught elementary school for twenty-one years, fourteen of them at the fourth-grade level. Ms. Freeman has been involved in summer social studies curriculum for her school district for a number of summers, drawing up a social studies curriculum for grades K–12, and developing a kit on Oregon history for use in fourth-grade classrooms in the district. Ms. Freeman is the author of a number of professional articles, which have appeared in *Learning, Teacher, Instructor,* and the *Phi Delta Kappan.*

Rosemary Dimoff currently teaches history at McLoughlin Jr. High School in Milwaukie, Oregon. She is a former fourth-grade teacher. Ms. Dimoff received her undergraduate, Master's, and Principal's credentials from Lewis and Clark College in Portland, Oregon. For the past 10 years, Ms. Dimoff has served as a writer–consultant for her district's curriculum department. She has developed several social studies projects for classroom teachers in grades 4–8. She recently represented her building at the National Recognition of Secondary School ceremonies in Washington, D.C.

Photo and art credits are on page 288.

Printed in the United States of America
ISBN: 0-03-001567-7
6789 039 98765

CRITICAL READERS

The following people served as critical readers for the OUR OREGON Pupil Edition:

GEOGRAPHY AND
ECONOMICS
James G. Ashbaugh, Ph.D.
Professor of Geography
Portland State University
Portland, Oregon

HISTORY AND
POLITICAL SCIENCE
Gordon B. Dodds
Professor of History
Portland State University
Portland, Oregon

HISTORY AND
WOMEN'S ISSUES
MaryJo Wagner
University of Oregon
Eugene, Oregon

The following person served as a critical reader for the OUR OREGON Teacher's Edition:
Julie L. Reynolds
Bellview Elementary School
Ashland, Oregon

TABLE OF CONTENTS

HISTORIC OREGON
BARLOW ROAD
FIRST ROAD BUILT OVER CASCADE RANGE
IN 1845 – 1846 BY
SAMUEL K. BARLOW (1792-1867)
AN OREGON PIONEER FROM KENTUCKY
WAMIC MILES 32
DALLES CALIFORNIA HIGHWAY 38
MAUPIN 48

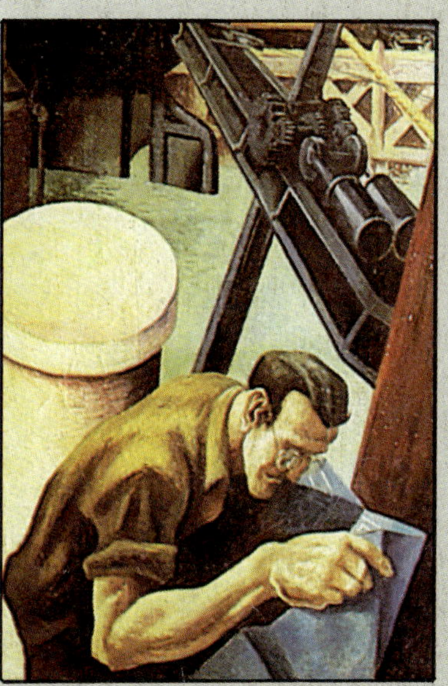

MAPS

reviewing GEOGRAPHY skills

If you visited a new city, how would you find your way around? You might use a street **map.** A street map shows street names. It also shows the locations of important places.

A street map is only one of the many kinds of maps that can help you learn about places on the earth. In this book, you will find both **globes** and maps. Most are easy to use once you learn about them.

Using a Globe

You know that the earth is like a big ball or sphere. A globe is a model of the earth. A globe shows the shape of all the earth's land and water areas.

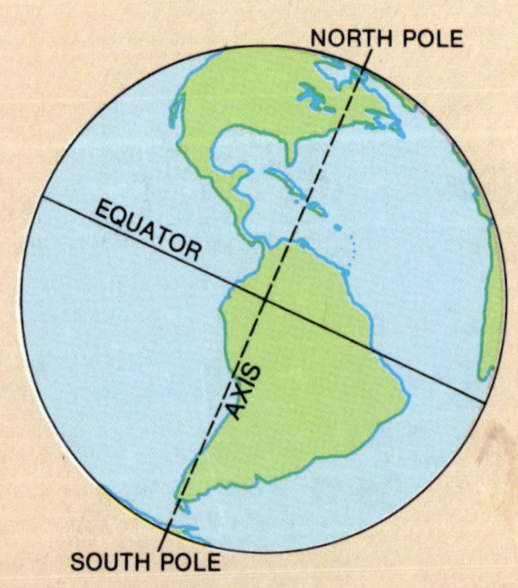

Look at the drawing of the globe at the left. See the lines drawn on it. The top of the globe shows where the **North Pole** is. The North Pole is the most northern place on a globe. The direction north is always toward the North Pole. The bottom of the globe shows the **South Pole.** The South Pole is the most southern place on the globe. The direction south is always toward the South Pole.

The dotted line on the drawing of the globe is called an **axis.** The axis is an imaginary line. It goes through the center of the earth from one pole

to the other. The earth makes one turn on this axis every 24 hours. This creates day and night.

Another imaginary line on a globe is the **equator.** The equator divides the earth into two halves, or **hemispheres.** (*Hemi-* means "half," so "hemisphere" means "half of the sphere.") Above the equator is the Northern Hemisphere. Below the equator is the Southern Hemisphere. Look at the drawing of the globe at the left. In which hemisphere is the United States?

The earth can also be divided along another imaginary line. This imaginary line runs from the North Pole to the South Pole. It divides the world into the Western and Eastern hemispheres. Look at the drawing of the globe at the right. In which of these hemispheres is the United States?

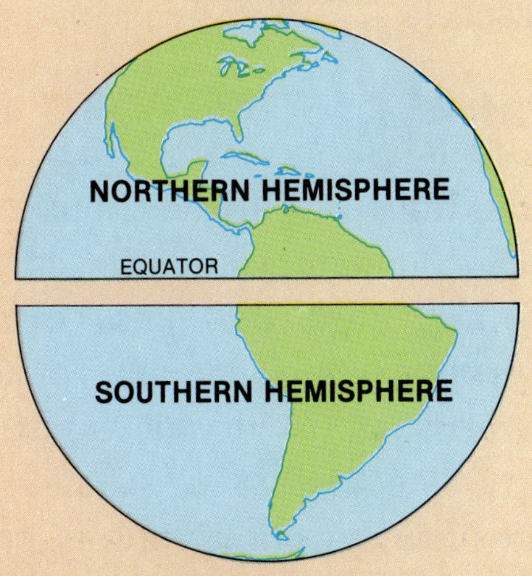

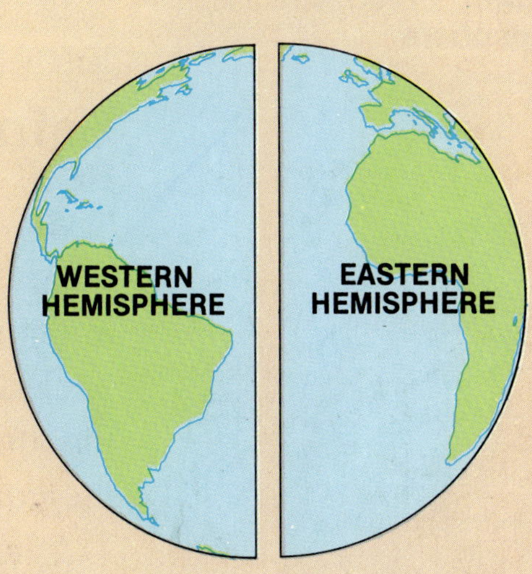

On a globe, you can see that most of the earth is covered by water. The largest bodies of water are called **oceans.** The rest of the earth is land. The largest areas of land are called **continents.** There are four oceans and seven continents. Find the names of the continents and oceans on the globes on this page. Which continents are in the Eastern Hemisphere? Which are in the Western Hemisphere? Which is in both hemispheres? Which ocean is only in the Eastern Hemisphere?

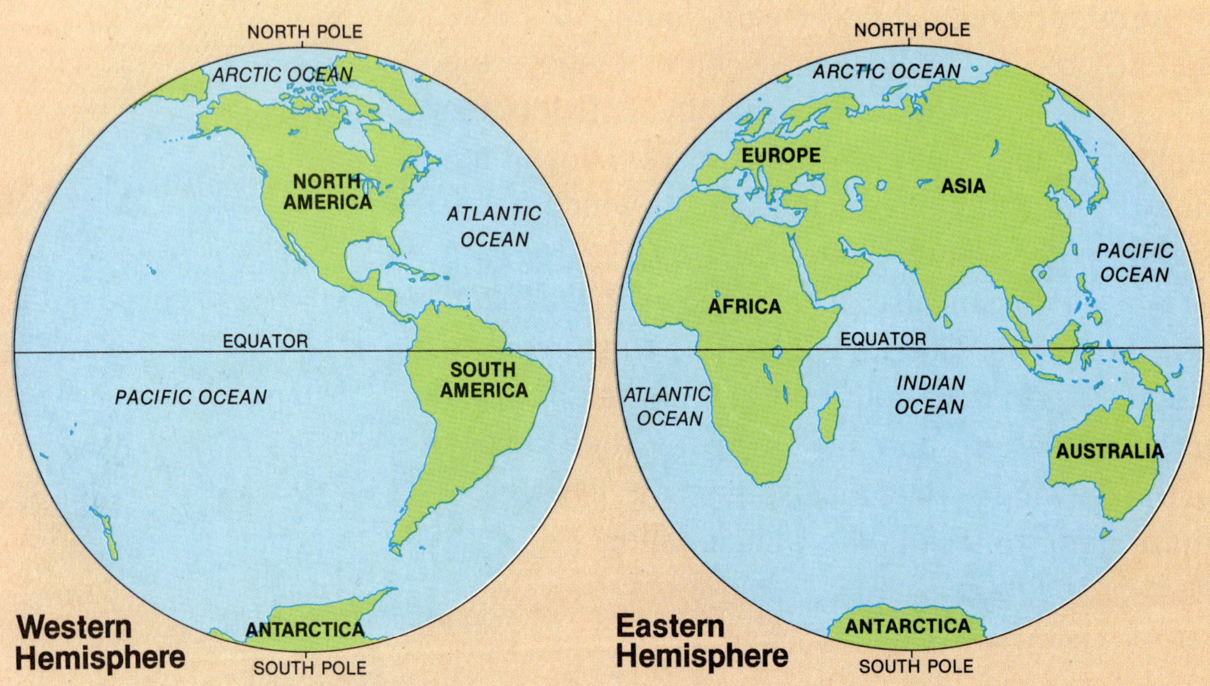

Using a Flat Map

On a globe, you cannot see all the continents at once. To see all of the earth, you use a flat map. Imagine that the outside of the earth could be peeled off and flattened out. It might look like the drawing on page 11. Now you can see all the continents.

A flat map can show the whole earth or part of it. The map on page 11 shows the continent of North America.

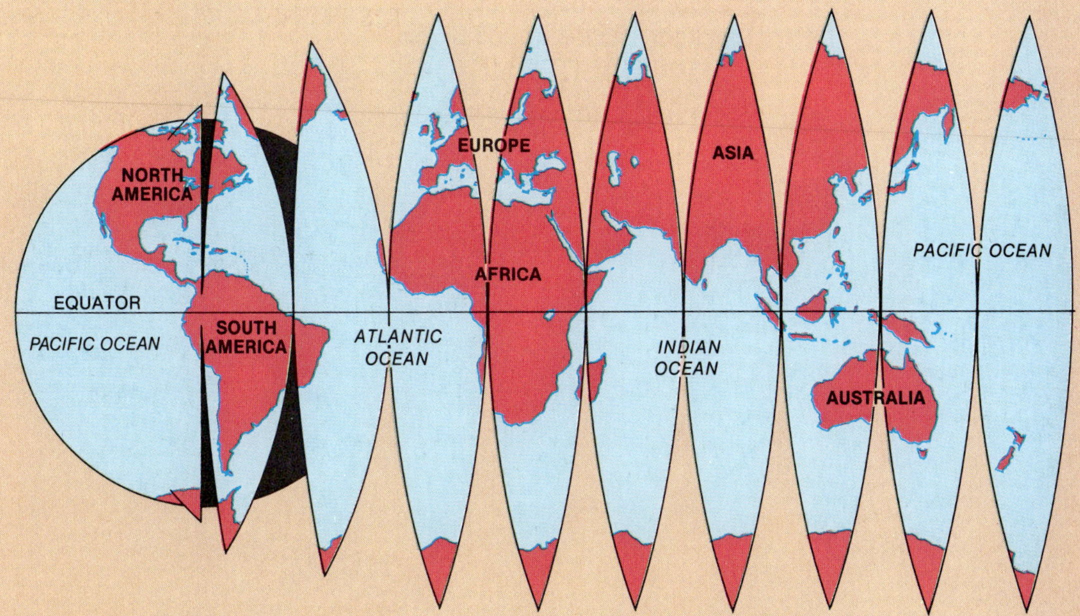

Using Symbols

Symbols are used on maps to stand for real things. Symbols can be colors, shapes, or designs. On most maps, blue is the symbol for water. Brown or green is the symbol for land. A dot might stand for a city.

Map symbols are on a **map key.** The map key tells what the symbols on a map mean. Look at the key on the map of North America. This symbol ⊛ means national capital. What does this ——— mean?

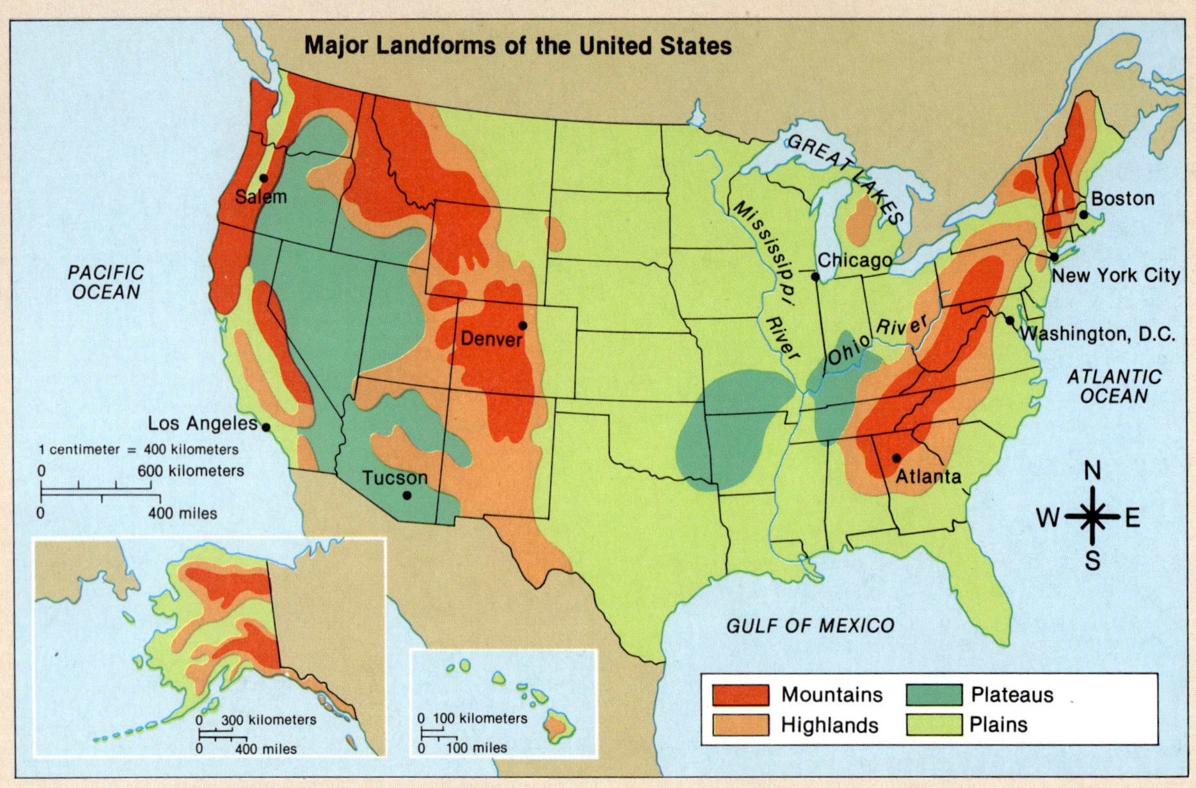

The map on this page is a **landforms map** of the United States. A landforms map uses colors to show the height and form of the land. The map key above lists four landforms. They are mountains, highlands, plateaus, and plains. What colors show mountains? plains? plateaus? highlands?

You can see that there are many plains in the center of the United States. And the country has two mountain regions. There is one in the East and one in the West.

Finding Directions

You know that north, south, east, and west are the main directions. In between the four main directions are northwest, southwest, northeast, and southeast. On a globe, north is the direction of the North Pole. South is the direction of the South Pole. On flat maps, directions are shown with a **compass rose.**

Find the compass rose on the landforms map on page 12. Notice that Boston is northeast of New York City. In which direction is Salem, Oregon, from Chicago, Illinois?

Finding Distance

A map is a very small picture of the land it shows. A **distance scale** shows how close or how far apart things are on a map. On a distance scale, centimeters or inches stand for kilometers or miles. Look at the distance scale on the right. How many kilometers does each centimeter stand for?

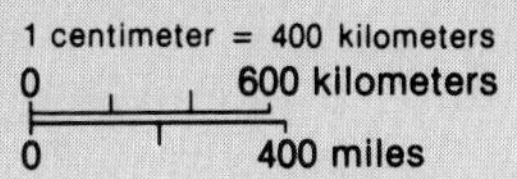

This is how you find distance on a map. Use a ruler to measure the number of centimeters or inches between points. Then multiply this distance by the kilometers or miles each centimeter or inch stands for.

Look at the distance scale on the landforms map. Notice how many kilometers each centimeter stands for. Now, on the map, use a ruler to measure the distance between Denver, Colorado, and Salem, Oregon. The distance on the map is 4 centimeters. What, then, is the distance between Denver, Colorado, and Salem, Oregon?

On the next two pages is a map of the United States. The map has all the tools you will need to read it. It has a map key, a compass rose, and a distance scale. Which will you use to tell how far Portland is from Seattle?

THE UNITED STATES OF AMERICA
PACIFIC OCEAN
WASHINGTON
Seattle
Olympia
Portland
Columbia R.
Salem
OREGON
MONTANA
Helena
Yellowstone R.
Snake R.
Boise
IDAHO
WYOMING
North Platte R.
Cheyenne
Sacramento R.
Sacramento
Carson City
NEVADA
Great Salt Lake
Salt Lake City
UTAH
San Francisco
Denver
COLORADO
CALIFORNIA
Colorado R.
Los Angeles
San Diego
ARIZONA
Phoenix
Gila R.
Santa Fe
NEW MEXICO
Pecos R.
Rio Grande
MEXICO
HAWAII
Honolulu
PACIFIC OCEAN
0 100 200 km
0 100 200 miles
ASIA
ARCTIC OCEAN
Yukon R.
CANADA
ALASKA
Juneau
PACIFIC OCEAN
0 200 400 km
0 100 200 300 miles
N
S
E
W

CANADA
NORTH DAKOTA
Bismarck
MINNESOTA
St. Paul
Minneapolis
Lake Superior
MICHIGAN
Lake Huron
Lake Michigan
WISCONSIN
Madison
Milwaukee
Lansing
Detroit
Pierre
SOUTH DAKOTA
IOWA
Des Moines
NEBRASKA
Lincoln
Chicago
Illinois R.
Springfield
ILLINOIS
INDIANA
Indianapolis
OHIO
Columbus
Cleveland
Cincinnati
Ohio R.
Lake Erie
Lake Ontario
Buffalo
NEW YORK
New York City
Newark
Albany
Hudson R.
St. Lawrence R.
Montpelier
MAINE
Augusta
NEW HAMPSHIRE
VERMONT
Concord
MASSACHUSETTS
Boston
RHODE ISLAND
Hartford
Providence
CONNECTICUT
Trenton
NEW JERSEY
Philadelphia
PENNSYLVANIA
Pittsburgh
Harrisburg
Baltimore
Dover
DELAWARE
Annapolis
MARYLAND
Washington, D.C.
WEST VIRGINIA
Charleston
Richmond
VIRGINIA
Frankfort
KENTUCKY
Kansas City
Topeka
KANSAS
Missouri R.
Jefferson City
St. Louis
MISSOURI
Kansas R.
OKLAHOMA
Oklahoma City
Canadian R.
ARKANSAS
Little Rock
Mississippi R.
Tennessee R.
Nashville
TENNESSEE
Raleigh
NORTH CAROLINA
Columbia
SOUTH CAROLINA
Savannah R.
Atlanta
GEORGIA
ALABAMA
Montgomery
MISSISSIPPI
Jackson
Red R.
Dallas
Sabine R.
LOUISIANA
TEXAS
Austin
Houston
San Antonio
Baton Rouge
New Orleans
Tallahassee
FLORIDA
Miami
ATLANTIC OCEAN
GULF OF MEXICO
0 100 200 300 400 500 kilometers
0 100 200 300 400 500 miles
National capital
State capital
City
100° 95° 90° 85° 80° 75° 70°
45° 35° 30° 25°

WASHINGTON
Columbia R.
PACIFIC
OCEAN
Astoria
Seaside
St. Helens
Scappoose
PORTLAND
BEAVERTON
HILLSBORO
Troutdale
Hood River
The Dalles
Forest Grove
Cornelius
Milwaukie
Lake Oswego
GRESHAM
Tillamook
Tigard
Tualatin
Gladstone
Sandy
Newberg
Wilsonville
Oregon City
West Linn
Canby
McMinnville
Molalla
Woodburn
Deschutes R.
Keizer
Silverton
Lincoln City
Dallas
Salem
Monmouth
Independence
Stayton
Detroit Lake
Newport
Toledo
ALBANY
CORVALLIS
Lebanon
Willamette R.
Sweet Home
Prineville
Crooked R.
Redmond
Junction City
Florence
SPRINGFIELD
EUGENE
Bend
Cottage Grove
Reedsport
Oakridge
Umpqua R.
North Bend
Coos Bay
Sutherlin
Coquille
Roseburg
Winston
Diamond
Lake
Myrtle Creek
Crater Lake
Summer
Lake
Rogue R.
Grants Pass
Upper Klamath
Lake
Central Point
MEDFORD
Ashland
Klamath Falls
Brookings
124°
122°

46°
Grande Ronde R.
Hermiston
Milton-Freewater
Pendleton
Snake R.
Wallowa R.
La Grande
Wallowa
Lake
N
W
E
S
Powder R.
John Day R.
Baker
IDAHO
Malheur R.
Ontario
44°
0
160 kilometers
0
100 miles
Lake
Owyhee
Malheur Lake
Harney Lake
OREGON
Population
3,000 to 10,000 people
10,000 to 25,000 people
25,000 to 50,000 people
50,000 to 100,000 people
Over 100,000 people
Lake
Abert
120°
118°
42°
NEVADA

UNIT 1

Oregon's Geography and Economics

CHAPTER 1 Geography

Mt. Hood from Trillium Lake

Oregon is a state of great natural variety. It has stretches of rugged shoreline where steep cliffs meet the ocean. There are towering mountains and green forests. Oregon has hundreds of waterfalls and many clear, cool lakes. There is much scenic beauty to enjoy.

At the end of this chapter, you should be able to:

- ○ Locate Oregon within the United States.
- ○ Name and describe the land regions of Oregon.
- ○ Name and locate important rivers in the state.
- ○ Explain how Oregon's location and landforms affect its climate.
- ● Read a climate regions map.
- ○ Describe the plant life, animal life, and the scenic beauty of Oregon.
- ● Read a road map.

1 Location and Size

Oregon is one of the 50 states in the United States. The United States is a large country on the continent of North America.

Location

Oregon is in the northwest part of the country. It lies between the Pacific Ocean on the west and the state of Idaho on the east. Its neighbor to the north is the state of Washington. South of Oregon are the states of California and Nevada.

The Snake River forms part of the boundary between Oregon and Idaho.

boundary
a line on a map that separates one state or country from another

Lines separate Oregon from other states on the map. A line on a map that separates one state or country from another is called a **boundary.** Boundaries are also called borders. Sometimes a river forms a boundary. Part of the northern boundary of Oregon follows the path of the Columbia River. This is what causes the dips and curves in the state's northern boundary. Find the Snake River on the map on pages 16 and 17. It is part of Oregon's eastern boundary. It separates the states of Oregon and Idaho.

Geographic Regions

region
an area of land

Oregon is part of the geographic **region** known as the Pacific Coast region. A region is an area of land. States in the United States can be grouped into six geographic regions. The states in each region have something in common.

The Pacific Coast region is made up of five states. They are Alaska, California, Hawaii, Oregon, and Washington. All of these states border the Pacific Ocean.

Size

Oregon is almost in the shape of a square. It is a little wider than it is long. At its greatest width, from east to west, Oregon is 604 kilometers (375 miles) wide. You would travel 475 kilometers (295 miles) at its greatest length.

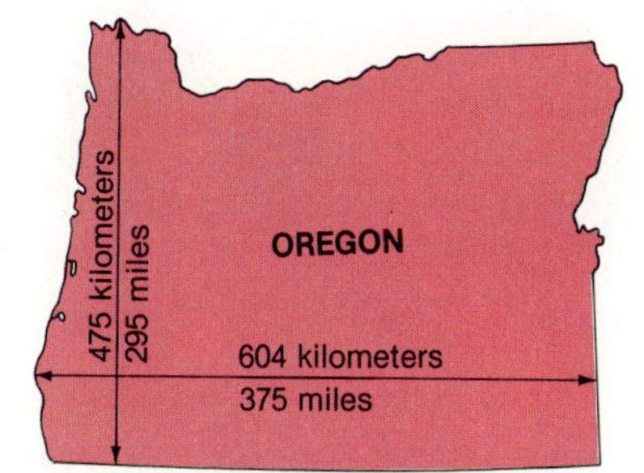

The state of Oregon is the tenth largest of the 50 states in land size. It has 251,180 square kilometers (96,981 square miles) of land area. This includes 2,064 square kilometers (797 square miles) of inland water. The largest state in the United States is Alaska. It is six times larger than Oregon.

Oregon is thirtieth in population among the states. This means that it is not a crowded state. The state with the greatest population is Oregon's southern neighbor, California. In 1980, 23,667,902 people were living in California. In the same year, 2,633,105 people were living in Oregon. Even though California is larger than Oregon in land area, its large population makes some areas of the state very crowded.

Section Review

Write your answers on a sheet of paper.

1. Name the states that border Oregon.
2. What rivers form part of Oregon's boundaries? Of which boundaries do they form a part?
3. In which geographic region of the United States does Oregon lie?
4. How does Oregon compare to the other 50 states in land size and population?

A break in the earth's surface

fault
a break in the earth's surface with a shift in the level of the land

fold
a buckle, or bend, in the earth's surface

volcano
an opening in the earth's surface through which hot liquid rock and other materials are forced out

lava
hot liquid rock that flows out of volcanoes

erosion
the wearing away of land by wind and water

2 A Varied Land

Over thousands of years, the forces of nature have shaped Oregon's land. The land has been built up and worn down. Some changes have happened rapidly. Others have happened very slowly.

The Blue Mountains and the Klamath (**kla**-muth) Mountains are older than the other mountains in the state. These mountains were formed by movements of rock deep below the surface of the earth. This movement caused the earth's surface to buckle and break. Sometimes the land along a break line shifted up or down. A break with a shift in the level of the land is called a **fault.** A buckle, or bend, in the earth's surface is called a **fold.** The older mountains in Oregon were formed by faulting and folding.

The Cascade and Coast mountains are younger mountains. But "younger" still means thousands of years old. The Coast Range was formed by folding. The Cascades were formed by folding and volcanoes. A **volcano** is an opening in the earth's surface through which hot liquid rock and other materials are forced out. The hot liquid rock, called **lava,** spread and cooled in layers, forming mountains. Lava flows can be found in many parts of Oregon.

The land of Oregon has also been shaped by wind and water. Over thousands of years, these forces have slowly worn away or changed the surface of the land. This wearing away of the land by wind and water is called **erosion** (ee-**roh**-shun). Much of Oregon's shoreline has been shaped by erosion.

Land Regions

Imagine that you are flying over Oregon in an airplane. As you look out, you can see that the land changes from place to place. There are six major land regions in the state. Look at the map on this page to find the name and location of each region.

Flying along the edge of the Pacific Ocean, you can see a group of low, rolling mountains. This is the Coast Range. A group of mountains is called a **mountain range.** Much of the area is covered with evergreen forests. Steep cliffs drop down to the ocean. In some areas, the wind and the ocean waves have formed sand dunes and beaches.

mountain range
a group of mountains

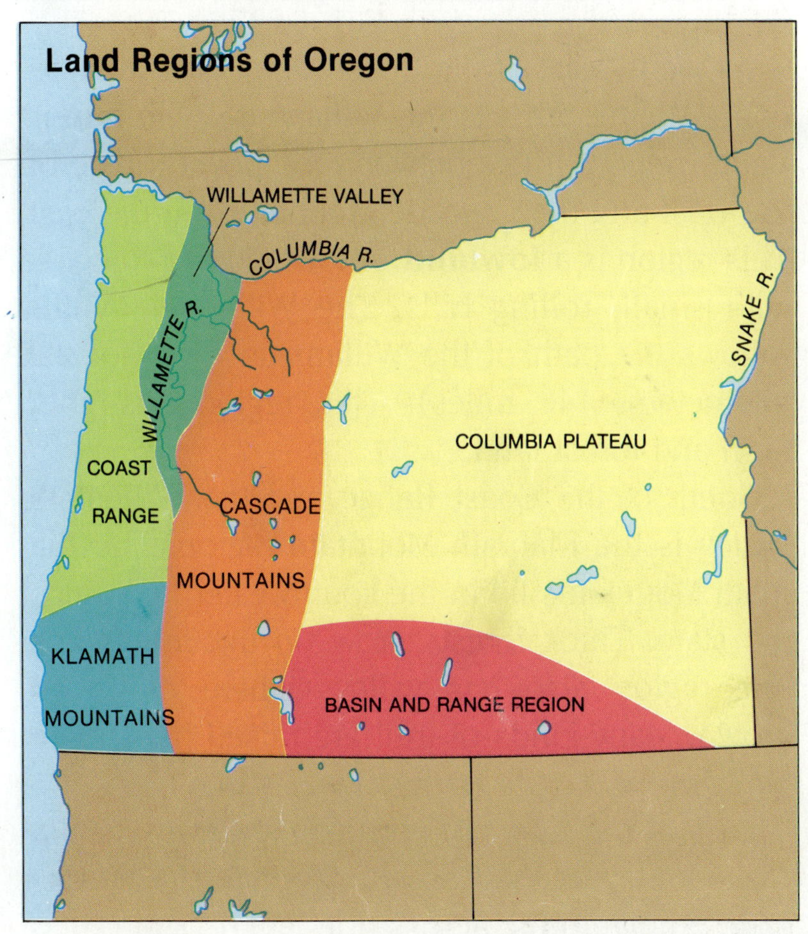

The Coast Range and Oregon coast

As we fly east of the Coast Range, the land becomes flatter. This is the Willamette (wih-**lam**-it) Valley region. It lies between the Coast Range on the west and the Cascade Mountains on the east. This region is a **lowland.** A lowland is a low area with small, rolling hills. The Willamette Valley follows the path of the Willamette River for 225 kilometers (140 miles). This region has good farm and forest land.

lowland
a low area with small, rolling hills

South of the Coast Range and the Willamette Valley is the Klamath Mountain region. The Klamath Mountains lie in the southwestern corner of the state. Thick forests grow on the mountains. The region also has valleys where crops are grown. Many kinds of fruit are raised here, especially in the Rogue (**rohg**) River Valley.

East of the Klamath Mountains and the Willamette Valley lie the Cascade Mountains. The Cascade Range runs across the entire state in a north–south direction. Mount Hood is the tallest mountain in Oregon. It is 3,426 meters (11,239 feet) high. The sides of the mountains are covered with thick forests. There are many beautiful waterfalls in the mountains.

The region that makes up most of eastern Oregon is called the Columbia **Plateau** (plah-**toe**). A plateau is an area of flat land higher than the land around it. Its surface is cut by many **canyons.** A canyon is a deep valley with steep sides. In the northeastern part of this region are the Blue and Wallowa (wah-**la**-wah) mountains. They are 610 to 1524 meters (2,000 to 5,000 feet) tall.

South of the Columbia Plateau is the **Basin** and Range region. A basin is an area of land that is surrounded by higher land. Small mountain ranges cut across the basin in a north–south direction. Much of the land is lava from very old volcanoes.

Look again at the map on page 25. Find the land regions of Oregon. The features of each region affect how the land is used.

plateau
an area of flat land higher than the land around it

canyon
a deep valley with steep sides

basin
an area of land that is surrounded by higher land

Section Review

Write your answers on a sheet of paper.

1. What are the names of the older mountain ranges in Oregon? How were they formed?
2. Where is the Willamette Valley located?
3. What is the tallest mountain in Oregon? In which mountain range is it located?
4. What is a plateau?
5. If you were a fruit farmer from California and were thinking of moving to Oregon, in which region would you settle? Why?

3 Rivers and Lakes

tributary
a river or stream that flows into a larger river or stream

gorge
a deep, narrow pass between mountains

mouth
the place where a river empties into a larger body of water

Oregon's most important river is the Columbia River. It starts in the Canadian Rocky Mountains and flows south through Canada and the state of Washington. Along its route, many streams and rivers, called **tributaries** (**trib**-yuh-terr-eez), flow into it. The main tributary of the Columbia is the Snake River. The Snake River flows into the Columbia River near Pasco, Washington. South of Pasco, the Columbia turns west and begins to form the northern boundary of Oregon.

As the Columbia moves west, it is fed by many of Oregon's streams and rivers. The John Day River in eastern Oregon and the Deschutes (deh-**shoots**) River in central Oregon flow north to meet the Columbia. About a dozen waterfalls tumble into the Columbia River **Gorge.** This is a narrow pass that the Columbia River has cut through the Cascade Mountains. Some of the waterfalls along the gorge are over 61 meters (200 feet) high.

The largest tributary of the Columbia west of the Cascades is the Willamette River. The Willamette River begins in the Cascades east of Cottage Grove, Oregon. It flows north through Salem and meets the Columbia River near Portland.

The waters of the Columbia enter the Pacific Ocean at Astoria. This is the river's **mouth.** The mouth of a river is the place where the river empties into a larger body of water. From its source in the Canadian Rockies to its mouth at the Pacific Ocean, the Columbia is about 2,000 kilometers (1,243 miles) long.

Not all of Oregon's streams and rivers flow into the Columbia. The Rogue, Umpqua (**ump**-kwah),

Circle irrigation

White-water rafting on the Rogue River

and Coquille (koh-**keel**) rivers cut their way through the Coast Range to the Pacific. The Malheur (**mal**-hoor) and Owyhee (o-**wah**-hee) rivers in southeastern Oregon are tributaries of the Snake River.

Nature has provided Oregon with many valuable things that people need and want. These valuable things are called **natural resources.**

natural resource
something from nature that people need or want, such as water, coal, soil, and forests

Water is a natural resource. Oregon's rivers give the state plenty of water. They provide drinking water and water for **irrigation.** Irrigation is supplying water to dry land through pipes, ditches, or canals. Goods can be carried from one part of the state to another on some of the rivers. Finally, Oregon's rivers are used for recreation. Many Oregonians and visitors to the state enjoy fishing. Other people can enjoy a wild raft ride down one of the state's swift rivers.

irrigation
supplying water to dry land through pipes, ditches, or canals

Lakes

Oregon has many lakes. One of the most beautiful is Crater Lake in the Cascade Mountains. It lies in the sunken volcanic crater of Mount Mazama. Its waters are very clear, unbelievably blue, and 589 meters (1,932 feet) deep. Crater Lake is the deepest lake in the United States. There are hundreds of smaller lakes in the Cascade Range.

Wallowa Lake in northeastern Oregon is known for its sparkling, clear water. Many of the lakes in southeastern Oregon, however, are shallow and salty. They have no outlet to the ocean. Some of these lakes dry up during the summer. Two large lakes in this region that have water all year round are Harney Lake and Malheur Lake. A number of other lakes in southeastern Oregon that were formed when dams were built also have water all year round. They are not shallow or salty.

Crater Lake

Wallowa Lake

There are many small lakes near the Oregon coast. Many of them were formed when sand and soil blocked the mouths of streams. This kept the streams from emptying into the ocean.

A lot of people enjoy fishing, boating, or water-skiing on Oregon's lakes. Other people visit the lakes for their quiet beauty.

Section Review

Write your answers on a sheet of paper.

1. Where does the Columbia River start? Where is its mouth?
2. What are tributaries? Name two Oregon rivers that are tributaries of the Columbia.
3. How are Oregon's rivers important to the state?
4. Suppose you wanted to take a trip to Crater Lake. To what region would you go, and what would you expect to see?

4 Climate and Weather

What is it like outside today? Is it warm and sunny? Is it cold and rainy? When you answer these questions, you are talking about the **weather.** Weather is what the air is like at a certain time or place. The kind of weather a region has over many years is its **climate.**

weather
the condition of the air at a certain time or place

climate
the kind of weather a region has over a long period of time

temperature
the measure of how hot or cold a place is

Describing Climate

We use several words to describe climate. One of these words is **temperature,** a measure of how hot or cold a place is. Places that have fairly high temperatures over a long period of time have warm climates. Places that have fairly low temperatures have cold climates. The charts below show differences in temperature in different parts of Oregon.

Average Monthly Temperatures									
PORTLAND					PENDLETON				
	C°		F°			C°		F°	
	High	Low	High	Low		High	Low	High	Low
JAN.	7	2	44	35	JAN.	4	−3	39	26
FEB.	10	3	50	38	FEB.	8	0	47	32
MAR.	13	5	56	41	MAR.	12	1	53	34
APR.	17	7	62	45	APR.	16	4	61	39
MAY	21	10	69	50	MAY	22	8	71	46
JUNE	23	12	73	54	JUNE	27	12	80	53
JULY	26	14	79	58	JULY	32	15	89	59
AUG.	26	14	79	58	AUG.	30	14	86	58
SEPT.	23	12	73	54	SEPT.	25	11	77	51
OCT.	18	9	64	49	OCT.	18	5	64	41
NOV.	12	6	53	42	NOV.	9	1	49	33
DEC.	8	3	47	38	DEC.	6	−1	43	30

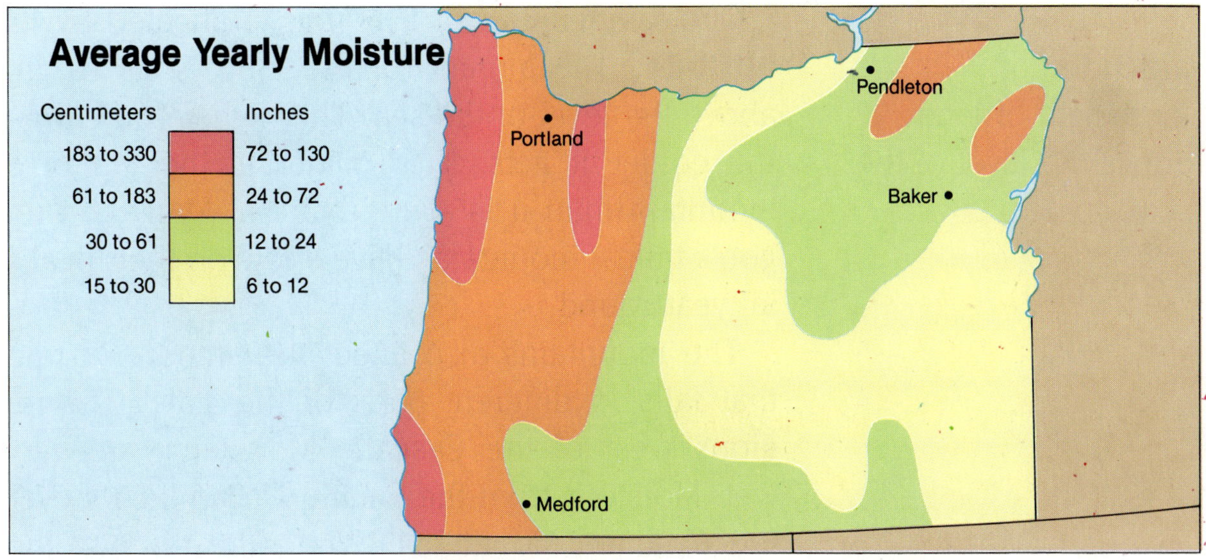

Climate can also be described as wetness and dryness. Some parts of Oregon receive a great deal of wetness, or **moisture.** Rain, snow, hail, and fog are forms of moisture we can see. There is also a form of moisture we cannot see. This moisture makes the air feel damp, or **humid.** The map on this page shows the amount of rain and snow that falls in different parts of Oregon.

moisture
water in the air or on the ground; wetness

humid
moist or damp

Influences on Climate

Why do different regions have colder temperatures than others? Why do some parts of the state get more rain than others? There are many things that influence climate.

The climate of Oregon is affected by the Pacific Ocean. In the winter, the air over the ocean is warmer than the air over the land. In the summer, the air over the ocean is cooler than the air over the land. Winds from the Pacific blow east over the land. Because of these winds, the western regions of the state have a mild climate. The winds from the ocean do not have as much influence on temperature in the eastern regions of the state. They are blocked by the Cascade Mountains.

altitude
the height of land above the level of the sea

The temperature of a region is affected by its **altitude.** The altitude of the land is its height above the level of the sea. The higher you climb, the colder it gets. It is colder at the top of a mountain than it is at the bottom. Many of Oregon's tallest mountains have snow on their peaks all year round.

The mountains also affect the amount of rain that falls in different parts of the state. The regions west of the Cascade Mountains are very wet. Moist air from the Pacific Ocean blows over the Cascade Mountains. When the air hits the mountains, rain or snow falls. The drawing on this page shows this. The western side of the Cascade Mountains gets more than 250 centimeters (100 inches) of rain or snow each year. The land on the eastern side of the Cascades gets very little rain. Only about 13 to 38 centimeters (5 to 15 inches) of rain fall each year.

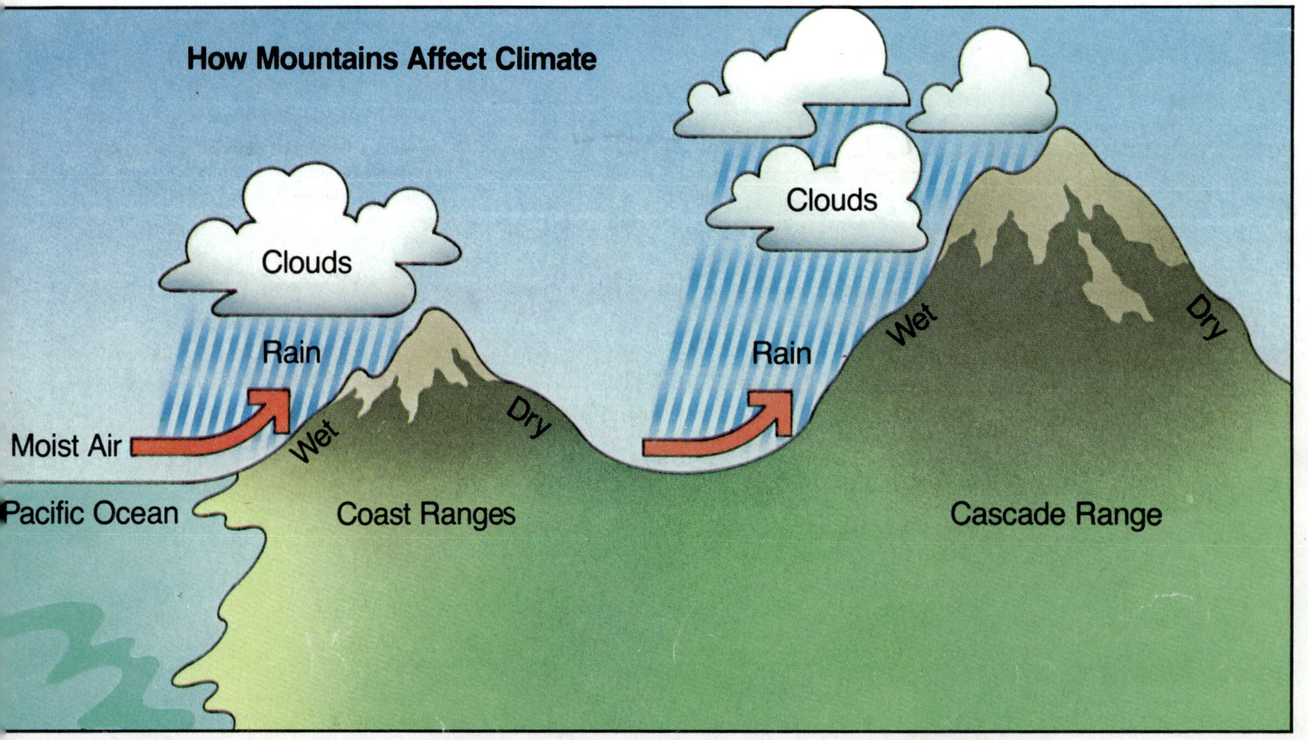

The Alvord Desert in southeastern Oregon (left) receives little rain. West of the Cascades (right), the land receives a much greater amount of moisture.

The temperature of a place is also influenced by how far it is from the equator. The sun's rays shine directly on areas near the equator. Regions close to the equator get more heat from the sun. The areas furthest from the equator are the North and South poles. The poles receive the least heat from the sun. They are cold all year round. Oregon lies about halfway between the equator and the North Pole. The state has cool winters and warm summers.

Section Review

Write your answers on a sheet of paper.

1. What is the difference between weather and climate?
2. Explain how the mountains affect the amount of rain that falls in different parts of Oregon.
3. Name three things that affect the temperature of a region.
4. Describe the climate in the region where you live. How does the climate affect what you wear and what you do in your free time?

SOCIAL STUDIES SKILLS

Reading a Climate Regions Map

What is the climate in Oregon? Is it hot in summer? Is it cold in winter? Is it humid and cool most of the year? Do different parts of the state have the same climate? You can find out something about the climate of a state by reading a climate regions map.

The map on the next page shows the eight climate regions of the United States. Each color on the map key describes a different climate. What is the climate in the states colored purple? in the state colored yellow? What section of the country has a mild, humid climate?

What can you learn about the climate of Oregon from the climate map? Do the Pacific Coast states have the same climate? Do any states on the east coast have the same climate as Oregon? What climate region do you live in?

Practice Your Skills

1. What part of Oregon has a mild, humid climate?
2. What other states have mild, humid climates?
3. What part of Oregon has cold, dry winters?
4. How do summer temperatures in eastern Oregon compare to summer temperatures in western Oregon?
5. What kind of landform separates the two kinds of climate found in Oregon?

GREAT LAKES
PACIFIC OCEAN
ATLANTIC OCEAN
GULF OF MEXICO
PACIFIC OCEAN
PACIFIC OCEAN
N
W
E
S
0 600 kilometers
0 400 miles
Tropical climate: Hot summers, warm winters, rainy
Desert or arid climate: Hot summers, warm winters, very dry
Semiarid climate: Hot summers, cold winters, dry
Polar climate: Cool summers, cold winters, very dry
Warm humid climate: Hot summers, mild winters, rainy
Cool humid climate: Cool to warm summers, cold winters, dependable rainfall
Mild humid climate: Cool summers, mild winters, rainy
Warm humid/dry climate: Warm dry summers, mild moist winters

Douglas fir

5 Plant and Animal Life

As you have read, the climate in Oregon changes from region to region. Differences in climate affect the plant and animal life in each region. Some plants grow well in cool, wet climates. Others are more suited to warmer and drier climates. Animals live in areas where they feel safe and where they can find food. Some can live in colder climates better than others. Many different kinds of animals live in the state's forests, on its grasslands, or on its dry plateaus. Many kinds of fish can be found in the state's rivers and lakes.

Plant Life

cedar
a kind of evergreen tree found in the western regions of Oregon

Forests cover nearly half the state of Oregon. The trees are mostly evergreens. Douglas fir, spruce, hemlock, and red **cedar** cover the Coast Range. These trees and some pine also grow in the western Cascade Mountains. Ponderosa pine is found in the eastern Cascade Mountains. In 1939, the Douglas fir was chosen as the state tree. The largest trees growing in the state are Sitka spruce. The largest Sitka spruce in the United States is found near the town of Seaside, Oregon. Its trunk measures 16 meters (52.5 feet) around. It is thought that this tree is about 700 years old!

Grasslands cover much of eastern Oregon. They are used as pastures for sheep and cattle. Short desert plants can be found in the southeastern part of the state.

Oregon has many kinds of flowers. The state flower is the Oregon grape. It has yellow flowers in the early summer and a blue berry that ripens in the fall. The berry can be used in cooking.

Animal Life

The American beaver was named Oregon's state animal in 1969. The first people in Oregon trapped this animal for its fur. As a result, the beaver population in the state became smaller. Efforts were made to save the remaining beavers and the places where they lived. Over the years, their numbers have increased. The dams they build are important to natural water flow and erosion control.

Many small animals live in Oregon. They include rabbits, chipmunks, raccoons, and foxes. Many of Oregon's larger animals belong to the deer family. Other large animals, such as black bears and cougars, still roam some mountain regions. A few bighorn sheep can be found in the Wallowa Mountains.

In 1927, Oregon's schoolchildren chose the Western meadowlark as the state bird. This bird can be found in the western regions of North America. It is known for its beautiful song.

Oregon grape

Western meadowlark

An American beaver family

Chinook salmon

Oregon swallowtail

Fish have always been important to the people of Oregon. Long before Europeans came to America, fish was the most important food for many Indian groups in the Pacific Northwest. The Chinook salmon is the Oregon state fish. Record catches of salmon up to 132 centimeters (52 inches) long and weighing as much as 57 kilograms (126 pounds) have been reported.

The Oregon swallowtail is the Oregon state insect. This beautiful butterfly is at home in the dry canyons along the Columbia River. It is a strong flier and not easily caught.

As more people move to a region, the animals are disturbed. Not long ago, the nesting areas of the sandhill cranes were disappearing. The cranes were laying fewer eggs. Many people feared that these birds would die out. Efforts were made to protect the cranes and their nesting areas. Slowly the number of sandhill cranes in Oregon is increasing.

Section Review

Write your answers on a sheet of paper.

1. How does climate affect plant and animal life?

2. What is the Oregon state tree? Where can it be found?

3. What is the Oregon state animal? How was it important in the past? How is it important today?

4. Why is it important to protect Oregon's plant and animal life? What do you think should be done to protect it?

6 Scenic Beauty

Many people have come to Oregon to view its scenic wonders. Large parts of Oregon have been preserved in their natural state. Oregonians are very proud of their beautiful state.

Along the Oregon Coast

In many places along the coast, the mountains drop down to the ocean. Ocean waves crash against the cliffs sending showers of ocean spray high in the air. Driftwood and rocks lie along the beaches. Golden sand dunes cover an 80 kilometer (50 mile) stretch of the Oregon coast. On clear days, beautiful sunsets can be seen over the ocean.

Driftwood and rocks along the Oregon coast

Mt. Hood

Scenic Mountains

Oregon's mountains add much beauty to the state. The peaks of Mt. Hood, Mt. Jefferson, and other mountains in the Cascade Range are covered with snow. They rise high above the clouds.

The beautiful Ochoco (**o**-cho-co) Mountains are in the center of the state. East of the mountains are the Painted Hills. These treeless hills appear to be painted with many colors. Mirrorlike lakes in the Wallowa Mountains reflect the beauty of the mountains. Oregon Caves National Monument is in the mountains of southwestern Oregon. These caves have beautiful marble in them.

Many beautiful waterfalls can be seen in Oregon's mountains. Silver Creek, with its many tributaries, has 14 falls. The waters of Multnomah Falls drop 189 meters (620 feet) into the Columbia River.

Over thousands of years, Oregon's rivers have cut gorges through the mountains. Layers of different kinds of rock give the walls of the gorges different colors. On the eastern boundary of Oregon, the Snake River has cut the deepest gorge in the United States. It is called Hells Canyon. Hells Canyon is over 2.5 kilometers (1.5 miles) deep.

The Painted Hills

Parks and Recreation

Crater Lake National Park is the state's only national park. The park is owned and run by the United States government. Laws relating to the operation of this park are made in Washington, D.C.

Oregon has over 225 state parks. These parks are owned and run by the state of Oregon. Lawmakers in Salem decide how these parks may be used. Many of the parks allow overnight camping. They also contain areas where people can enjoy hiking, bicycling, swimming, and boating.

Many cities also have parks. Portland is nicknamed the "City of Roses" because of its many beautiful public and private rose gardens. Many city parks may also be used for outdoor recreational activities.

Roses in Portland's Washington Park

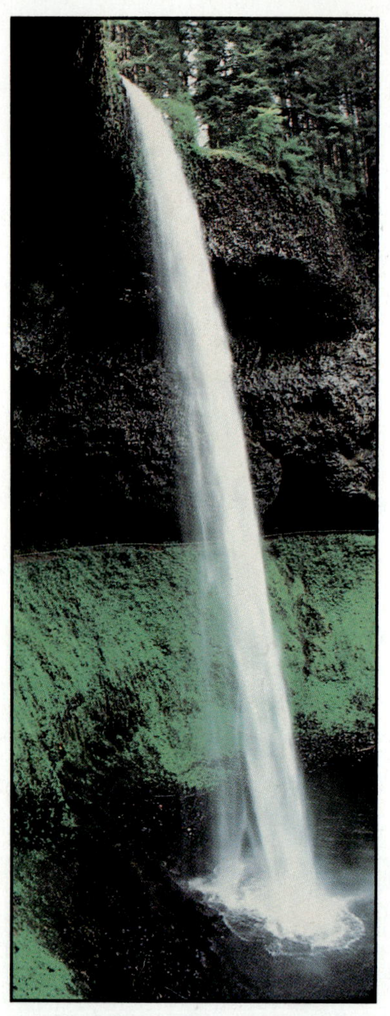
Silver Falls State Park

Protection and Use

In addition to creating state parks, Oregon has set aside its beaches for public use. No one may own any land along a strip of land within 4.9 meters (16 feet) of the ocean's edge. This land is to be used and enjoyed by everyone. To protect the beaches, laws were passed to limit the use of motor vehicles on the beaches.

Laws have also been passed to cut down on the amount of litter found along Oregon's roads and beaches. One of these laws is the Bottle Bill. This law says that soft drinks and beer cannot be sold in Oregon in non-returnable bottles or cans. It has helped reduce litter and preserve the state's beauty.

Some of Oregon's rivers have been named scenic waterways. Programs have been developed to preserve the beauty and protect the animal life of these rivers.

The scenic wonders of Oregon delight thousands of people every day. Efforts to protect the natural surroundings will help to keep Oregon a beautiful place to live and visit.

Section Review

Write your answers on a sheet of paper.

1. Describe the scenic beauty that can be found along Oregon's coast.
2. What kinds of activities can be enjoyed in Oregon's state parks?
3. What laws have been passed regarding Oregon's beaches?
4. What might the people in Oregon do to keep the state beautiful?

FAMOUS OREGONIANS

TOM McCALL

Tom McCall was governor of Oregon between 1967 and 1975. He cared about protecting Oregon's natural beauty.

Before McCall was governor, he wrote for a newspaper in Portland. Later he became a news reporter on radio and television. McCall often spoke about cleaning up Oregon's dirty rivers and roadways. He even won an award for a film he made about cleaning the Willamette River.

During his two terms as governor, McCall worked to improve life in Oregon. He helped ban throwaway bottles and cans, which had littered Oregon's roadsides. He also helped clean up the state's rivers. They were made safe for boaters, swimmers, and fish.

During a power shortage in Oregon, McCall asked people to follow his plan to save energy. Machines and lights in state buildings were shut off for short periods of time during the workday. Only half of the streetlights were left on at night. McCall's plan worked. Everyone had enough power during the shortage. The governor's ideas were soon used in other states.

In 1983, Tom McCall died of cancer. Yet his wishes for a better Oregon are still coming true.

SOCIAL STUDIES SKILLS

Reading a Road Map

Suppose you are on a sightseeing tour of Oregon. You can use road maps to figure out how to get from one place to another. You also can use them to figure out the distance between places. One way of doing this is to use the map scale to find how many kilometers or miles it is from one place to another. For example, the distance between Wallowa and Enterprise is about 30 kilometers, or 20 miles.

Another way of figuring distances on a road map is by adding up the numerals that appear along a road or highway between different places. The road map on page 46 shows a part of northeastern Oregon near Pendleton and La Grande. Look closely at Highway 84. The little squares show you where the highway exits are. Notice the little numerals between the exits. These numbers tell how far it is from each exit to the next. How far is it from the North Powder exit to the Baker exit? Along the smaller roads you can see other tiny numerals. These tell how far it is from one town to another. Find Highway 82. How far is it from Imbler to Elgin?

The scale of this map is 30 kilometers (almost 20 miles) to 2 centimeters (almost 1 inch). Use the scale to find the distance from Baker to La Grande. Now add up all the numbers along the route. The distances should be about the same.

Practice Your Skills

1. Suppose you wanted to travel from Medical Springs to Union along Route 203. How far is it from Medical Springs to Union?
2. Traveling along Route 82, how far is it from Elgin to Enterprise?
3. Traveling on Highway 84, how far is it from North Powder to Meacham?

CHAPTER 2 Resources and Economics

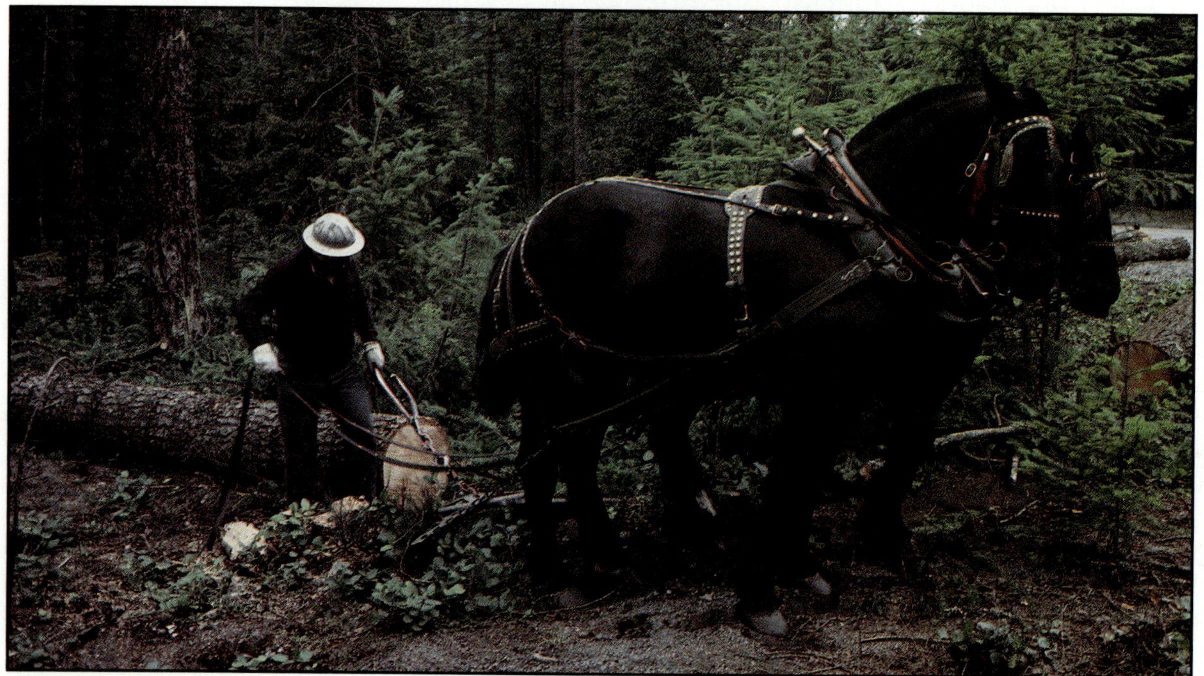

Oregon is a state rich in natural resources. Many people in Oregon use these resources to make their living. They make the things that people need or want. Today Oregon is trying to bring new and different businesses to the state. These new businesses will create more and different kinds of jobs for the people of Oregon.

At the end of this chapter, you should be able to:

○ Describe the natural resources of Oregon.

○ Explain the way people in Oregon make a living through the use of resources.

○ Describe the industries in Oregon.

● Read a pie graph.

● Read an economic activity map.

1 The Timber Industry

Forests are one of Oregon's most important natural resources. There is enough **timber,** or wood, in Oregon to rebuild every house in the United States! The timber from the forests can be made into many useful things. Cutting down trees and making useful things out of the wood is a big business in Oregon. It is an important **industry.**

timber
wood from trees that can be made into something useful

industry
a big business

Most of Oregon's timber comes from the thick forests that cover the sides of the mountains. Almost 8 billion board feet of timber are cut in Oregon each year. A board foot is 1 foot long, 1 foot wide, and 1 inch thick. Oregon produces more things from timber than any other state in the United States.

Many people work in Oregon's timber industry. One of the most important things made from timber is lumber. Much of the lumber produced in Oregon is used to build new homes or other buildings. In recent years, Oregon's lumber industry has suffered because fewer new buildings have been built. But the timber industry is still one of Oregon's most important industries.

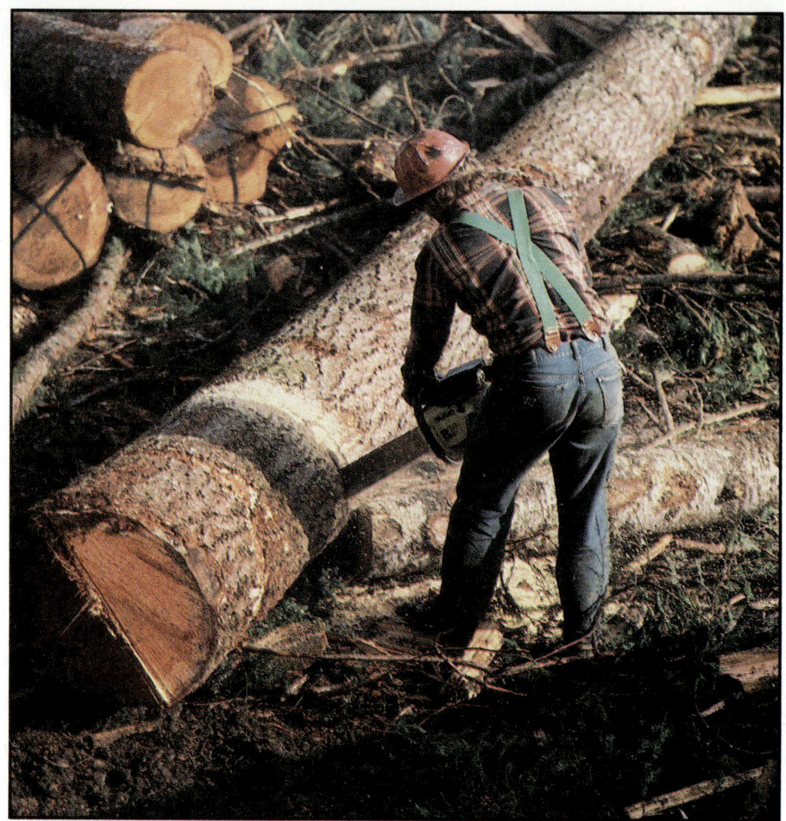

logger
a person whose work is cutting down trees, cutting them into logs, and sending them to the sawmill

forester
a scientist trained in growing crops of trees

Cutting Down Trees

The trees are cut down by workers called **loggers.** Before the loggers go into the woods, a **forester** decides which trees should be cut. A forester is a scientist trained in growing trees. Once the trees are marked, the loggers use heavy power saws to cut them down. These saws can slice through a tree in just a few seconds.

Transporting Logs

Loggers use tractors and long cables to move the logs to a central place in the woods. This place is called the landing. Usually the logs are hauled over the ground. But sometimes large balloons or helicopters are used to lift logs out of canyons. Balloons and helicopters solve the problem of getting logs out of hard-to-reach places.

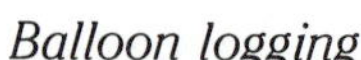

Balloon logging

The logs are piled at the landing until they can be moved to the mills or factories. If the landing lies near a road, the logs are loaded on trucks. If it lies on the bank of a river, loggers use chains to bind the logs together. The log rafts then float along the rivers to the mills. Sometimes the logs are transported on railroad cars or on large boats with flat bottoms called **barges.**

barge
a large, flat-bottomed boat

At the Sawmills

When the logs arrive at the mill, they are sometimes kept in a nearby pool of water. This pool is called a log pond. Workers wearing spiked boots walk about on the wet logs. They use long poles to sort the logs by size. In other mills, the logs are stored on dry land. Here they are handled by loading machines.

In many mills, a machine removes the bark from a log before it is sawed. The log is then loaded onto a moving platform called a carriage. The carriage moves the log into the teeth of the first saw. This saw slices the log into boards. Moving belts carry the boards to other saws that trim off rough edges and make the sides straight.

Logs are loaded onto trucks that carry them to the sawmills.

Rolls of paper at a paper mill

At the Paper Mills

In order to make paper, logs must first be made into **wood pulp,** which is ground-up wood fibers from logs. The wood pulp then passes through other machines that wash it and break down its wood fibers even more. Finally the wood pulp goes into a huge machine called a fourdrinier (foohr-**drih-**nee-ur). This is a long paper-making machine that presses the pulp into a sheet. A set of rollers at the end of the machine gives the paper a smooth finish.

wood pulp
ground up wood fibers from logs

plywood
thin sheets of wood that have been glued together

Other Forest Products

Logs that are not cut into thick boards or made into paper may be made into **plywood.** Plywood is thin sheets of wood that have been glued together.

Bark and other small pieces of wood from the lumber mills are made into useful things. Gardeners buy bark chips to place around plants. Small pieces of wood can be ground up and formed into bowling balls. Sawdust is made into small logs for fuel.

Section Review

Write your answers on a sheet of paper.

1. Where does the wood for Oregon's forest product industries come from?
2. Describe how logs are moved from the forests to mills and factories.
3. What is wood pulp? What is made from wood pulp?
4. Why is timber important to Oregon?

2 Agriculture

One third of Oregon's land is farmland. Most of the farms average 197 hectares (486 acres) in size. Farms in eastern Oregon are usually larger. The period of time during which it is warm enough for crops to grow is called a **growing season.** Differences in climate affect growing seasons in Oregon. When soil is good for growing plants, it is called **fertile.** Much of Oregon's land is fertile. Dry soil has been made into fertile farmland by irrigation.

Cattle, wheat, dairy products, and potatoes are Oregon's most valuable farm products. But differences in climate and soil make it possible for Oregon's farmers to raise a wide variety of farm goods.

growing season
the period of time during which the weather is warm enough for crops to grow

fertile
good for growing plants and crops

Harvesting cauliflower

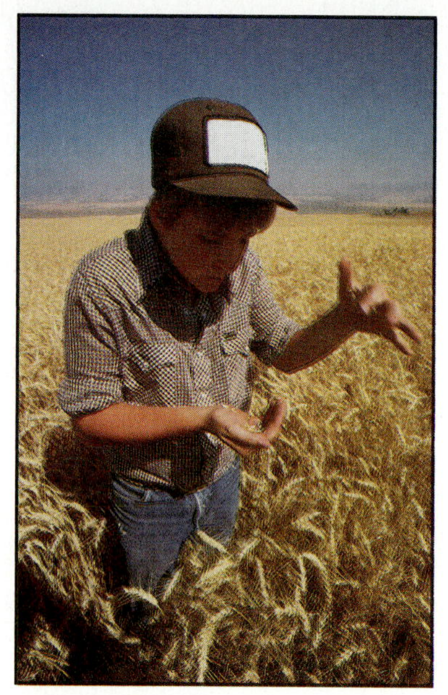

Wheat is Oregon's most valuable crop.

Large herds of livestock are raised in Oregon. Beef cattle are the state's most valuable farm product. They bring in nearly $273 million of income a year. Most of the cattle are raised in the dry, open regions east of the Cascades. Dairy cattle are found in western Oregon. Southeastern Oregon is a sheep-raising area. Sheep can also be found grazing in the Willamette Valley. Farmers in the Willamette Valley raise most of the state's chickens. More hogs are raised in Umatilla (you-mah-**til**-lah) County in northeastern Oregon than in any other county in the state.

Oregon's most valuable crop is wheat. Most of it is sold outside the state. Oregon wheat has been sold to Japan, Korea, Taiwan, and the People's Republic of China. Most of Oregon's wheat is grown on the Columbia Plateau. Other important grain crops grown in this region are barley and oats. Hay is grown as feed for animals.

Driving cattle in eastern Oregon

The main vegetable-growing region in the state is the Willamette Valley. Green peas, onions, and corn are grown there. Oregon is one of the leading states in the production of snap green beans. Potatoes are an important crop grown in the eastern regions of the state. Long irrigation pipes are used to water the potato vines. The state also grows hops, which are used in making beer.

An apple orchard in Banks, Oregon

Many kinds of fruit are raised in Oregon. The Hood and Rogue river valleys are famous for their pears. Apples also grow well in the Hood River valley. Peaches, plums, and sweet cherries are grown in the northern and western regions. Oregon is one of the leading states in strawberry production.

Oregon's farmers raise several crops that are not widely grown in other states. Nearly all of the country's hazelnuts come from Oregon. Many kinds of grass seed are raised in the northwestern regions of the state. Oregon has, at times, grown more peppermint than any other state. Flower bulbs and ornamental trees and plants are also important farm products.

Section Review

Write your answers on a sheet of paper.

1. What is Oregon's most valuable agricultural product?
2. What is Oregon's most valuable crop? Where is most of it grown?
3. What crops are grown in Oregon that are not widely grown in other states?
4. Why do you think some farm products grow well in one region and not in another?

SOCIAL STUDIES SKILLS

Reading a Pie Graph

pie graph
a drawing of a circle divided into parts

The graph on this page is called a **pie graph.** It is divided into sections like the slices of a pie. A pie graph shows a whole thing divided into parts. The circle stands for the whole. The slices stand for parts of the whole. What does the whole of the pie graph on this page stand for? What does each part, or slice, represent?

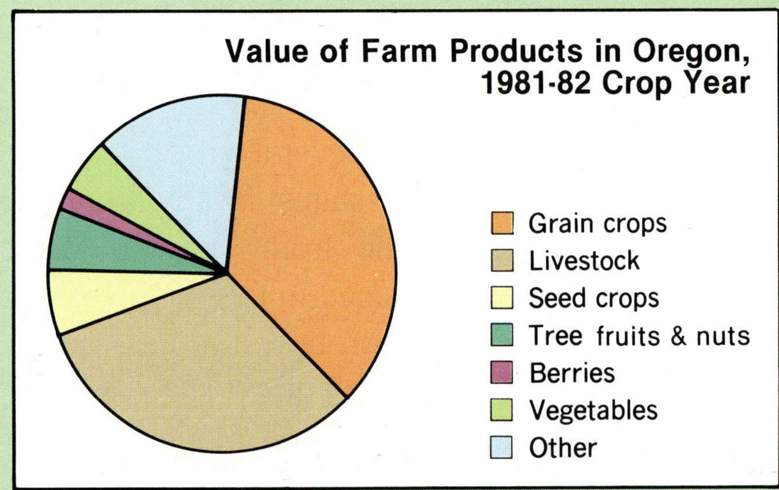

Practice Your Skills

1. For what crop year does this pie graph show the value of farm production in Oregon?
2. Into how many parts is this pie graph divided? Name the farm products each slice represents.
3. What farm products had the greatest value in the year shown?
4. Which farm products were more valuable in the year shown—vegetables or berries?

3 Manufacturing

As you have read, wood is used to make lumber. In its natural state, wood is called a **raw material.** Using a raw material, such as wood, to produce a finished product, such as lumber, is called **manufacturing.**

raw material
a material in its natural state used in making finished goods

Almost one out of every five workers in Oregon works in manufacturing. The Willamette Valley is the state's most important manufacturing region.

manufacturing
making finished goods from raw materials

Manufacturing Industries

Oregon's most important manufacturing industry is **wood processing.** In the wood-processing industry, wood is made into lumber, plywood, and other wood products. Many cities in Oregon have factories and sawmills that make things out of wood.

wood processing
changing wood into useful wood products

Food processing is the second most important manufacturing industry in Oregon. In the food-processing industry, a farm product such as milk is turned into another product, such as cheese or butter. Other farm products may be canned or frozen.

food processing
changing farm products into food products

Making cheese in Tillamook, Oregon

The electronics industry

textile
cloth made from cotton, flax, or other materials

Oregon's many crops helped to make food processing an important industry in the state. Over 40 different crops are processed. Canning and freezing plants pack fruits and vegetables. There are also several plants that pack meat. Many kinds of fish are processed in Coos Bay and The Dalles (**dalz**). Tillamook County is famous for its cheese.

The third most important industry in the state is the manufacturing of paper. Large paper mills can be found in Gardiner, Springfield, and Toledo.

Other factories in the state make cloth. Clothmaking is called **textile** manufacturing. Oregon flax is made into linen. Woolen and knitting mills can be found in Portland, Pendleton, and Eugene. Sports clothes made in Oregon are sold all over the world.

Electronic goods and transportation equipment are also made in Oregon. More people work for an electronics company outside Portland than work for any other company in the state!

The textile industry

Metal production is another important industry. Steel is made in small plants around Portland. Aluminum is also made in Oregon. Large amounts of electricity are needed to make aluminum. Low-cost electricity helped in bringing this industry to the Pacific Northwest.

Making Electricity

Electricity is used to run machines in almost all the manufacturing industries in Oregon. The rivers in the Pacific Northwest help make electricity. This power, or energy, that produces electricity is called **hydroelectric** (hie-droe-ih-**lek**-trik) **power.**

hydroelectric power energy produced by waterpower

Along the rivers, dams have been built to control the water. These dams make it possible to use the water for hydroelectric power. Some of the water behind a dam is allowed to enter large pipes that pass through the dam. These pipes lead to the power plant. As the water passes through the plant, it turns the machines that make electricity.

Hydroelectric power plant

Hydroelectric power usually costs less than power made in other ways. The water used to turn the machines in the power plant is never used up. After passing through the power plant, it flows back into the river. In some areas of the country, there is not enough waterpower to make electricity. Fuels like oil, coal, or uranium are burned to turn the machines in the power plants. The electricity that is produced by burning these fuels often costs more than hydroelectric power.

Section Review

Write your answers on a sheet of paper.

1. Name Oregon's three most important manufacturing industries.
2. Explain how dams help produce hydroelectric power.

FAMOUS OREGONIANS

BEATRICE CANNADY

In 1912, Beatrice Morrow Cannady became the first black woman to be an editor of a newspaper in Oregon. Ten years later, she became the first black woman in Oregon to earn a law degree as well.

The newspaper that Cannady worked on was called the *Advocate.* The paper printed stories of interest to all blacks.

Beatrice Cannady used her position on the newspaper to help others of her race. She wrote about the unfair things that were happening to black people. She made her readers aware that young blacks out of high school and college were getting poor-paying jobs.

She criticized schools that separated black children from white children. She reported on businesses that refused to serve black customers. Cannady encouraged her readers to insist on their right to buy seats in any part of a theater.

As an editor, Beatrice Cannady helped blacks find courage and not feel alone. Soon blacks were fighting for their rights and winning.

Beatrice Cannady was proud to be black and wanted others to know why. Through her efforts, black history is now taught in Oregon high schools.

SOCIAL STUDIES SKILLS

Reading an Economic Activity Map

economic activity
a way that people use their resources to make money

Oregon is a leading producer of lumber. It is also a manufacturing and farm state. You can learn more about Oregon's many **economic activities** from a map such as this. Economics has to do with how people use resources to make money. Study the map and the map key. Then name some of the activities that help make Oregon a rich state. Describe the parts of the state in which each activity takes place. Are the activities near mountains? rivers? cities?

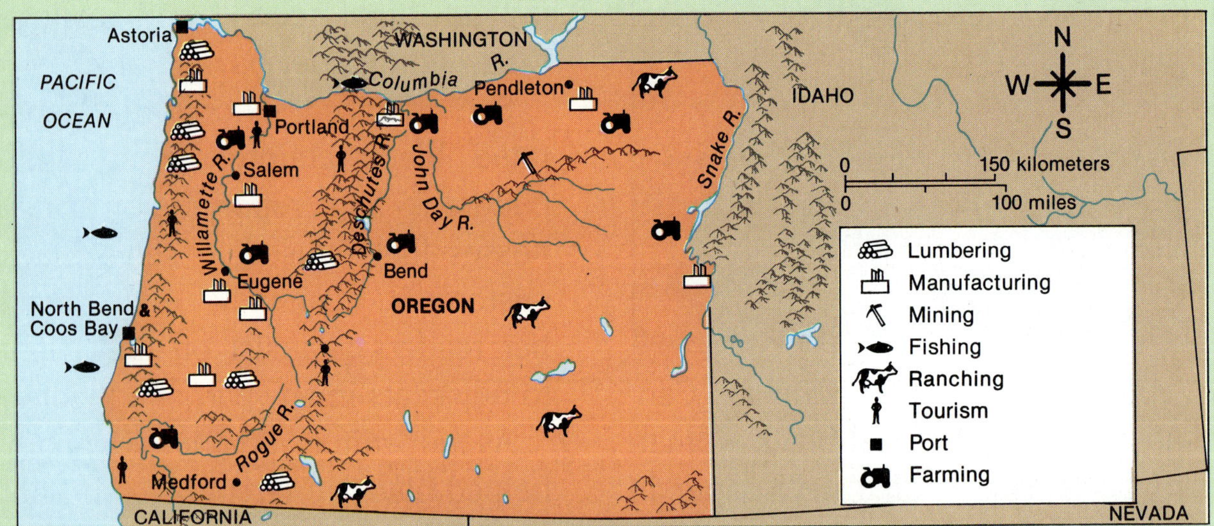

Practice Your Skills

1. In what parts of the state is farming an important activity?
2. What economic activities are people involved in along the Oregon coast?
3. In what parts of the state is lumbering an important economic activity?

4 Fishing

Many kinds of fish live in Oregon's rivers and in the waters off the coast. About 8,000 people in the state make their living by catching and selling fish. These people work in the **commercial fishing** industry. Other people fish because they enjoy it. They do not sell the fish they catch. This kind of fishing is called sport fishing. Both commercial and sport fishing are big business in Oregon.

commercial fishing
catching fish for the purpose of selling them

Commercial Fishing

Salmon are Oregon's most valuable commercial fish. For thousands of years, salmon have been making the same journey up and down the Columbia River.

salmon
an important fish found in Pacific Northwest waters

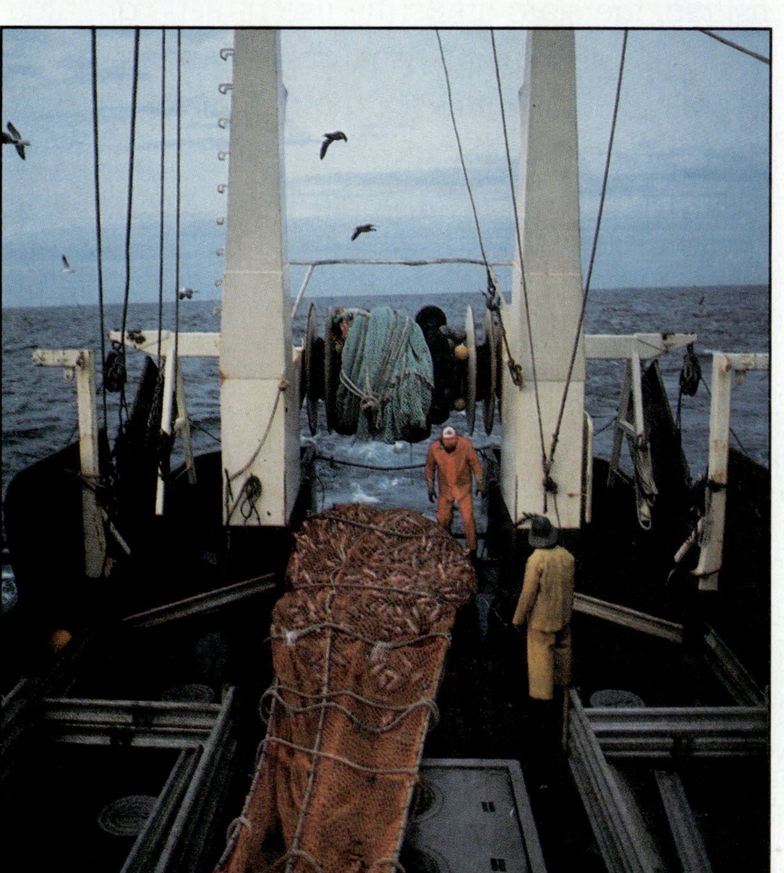

Fishing off the coast of Oregon

fish ladder
a series of small waterfalls built to allow fish to get around a dam

Each year, thousands of salmon leave the ocean to lay their eggs. They swim back to the freshwater streams where they were hatched. It is a hard journey. They must swim against the current of the river. Near Bonneville Dam, a **fish ladder** has been built. The ladder is a group of little waterfalls. The salmon can jump these falls to pass by the dam.

After the salmon lay their eggs, they die. When the young salmon are about one year old, they try to swim down the river to the ocean. They have trouble getting by the dams. Those that make it to the ocean stay there until it is time for them to lay their eggs. Then they return to the river.

About 2 million salmon are caught each year. Chinook (shi-**nook**) and Coho are the main kinds of salmon that are caught. To help prevent overfishing, the state limits the use of nets for catching fish. Nets may be used only on the lower 322 kilometers (200 miles) of the Columbia.

Tuna is Oregon's second leading commercial fish product. Large schools of this fish can be found in the waters off the coast during the summer months. Oysters, crab, and cod are other important foods from the sea.

Salmon in a fish ladder

Sport Fishing

Many Oregonians and people who visit the state enjoy sport fishing. Steelhead trout are a prized catch. Rainbow and eastern brook trout can be found in the Deschutes River. The waters of Oregon also have perch and striped bass.

Sport fishing is also a big business. People spend thousands of dollars a year for equipment, fishing licenses, and places to stay while on fishing trips.

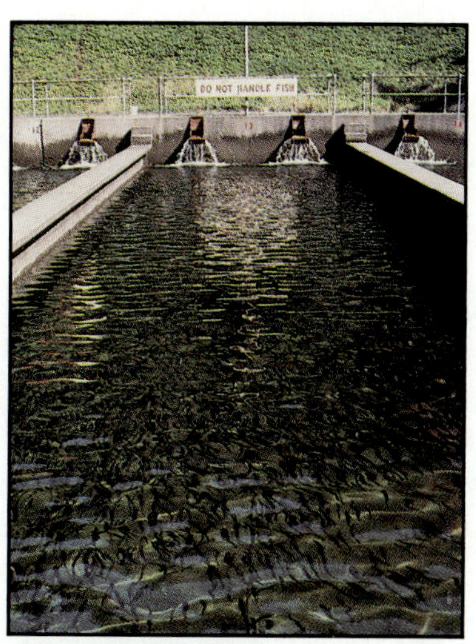

Fish hatchery

Raising Fish

Many of the fish living in Oregon's rivers and lakes were hatched in **fish hatcheries.** These are protected places where fish eggs are hatched. Oregon's 33 fish hatcheries produce almost 71 million fish a year. When the fish are big enough, they are put into the state's rivers and lakes. This is called **restocking.** Restocking makes more fish available for sport and commercial fishing.

fish hatchery
a protected place where fish eggs are hatched

restocking
building up the supply of something

Section Review

Write your answers on a sheet of paper.

1. What are Oregon's two most important commercial fish products?
2. How is sport fishing a big business?
3. Explain how Oregon restocks its rivers and lakes.
4. Why is the fish ladder near Bonneville Dam important? What do you think would have happened to the salmon if it had not been built?

ROBERT D. HUME

Robert D. Hume was born in Maine in 1845. Like many young Americans, he wanted to move west to seek a new life. At the age of 21, he set out for California. After working there for awhile, he moved to Oregon.

Beginning in 1868, Robert Hume and his brother bought and rented a number of salmon canneries on the lower Columbia River.

In 1876, Robert Hume sold his share of these canneries and headed for the rich valley and fine fish of the Rogue River. In Wedderburn, Oregon, he began to build the biggest cannery in the state. Soon he owned all of the land along both sides of the river.

But Hume did not limit his canning business to fish. He also started canning vegetables—mainly peas at first—and built more canneries.

Hume knew that the supply of salmon in the river would not last forever. He built special places, called hatcheries, where young salmon were raised. In time he restocked the rivers with the young fish.

Today we know the value of raising fish in hatcheries. Thanks to Robert D. Hume, we are still doing it.

5 Mining

You have read that the forests and rivers of Oregon are important natural resources. Oregon also has **mineral** resources. Materials, such as coal and iron, that are dug from the earth are called minerals.

Mineral resources are often found in large areas, or **deposits,** deep in the earth. Before these deposits can be used, they must be taken out of the earth. The process of doing this is called **mining.**

mineral
a material dug from the earth

deposit
large area deep in the earth where a mineral is found

mining
the process of taking mineral deposits from the earth

Mineral Resources

Oregon mines about $165 million worth of minerals a year. Stone, sand, and gravel make up most of the value of Oregon's minerals. Gravel and sand can be found in almost all parts of the state. These minerals are used to build roads. Deposits of limestone are found in some parts of the state. Limestone is a kind of rock used in making steel and in building. Some companies use limestone to make cement. It is also used to make farmland more fertile.

Gravel mining

Gold mining

Deposits of low-grade coal can be found near Coos Bay. It takes millions of years for coal to form. Heat and pressure deep in the earth turn decaying plants into coal.

The Blue Mountains are the center of the gold-mining industry in Oregon. Other metals found in Oregon are copper, nickel, silver, lead, mercury, and zinc. Zinc is used in making iron and paint.

Scientists are looking for more mineral deposits in the state. In 1979, they found the state's first deposit of natural gas. The discovery of new mineral deposits will help to make mining a more important industry in Oregon.

Section Review

Write your answers on a sheet of paper.

1. What minerals make up most of the value of Oregon's mineral resources?

2. Where are Oregon's coal deposits located?

3. Why do you think more people in Oregon work in industries like lumbering than work in mining?

6 Shipping

Each day ships arrive at Oregon **ports** to load and unload goods. They bring goods from other states and countries. They carry away the products of Oregon's farms, mines, and factories. Some of the ships dock at ports along the coast. But most of them go up the Columbia River to Portland.

port
a place where ships can load and unload goods

Portland's location has helped make it Oregon's most important port city. It lies near the point where the Willamette River meets the Columbia River. Many goods from eastern Oregon are shipped to Portland down the Columbia River. From there they can be shipped to ports all over the world.

The port of Portland

7 Tourism

tourist
a person who visits an area for pleasure

Each year millions of people tour Oregon on their vacations. These people are called **tourists.**

Tourism is an important industry in Oregon. Tourists spend over 1 billion dollars in the state each year. They enjoy the state's beauty and like to camp, swim, and fish in the state parks. Rodeos and fairs also draw tourists to Oregon. Many Oregonians work in jobs that provide services to tourists.

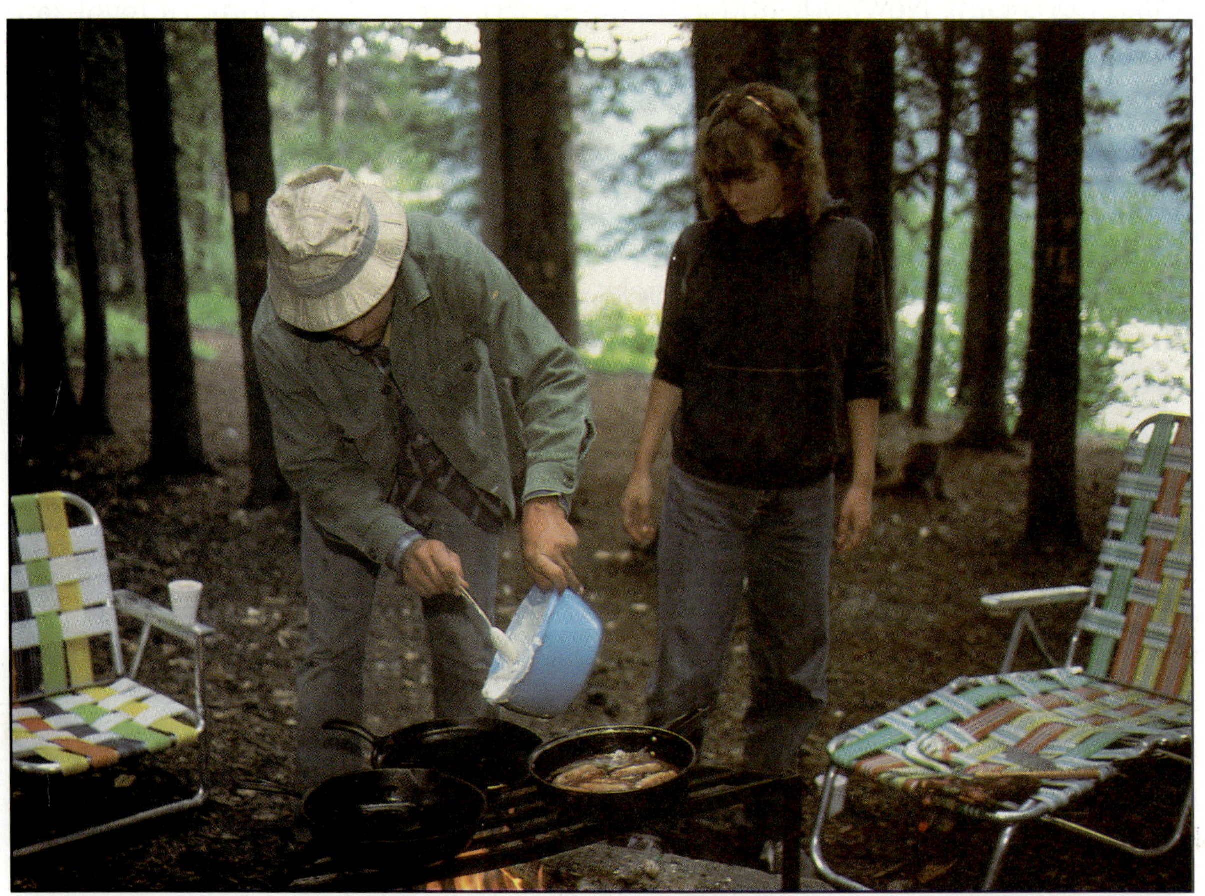

Vacation Resorts

Many vacation resorts can be found throughout Oregon. Resorts offer recreation and entertainment for many tourists. One of the best known resorts in Oregon is near the town of Madras. It

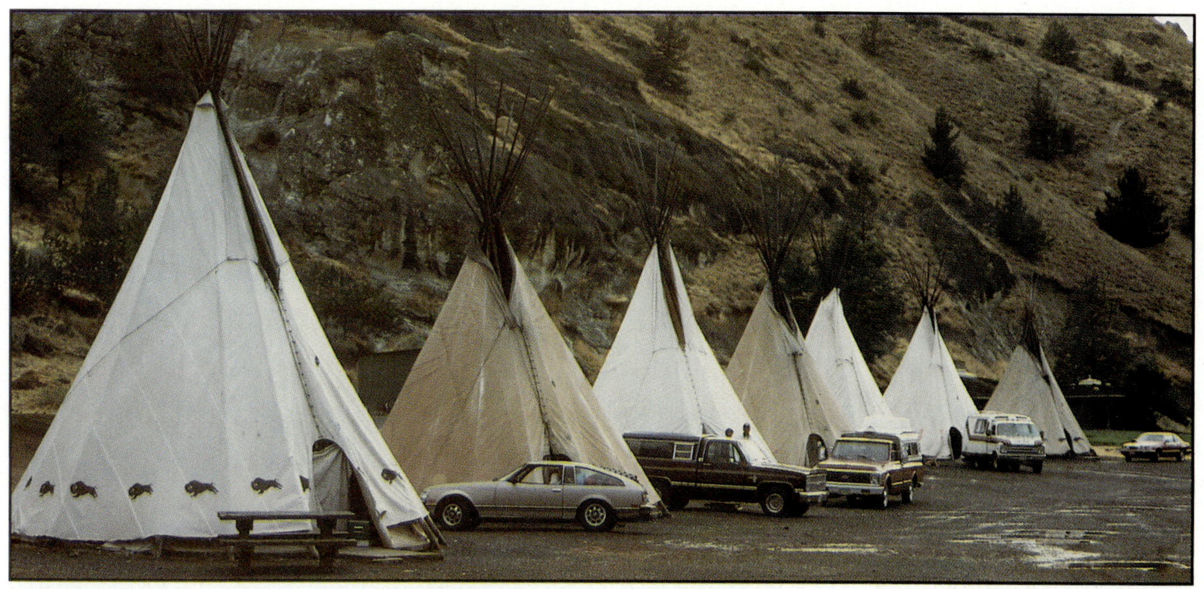

was developed by Northwest Indians on Indian-owned land. Visitors can swim, fish, play tennis, or enjoy a hot mineral bath. At night, they can sleep in a modern lodge or a tepee.

Ski resorts in the Cascade Mountains are popular in the winter. Horseback riding is a favorite activity at resorts in eastern Oregon. A few vacation resorts have been built along the Oregon coast.

Oregon Events

Rodeos, fairs, and festivals draw many tourists. They offer exciting entertainment. At rodeos, tourists can see cattle roping and bull riding. At the Shakespearean Festival in Ashland, they can see plays performed on an outdoor or indoor stage. Other yearly events are flower and harvest festivals, art fairs, and timber carnivals. There are more than 400 community and regional celebrations in the state each year.

These people are enjoying a roller coaster ride at the Oregon State Fair.

More Tourists

The state of Oregon would like to draw more tourists to Oregon. It would also like them to stay longer. This would bring more money into the state.

To bring more tourists to Oregon, the state prepares travel advertisements. These are placed in more than 1,000 newspapers and magazines each year. They draw tourists from all parts of the United States.

A tourist information center

Information Centers

The state has set up several information centers near its boundaries. The people who work in these centers give out travel information and maps. They also welcome visitors to the state. Several centers can be found near the boundary between Oregon and California. Almost four out of every ten visitors to Oregon are from California. Other centers can be found in Astoria, Ontario, and Portland.

Section Review

Write your answers on a sheet of paper.

1. How is tourism an important industry in Oregon?
2. What activities can tourists enjoy at vacation resorts?
3. How is Oregon trying to draw more tourists to the state?
4. What might Oregonians do to make out-of-state visitors feel welcome in Oregon?

Close-up on

Albany Timber Carnival Oregon's forests are one of the state's finest natural resources. They provide jobs and wood products for many people. The World Championship Timber Carnival held in Albany, Oregon, honors the workers of the lumber industry.

In 1941, the people of Albany wanted to reward loggers in some way for their hard work. They decided to hold contests. In this way loggers could show off their skills. From these first contests grew the biggest yearly event in the lumber industry.

Today loggers from around the world test their skills in the Timber Carnival for prizes and money. In 1941, a top prize was $100. Today people try to win prizes worth over $21,000.

The contests are difficult and have very strict rules. Major events include speed climbing, tree topping, standing block chop, bucking

OREGON

saws, and women's log rolling. Most events are timed against a clock. Log rolling requires fancy footwork. A contestant must stay on top of a floating log without falling into the water. Racing up a tall, swaying tree, cutting off its top, then racing down again is exciting to do. It is also thrilling to watch. Many people see such thrills every year at the Timber Carnival.

Working conditions are safer for loggers today than in the past. Yet the job is still a dangerous one. The Albany Timber Carnival salutes the skilled workers of the lumber industry.

UNIT REVIEW

Word Work

Write the sentences below on a sheet of paper. Fill in the blanks with the correct words from the list.

tributary	gorge	erosion
manufacturing	lava	plateau
growing season	port	altitude

1. A deep passage through mountains is called a ____.
2. The time during which crops can be raised is the ____.
3. ____ is the wearing away of land by water or wind.
4. Hot liquid rock that comes out of a volcano is called ____.
5. A ____ is a place where ships can load or unload goods.
6. Making finished goods from raw materials is called ____.
7. ____ is the height of the land above the level of the sea.
8. A river or stream that flows into a larger body of water is called a ____.
9. A ____ is an area of flat land higher than the land around it.

Knowing the Facts

Write your answers on a sheet of paper.

1. Name and describe the location of two rivers that form a part of Oregon's boundaries.
2. How were the Cascade Mountains formed?
3. Explain how Oregon's mountains affect its climate.
4. Name three products made from Oregon timber.
5. How have many dry regions in Oregon been turned into good farmland?
6. Describe how salmon and boats can get past the dams that have been built on Oregon's rivers.
7. Name and explain how three industries in Oregon use the state's rivers as a resource.
8. What activities can tourists enjoy in Oregon?

Using What You Know

Choose one of the following activities to do. Follow the instructions given here.

1. Make a picture poster of the places you would like to visit in Oregon.
2. Imagine you have just arrived in Oregon. In what region would you choose to settle? Tell why.
3. Write a story describing a boat trip today down the Columbia River.
4. Make a map showing the landforms in Oregon.
5. Design a travel advertisement to attract more tourists to Oregon.
6. Make a map showing where different farm products are raised in Oregon.

Skills Practice

Use the map on page 37 to answer the questions below. Write your answers on a sheet of paper.

1. What two kinds of climate does Oregon have?
2. Name two states that have the same kinds of climate as Oregon.
3. Which is generally warmer all year long, a desert or a semiarid climate?

Use the following road map to answer the questions below.

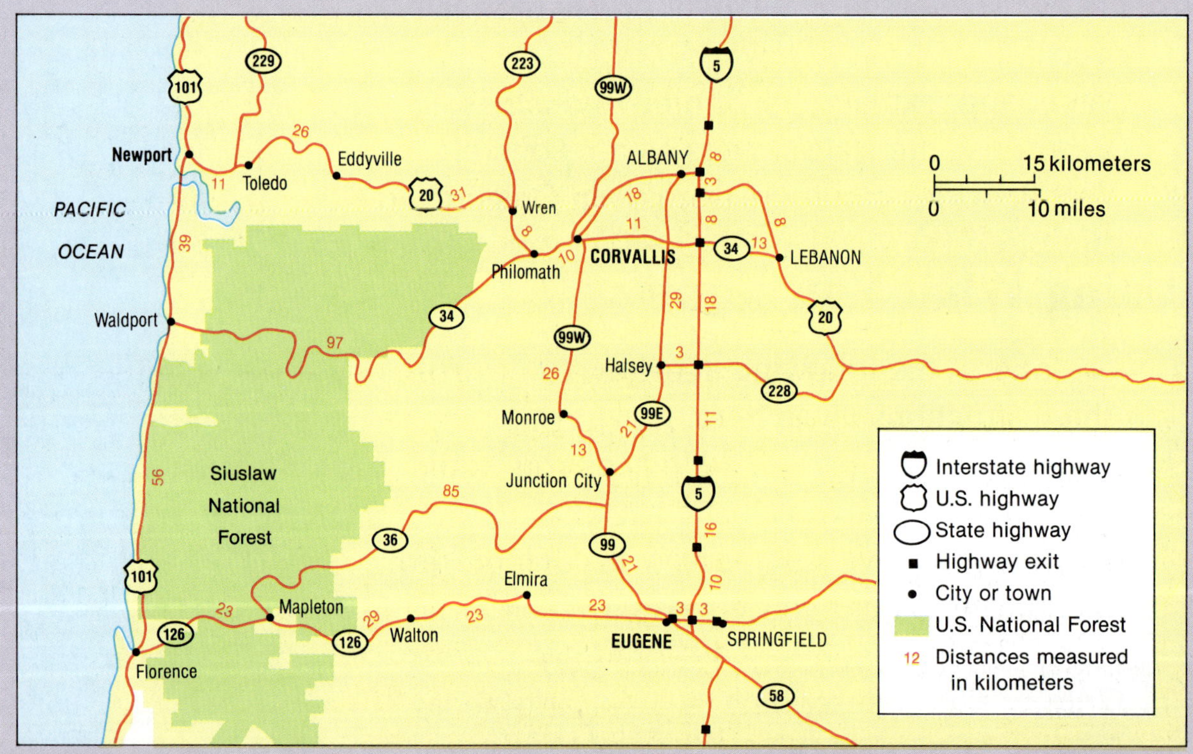

1. You are driving from Florence along Highway 101. How far is it to Newport?
2. Traveling along Route 99 W, how far is it from Corvallis to Junction City?
3. How far is it from Toledo to Albany along Highway 20?

Use the following pie graph to answer the questions below.

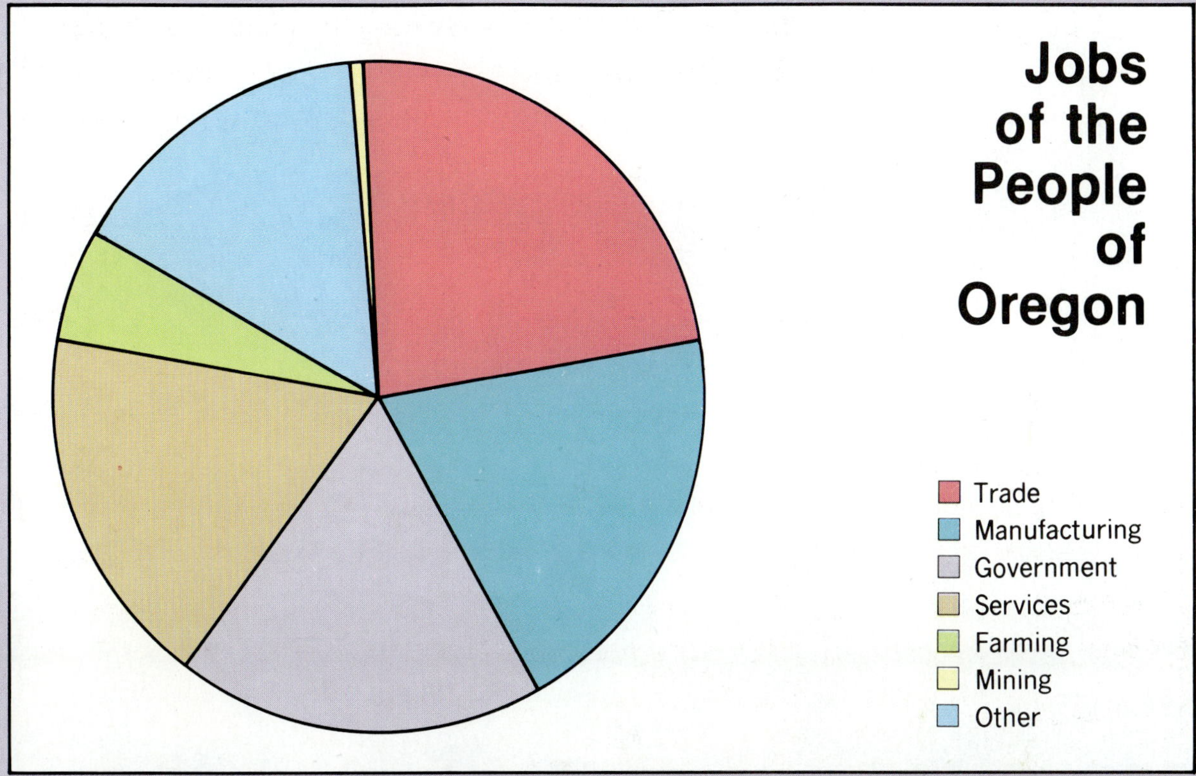

1. What does the whole pie graph stand for? What does each piece of the pie graph stand for?
2. Which job type employs the greatest number of people?
3. In which job area are there fewer people working than are working in agriculture?

Use the map on page 62 to answer the questions below.

1. Name three ports in Oregon.
2. In what parts of the state is mining an important economic activity?
3. What economic activities are people involved in around Eugene, Oregon?

UNIT 2 Oregon's Early History

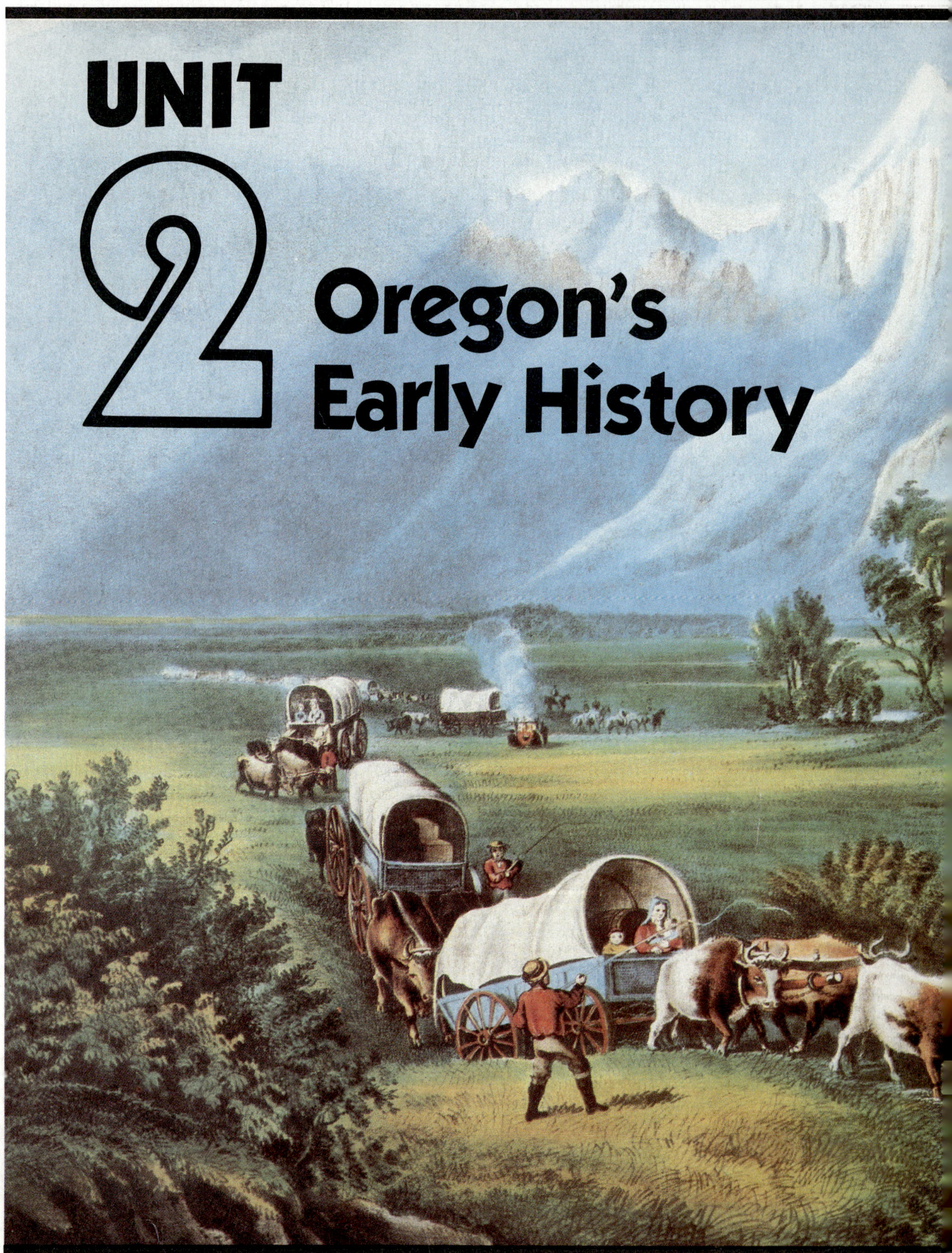

CHAPTER 3 Early Indians in Oregon

Northwest Coast Indians

Many scientists believe that the first people in Oregon were the Indians. The early Indians lived in different land regions. They used the natural resources in whichever region they lived. The resources of each region were different. So the Indians in each region had different ways of life.

At the end of this chapter, you should be able to:

- ○ Describe how scientists study the past.
- ○ Locate and describe the regions where the Coastal and Plateau Indians lived.
- ○ Describe how the Indians used the resources of the region in which they lived.

1 Records of the Past

When Christopher Columbus landed in America in 1492, he found people already living there. Columbus did not know he was in America. He thought he was in the East Indies. So he named the people he met "Indians." Many people still use the name Indians in talking about the first people in America.

Bone carvings found in Oregon

Indians Come to America

Most scientists believe that the first Indians came to North America from Asia sometime between 12,000 and 25,000 years ago. It is thought that they may have walked across a dry piece of land that connected Asia and Alaska. Today, this piece of land is covered by the Bering Strait. Slowly, over many years, the Indians moved south. In time, they settled in most parts of North and South America.

Indian Remains

The early Indians did not leave any written records of how they lived. Over the years, scientists have looked for and found things that were made and used by earlier people. Things that have been left by earlier people are called **artifacts.** Tools, weapons, and artwork may be artifacts. Scientists study the artifacts to get clues about where, when, and how early groups like the Indians lived. Scientists who study artifacts are called **archeologists** (ark-ee-**ahl**-o-jists). An important clue to where the first Indians came from was found near the Columbia River.

artifact
a weapon, tool, or other article made and used by people who lived long ago

archeologist
a scientist who studies artifacts

Rock pictures found on cliffs near the Columbia River

Rock Pictures

Indians who lived near the Columbia River carved pictures in the rocky cliffs. Rock pictures have been found all over the world. The ones that were found near the Columbia River were very much like ones that had been found in northern Asia. This led scientists to believe that the first Indians may have come to North America from Asia.

The rock pictures showed what the Indians did, as well as the things around them. These pictures were important clues as to how early Indians in this region lived.

Written and Spoken Records

journal
a written record of daily activities, like a diary

Many European explorers who came to America kept daily written records of what they did and saw. This kind of a written record is called a **journal.** Early journals tell us much about how early Indians lived.

The Indians told many stories that give us clues about their history and way of life. By studying these stories, we can get an idea of how the Indians lived and what was important to them.

Section Review

Write your answers on a sheet of paper.

1. From where do scientists think the first Indians came? Why do they think this?

2. Suppose you were digging in the ground and found an arrowhead in the middle of a group of small bones. What would you think about what you had found?

2 Coastal Indians

The Indians who lived in Oregon divided into two main **cultures,** the Coastal Indians and the Plateau Indians. A culture is a way of life shared by a group of people who have the same customs, beliefs, past, and often language. Look at the map on this page to find the names of Oregon Indian tribes that lived in each cultural region.

culture
a way of life shared by a group of people who have the same customs, beliefs, past, and often language

The Coastal Indians lived along the northern part of the Pacific coast. They lived on a narrow strip of land about 160 kilometers (100 miles) wide. In some places it was much narrower. The Coastal Indians lived in a rich **environment.** The land, climate, and living things of the region made it a good place for people to live.

environment
the land, climate, and living things surrounding a group of people

Finding Food

The Coastal Indians had no problem getting enough to eat. They lived in a region that was rich in food resources. Huge amounts of fish were easily caught. The Indians used hooks, nets, traps, and spears to catch many kinds of fish. Salmon were the most important fish to the Coastal Indians. In fact, they called all kinds of fish "salmon."

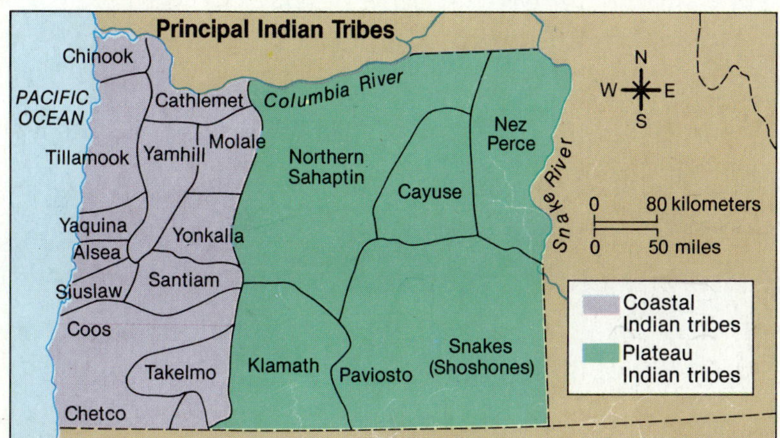

Large numbers of fish passed through the ocean waters only a few times a year. Most of the fish caught during a fish "run" were saved for times when fresh fish could not be easily caught. The Coastal Indians kept the fish from spoiling by smoking or drying them. Smoked and dried fish were an important part of the Coastal Indian diet.

A special kind of fish called a candlefish was also dried. This fish is rich in oil. When dried and threaded with a wick, it burns like a candle.

The Coastal Indians also hunted animals and gathered wild plants. They caught sea lions, whales, and porpoises (**por**-puh-sez) in the ocean. Land animals, such as deer and elk, added to the meat supply. Nuts, roots, and berries could be found all year round. The camas root was an important part of the Coastal Indian diet.

Many Uses for Cedar

Like their food, the clothing worn by Coastal Indians came from their surroundings. For most of the year, the Indians wore clothing made from the soft inner bark of cedar trees. The bark was woven into rain capes, umbrella-like hats, and skirts. In the very coldest weather, the Indians wore animal skins.

Most Coastal Indian homes were also made out of cedar. Their houses, called plank houses, were about 30 meters (100 feet) long. Usually 10 to 12 families lived in each plank house. Hanging mats or wooden chests were used to separate one family from another. Small fires were used for cooking and heating. There were no windows in the plank houses. The smoke from the fires escaped through holes in the roof.

Drawing of a Coastal Indian home

This picture of a Coastal Indian woman and a canoe was taken near Newport, Oregon, around the year 1900.

The Coastal Indians also used cedar to make boxes. They steamed and bent the wood to make the sides. The edges were tied together with roots. The boxes were often used to store dried fish.

Boats were made out of the cedar trees. The Indians used these boats for fishing or hunting sea animals. They also used them to travel up the Columbia River to trade with Indians who lived further east. The Coastal Indians seldom went into deep ocean waters because everything they needed was close to the shore.

Life Among the Coastal Indians

Like other American Indian groups, Coastal Indian men and women did different kinds of work. The men did the fishing and hunting. They built houses, boats, and boxes. Many men carved beautiful pieces of art out of wood. Women gathered roots, nuts, and berries. The women also dried or smoked the fish and made clothes, baskets, and mats. The older women were in charge of giving directions to the younger women.

This painting shows the flattened forehead of a Coastal Indian woman and her baby in a cradleboard.

Coastal Indian children received special care. Babies spent much of their first year of life strapped to their mothers' backs. They were carried in cradleboards. These were hollowed-out logs that were filled with small pieces of bark. Pads were placed under a baby's knees, neck, and across its forehead. The forehead pad was to make sure that the child grew up with a flat forehead that rose to a peak at the top of the head. Among the Coastal Indians, a wide forehead and pointed head were marks of importance.

Young children who were able to walk stayed in the village. There they were cared for by older family members. Young boys were taught what was considered men's work, and young girls learned what was thought of as women's work.

There was often more than one leader to a village. There might be a war leader, a hunting leader, and a fishing leader. The Coastal Indians used the word "leader" for anyone they thought of as important. Anyone who was the best at something might be called a leader.

Section Review

Write your answers on a sheet of paper.

1. Where did the Coastal Indians live? Describe the region in which they lived.

2. Name four ways the Coastal Indians used cedar trees.

3. What work was done by Coastal Indian men? by Coastal Indian women?

4. Why do you think the Coastal Indians never practiced farming?

3 Plateau Indians

Where people live influences the way in which they live. As you have read, the Coastal Indians lived in a rich environment. They had no problem finding food close to where they lived. They used the trees that covered much of the land to build their houses and boats. They also used the trees to make some of their clothing and many other useful things. The Coastal Indians' way of life was closely tied to the ready supply of natural resources found in the region in which they lived.

The Plateau Indians lived in a very different environment. They lived east of the Cascade Mountains on the Columbia Plateau. As you have read, this region gets much less rain than regions west of the Cascades. During the summer, daytime temperatures on the plateau are hot. The winters are cold. There are few forests in this region and, of course, there are no ocean waters. Like the Coastal Indians, the Plateau Indians were influenced by their environment.

An Umatilla Indian village on the Columbia Plateau

Following the Food

Food was not easy to find on the plateau. The Indians had to move from place to place looking for food. Every year, they moved in the same circle. They could not live in just one village.

Women were in charge of gathering roots, berries, seeds, and wild plants. These foods were an important part of the Plateau Indian diet.

At certain times of the year, the Indians moved to places where they could get fish or meat. Once a year, Plateau Indians would gather at Celilo (seh-**lie**-lo) Falls on the Columbia River to catch salmon and to trade. The men caught the salmon using nets and spears. Women smoked the fish so it could be eaten at a later time. During the salmon run, Coastal Indians would come up the Columbia River to trade. The Plateau Indians traded for shells and fish oil. During another part of the year, the Plateau Indians camped in the mountains. There the men hunted for deer, mountain sheep, and other animals to add to the meat supply.

An Indian woman drying meat on poles

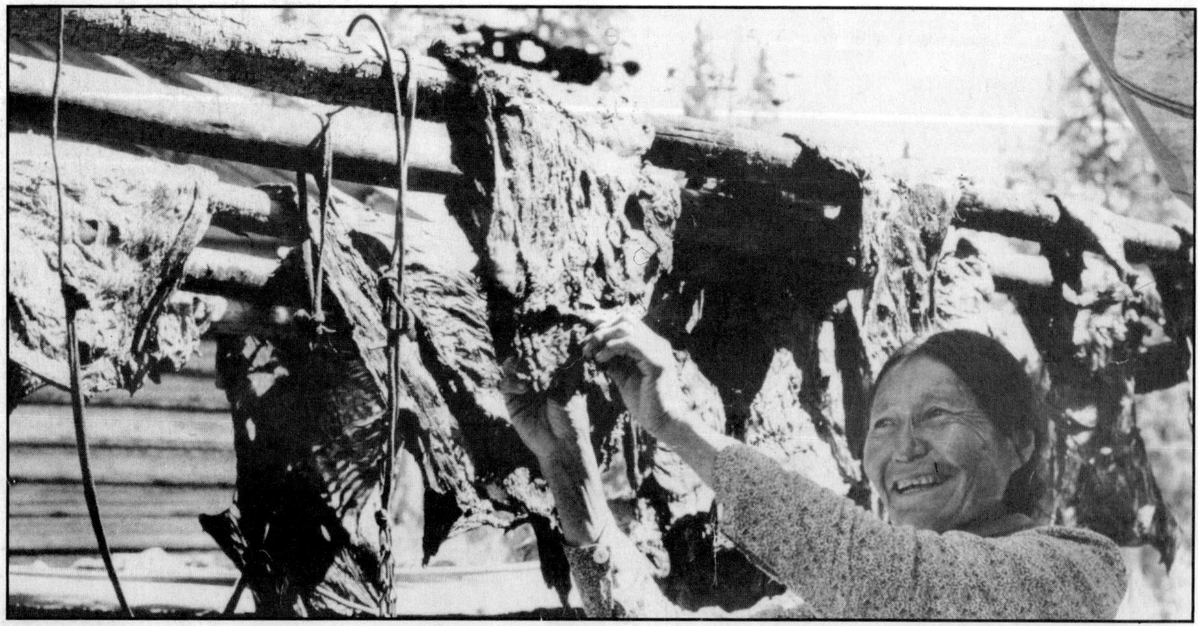

The Coming of Horses

Horses as we know them did not live in North America in early times. The first horses were brought to North America by Spanish explorers around the year 1500. The first horses reached the Plateau Indians in Oregon around 1740. Horses brought great changes to the Plateau Indians' way of life. By riding horses, the Indians could travel farther and faster.

This tepee lining shows the spotted Appaloosa horses raised by the Nez Perce Indians.

By 1750, many Plateau Indians in Oregon were going east to the Great Plains each year. They went to hunt buffalo and to trade with the people who lived there. They traded for eagle feather headbands and war clubs. New ideas and trade goods from the Plains Indians became part of the Plateau Indian culture.

The Plateau Indians also raised and traded horses. The Nez Perce (**nezz purss**) Indians raised spotted horses, now known as Appaloosas (ap-uh-**loos**-uhs). These horses were known for their great speed. They could also run for a long time without getting too tired. The Cayuse (**kie**-yoos) Indians were horse traders. The early Oregon settlers used the name "Cayuse" as another word for horse.

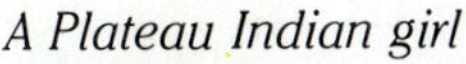

A Plateau Indian girl

Clothing and Shelter

The Plateau people had to wear warm clothing in the winter because of the cold weather. Men and women wore animal skins and furs. Snowshoes helped them move over deep snowdrifts. In the summer, they wore fewer clothes. Plateau Indian women wore basket hats, which they made from grass and plant fibers. Porcupine (por-**kya**-pine) quills, shells, and animal teeth were used to decorate clothing and make necklaces.

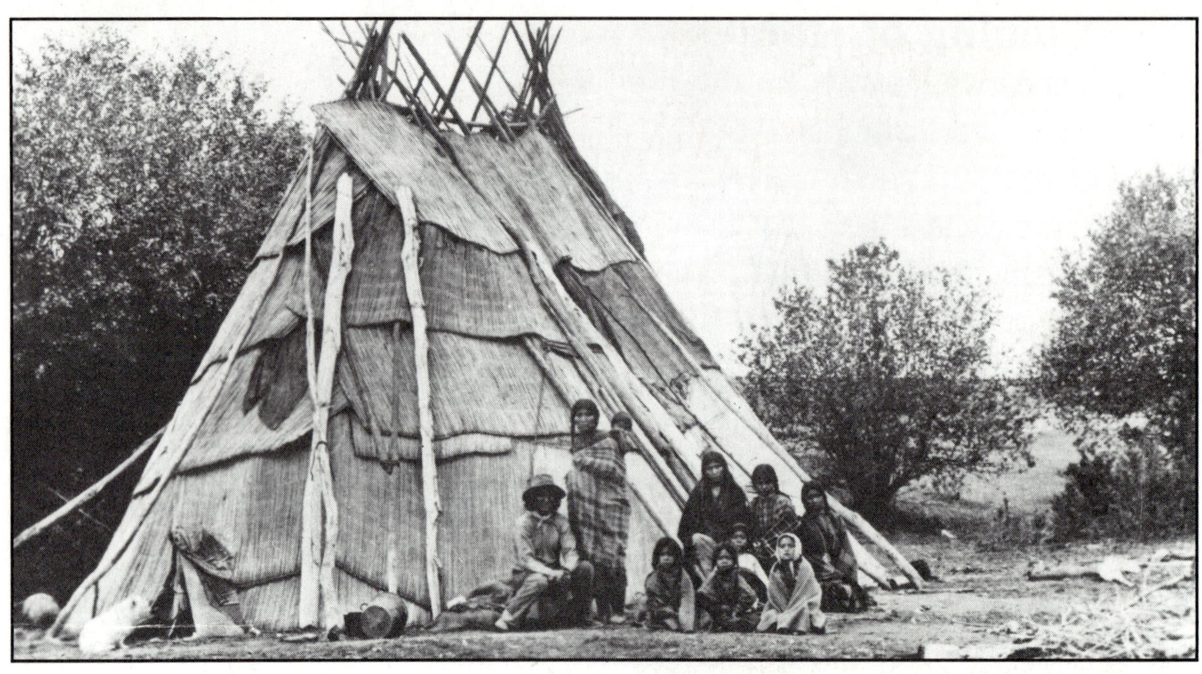

Grass-mat Plateau Indian home

Early Plateau Indians lived in grass mat homes. These were little more than long sticks covered with grass mats or brush. The Plateau people learned about tepees from the Plains Indians. Both tepees and grass-mat homes could be moved from place to place. This was important to the Plateau people because they never stayed in one place for very long.

Section Review

Write your answers on a sheet of paper.

1. Where did the Plateau Indians live? Describe the environment in which they lived.

2. Why did the Plateau Indians move from place to place?

3. How did Plateau Indian life change with the coming of horses?

4. Why do you think horses were more important to the Plateau Indians than they were to the Coastal Indians?

FAMOUS OREGONIANS

CHIEF JOSEPH

Chief Joseph was the leader of the Nez Perce Indian tribe, which lived in the Wallowa Valley of Oregon. Joseph was a wise chief who believed in and valued peace. His tribe was friendly toward all people.

As more settlers moved west, the government wanted to open the valley to farmers and miners. In 1876, the government ordered the Nez Perce Indians to move to Idaho.

The Nez Perce resisted. Chief Joseph knew that his tribe would never be able to defeat the United States Army. Rather than continue to fight, Chief Joseph decided to lead his people to safety in Canada.

The U.S. Army chased after the Nez Perce. But Chief Joseph was a skilled leader and managed to outrun the soldiers. With only 200 warriors, he moved over 650 men, women, and children 1600 kilometers (1,000 miles) in four months.

But only one day's march from the border, soldiers surrounded Chief Joseph's weary people. With a sad heart, he gave up to General Miles and swore "to fight no more forever." Chief Joseph and his people were sent to live on land in what is now Oklahoma. He is remembered by Indians and whites alike [illegible] one of the bravest and brightest Indian leaders in American history.

CHAPTER 4 Exploration and the Fur Trade

This painting shows Lewis and Clark meeting the Chinook Indians in Oregon.

It was only about 400 years ago that the first Europeans sailed toward the Pacific Northwest. In this chapter, you will read about what these early Europeans did and did not find in the Northwest. You will also read about something that they were surprised to find—a rich supply of furs to trade in other parts of the world.

At the end of this chapter, you should be able to:

○ Describe the Northwest Passage and explain its importance.

○ Identify Europeans and Americans who explored the Pacific Northwest.

● Read an altitude diagram.

○ Explain American and European involvement in the fur trade.

1 Early European Explorers

A person who goes to faraway places in search of something is called an **explorer.** The first European explorers reached the coast of the Pacific Northwest in 1542. At first, ships from Spain, Russia, and later, England explored only the waters along the coast. Most of these explorers were looking for the **Northwest Passage**—a water route through North America to Asia. In Asia, European traders could buy spices, silks, and other goods that were not available in Europe.

explorer
a person who goes to faraway places in search of something

Northwest Passage
an imaginary water passage that early explorers believed would lead through North America to Asia

The Northwest Passage

The green arrows on the map below show the route that Europeans had to take to reach Asia by sailing west. They had to sail around the tip of South America. The orange arrows show what Europeans hoped to find in the Pacific Northwest—a water route across North America. The explorer who found this water route would cut the journey from Europe to Asia in half!

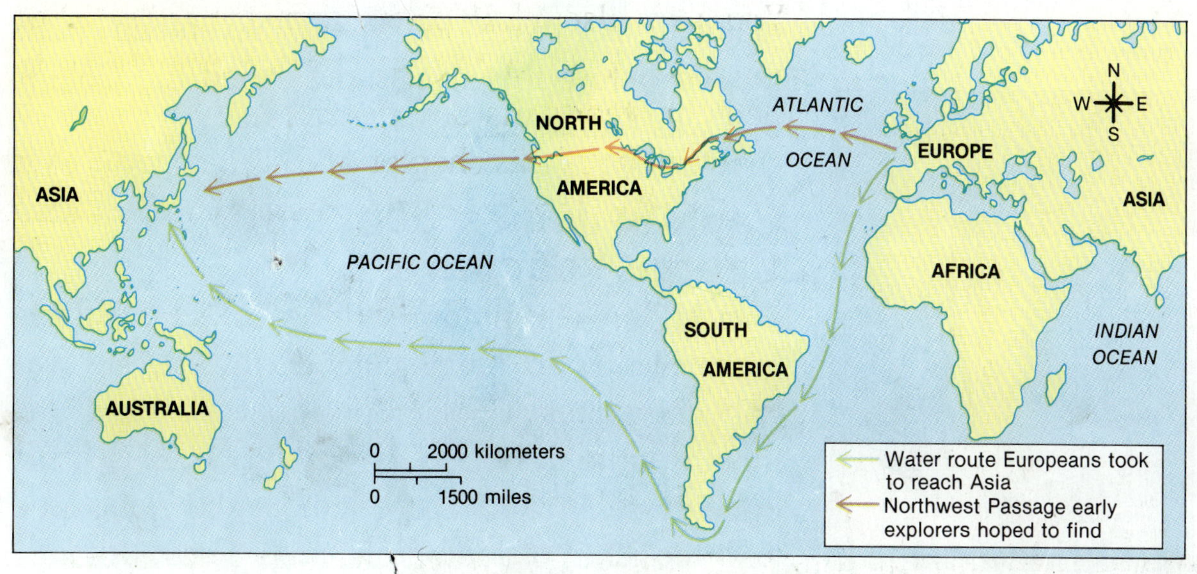

In 1579, Francis Drake sailed along the west coast of North America. He was one of England's most well-known explorers. Drake claimed the land for England and named it New Albion (**ahl**-bee-un). For almost 200 years, mapmakers used this name for the Pacific Northwest.

The first report of what might have been an entrance to the Northwest Passage came in 1592. An explorer named Juan de Fuca (**wahn day foo**-kuh) reported that he had found a wide opening along the northern coast. This opening was later named for him. You can find it on the map on page 99.

In 1775, a Spanish explorer named Bruno Heceta (hay-**zay**-tuh) discovered another large opening in the coast. The opening he found was south of the Strait of Juan de Fuca. Heceta sailed into a large body of water, which he named Assumption (ah-**sum**-shun) **Bay**. A bay is a body of water with land on at least two sides. The bay-water currents were very strong. This led Heceta to believe that he was at the mouth of a large river. Might this have been the Northwest Passage? He named the river the San Rogue and claimed the place for Spain. Seventeen years passed before this river, now called the Columbia, was found again.

bay
a body of water almost surrounded by land

Captain James Cook

Captain James Cook and George Vancouver

In 1778, Great Britain sent one of its most daring explorers to the Pacific Northwest. He was Captain James Cook. Cook never found the mouth of the Columbia River, and he missed the opening de Fuca had reported. He did claim land near the Strait of Juan de Fuca for Great Britain.

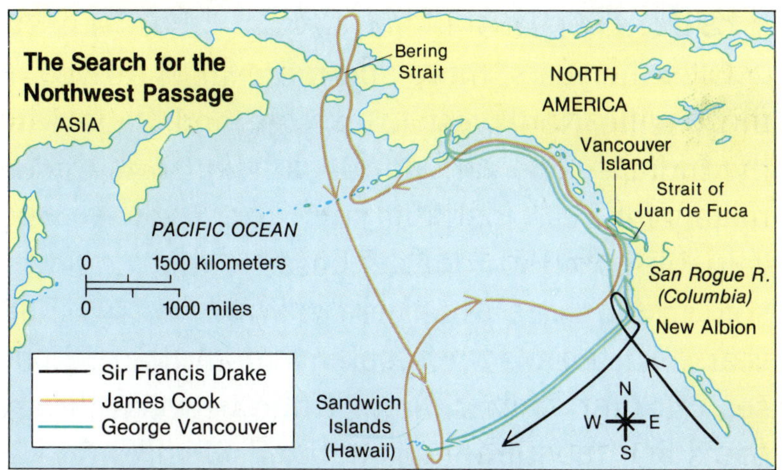

Great Britain sent George Vancouver (van-**koo**-ver) to strengthen its land claims in the Pacific Northwest. Vancouver sailed along the Pacific Northwest coast. He made maps of the coastline and described the beautiful land of Oregon in his journals. Vancouver was the first European to sail around the large island north of the Strait of Juan de Fuca. This island was named Vancouver Island in his honor.

Lieutenant William Broughton (**brow**-ton) commanded one of the ships that sailed with Vancouver. In 1792, he sailed about 160 kilometers (100 miles) up the Columbia River. He claimed the river for Great Britain. He also gave Mt. Hood its name.

Spanish Land Claims

Spanish explorers sailing along the coast of the Pacific Northwest also claimed the region for Spain. For many years, Spain and Great Britain could not agree on who would rule the new land. Finally they came to an agreement. Great Britain agreed to stop trading, fishing, or even sailing near Spanish settlements. Spain agreed that Britain could trade, fish, or settle lands not already occupied.

Trade Begins

Over the years, more and more ships arrived in the Pacific Northwest to explore and trade with the Indians. The early European explorers traded metals for fresh food and furs. The furs were very valuable to the Europeans because they could be sold in China at a high price. Within a few short years, Europeans were selling more than 12,000 sea otter furs a year there. Trade between the Indians and the Europeans in the Pacific Northwest got off to a good start. Each group had something the other wanted.

The Northwest Passage was not found as early explorers had hoped. Europeans still had to sail around North and South America to reach Asia. But in their search for the Northwest Passage, early European explorers did discover that the Pacific Northwest offered them a rich trade in furs.

Section Review

Write your answers on a sheet of paper.

1. What was the Northwest Passage? Why were Europeans looking for it?
2. What European explorer first discovered the Columbia River? For what country did he claim it?
3. Which explorers claimed land in the Pacific Northwest for Great Britain?
4. What source of trade did European explorers discover in the Pacific Northwest?
5. What do you think makes a person a good explorer?

Reading an Altitude Diagram

SOCIAL STUDIES SKILLS

The altitude of a place affects its climate. This diagram shows how climate changes on a mountain as altitude changes. The numbers on the left mark altitude in meters and feet. Each band shows different climate zones. You can see that the climate gets colder as the altitude gets higher. Plant life changes, too.

At the bottom of this mountain, you would be in a hot, desert climate where cacti and sagebrush grow. As you climb to a height of 1,500 meters (4,950 feet), the air would be colder. Grass would be growing on the ground. Above 2,500 meters (8,250 feet), you would find snow.

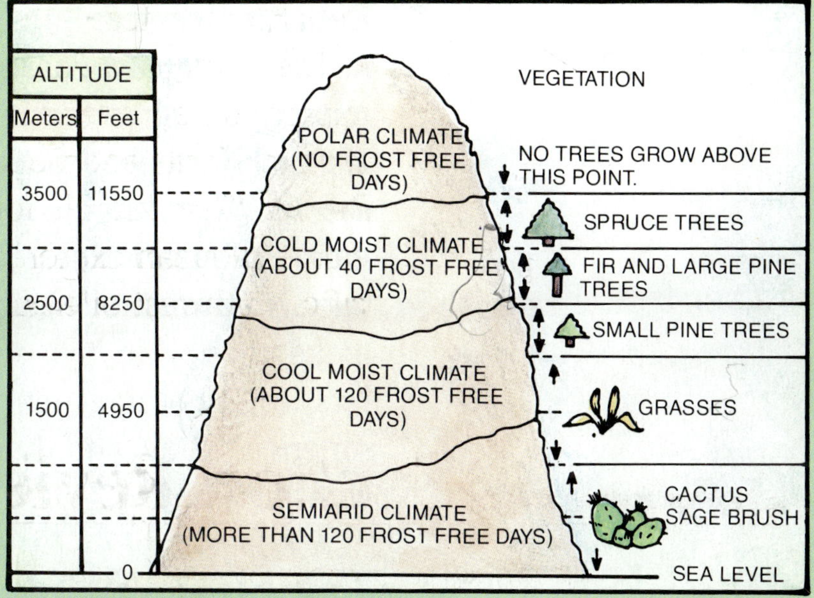

Practice Your Skills

1. How many climate zones does this mountain have?
2. In which two zones do trees grow on the mountain? In which zones are there no trees?
3. What is the climate like at 2,000 meters (6,600 feet)?

2 Robert Gray's Discovery

merchant
a person who buys and sells goods

Stories about the growing fur trade in the Pacific Northwest soon reached the new American cities of Boston and New York. By 1788, Boston **merchants** were prepared to send ships to the coast of Oregon. A merchant is a person who buys and sells goods. The merchants hired two sea captains, Robert Gray and John Kendrick, to find new sources of trade in furs.

Captain Robert Gray

Americans thought they could do better in the fur trade than the British. For one thing, the journey from the east coast to the west coast of North America was shorter than the trip from Great Britain to the Pacific Northwest. After getting the furs, they believed they could go to China and trade them for silks, spices, fine dishes, and tea to sell back in America. This meant that they could make money in two ways. They could sell the furs in China and then sell the Chinese goods in America. Gray and Kendrick sailed for Oregon with high hopes.

The First Voyage

Gray and Kendrick arrived along the southern coast of Oregon in August 1788. They began trading with the Indians near, what is today, the town of Tillamook. In return for metal goods like knives and axes, Gray and Kendrick received the sea otter skins they wanted to sell in China.

Moving north along the coast, they did not find as much trade as they had hoped. But they sailed for China with the furs they did have.

Unfortunately, by the time Gray and Kendrick arrived in China, many other fur traders had been there before them. They did not receive the high

Captain Robert Gray trading with Indians near the mouth of the Columbia River

prices they had expected for the furs. And on their way home, the tea they had traded the furs for was ruined by water. Although in some ways this first trip was a disappointment, in another way it was quite successful. Instead of returning to America the way he had come, Captain Gray sailed west from China all the way back to Boston. In doing this he became the first American to sail around the world.

The Second Voyage

By April 1792, Captain Gray was back in the Pacific Northwest on his second trip to find furs. This time he found the great river that people had been searching for ever since Bruno Heceta was said to have discovered it almost 17 years earlier. Was this the river that might finally prove to be the Northwest Passage?

Gray's ship, the Columbia

Powerful waves and a long sandbar made it hard to enter the river. But in May 1792, Gray was able to steer his ship, the *Columbia,* safely into the river. Gray's ship was soon surrounded by Indian canoes. The Indians had brought fresh fish and furs to trade.

Gray's second trip to the Pacific Northwest was important to the region and to the United States. Gray renamed the river Columbia, after his ship. He also helped to start trade between the United States and China. Finally, the United States used Gray's trip to make its claim to the Pacific Northwest.

Section Review

Write your answers on a sheet of paper.

1. Why did Americans think they could do better in the fur trade than the British?
2. What are two things Robert Gray was the first American to do?
3. How was Gray's second voyage important to the Pacific Northwest and the United States?
4. Why would the Northwest Passage be important to American traders?

3 The Lewis and Clark Expedition

In the early 1800's, Great Britain and the United States were the only countries trading in the Oregon Country. Britain had forced the Spanish out of the region. A real struggle for control of the Oregon Country now began between Great Britain and the United States.

The American President during this time was Thomas Jefferson. In 1803, the United States had bought the land between the Mississippi River and the Rocky Mountains from France. Jefferson wanted to learn more about this land called Louisiana (loo-eez-ee-**an**-na). He also wanted to find out, once and for all, if the Missouri (mih-**zoor**-ee) River connected with another river that went all the way to the West Coast. He thought that the other river might be the Columbia.

President Jefferson chose Meriwether Lewis and William Clark to lead the journey, or **expedition,** to Oregon. Both were experienced explorers. The President asked them to look for the Northwest Passage and draw maps of all the land and water features they saw along the way. They were also asked to keep careful records of the plant and animal life they found along the way. Even more important, Jefferson ordered Lewis and Clark to officially claim the lands of the Northwest for the United States.

expedition
a journey for a special purpose

To prepare for their journey, Lewis and Clark gathered explorers, soldiers, helpers, and supplies. They also collected all the scientific equipment they could find. By the spring of 1804, the Lewis and Clark expedition was ready to leave from St. Louis, Missouri.

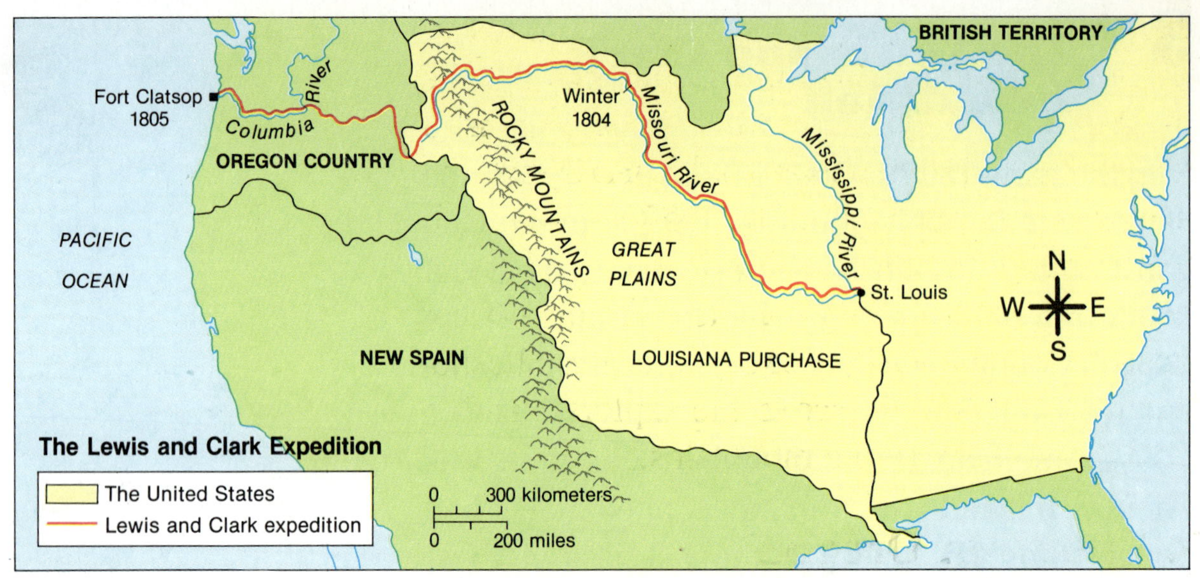

The Journey to Oregon

The Lewis and Clark expedition left St. Louis on May 14, 1804, by way of the Missouri River. Find St. Louis, Missouri, on the map on this page. The route the expedition followed is shown by a red line. Use the map scale to see how far the explorers had to go to reach the Pacific Ocean.

The journey was hard for everyone in the group. The weather was hot and humid all that summer. Mosquitoes and other bugs filled the air. It was a long and tiring trip.

The explorers spent the winter of 1804–1805 in a Mandan Indian village, in what is now North Dakota. There they were joined by a French-Canadian fur trapper and his Indian wife, Sacajawea (sack-uh-juh-**wee**-uh). Sacajawea was a Shoshone (shuh-**sho**-nee) Indian by birth. Lewis and Clark planned to go to the Shoshone country, but they could not speak the Shoshone language. They asked Sacajawea to go with them as a guide and to talk to the Indians for them.

In the spring of 1805, the Lewis and Clark expedition reached the Rocky Mountains. The explorers hoped to buy horses from the Shoshones to carry them across the mountains. But the Indians did not want any white people on their lands. Then the Shoshone leader heard that the explorers had a young Shoshone Indian woman with them. When he saw Sacajawea, he hugged her. She was his sister whom he had not seen for many years. Because of Sacajawea, the Shoshones agreed to sell horses to the explorers and to guide them through the mountains.

A Winter in Oregon

Finally, in the fall of 1805, the Lewis and Clark expedition reached the Pacific Ocean at the mouth of the Columbia River. They built Fort Clatsop (**klat**-sup) and settled in for the long winter on the Oregon coast.

This painting of the Lewis and Clark expedition shows Ben York, Clark's slave who was freed when the expedition was over, and Sacajawea, the Shoshone guide.

The winter was a cold and rainy one, and there was little good food to eat. But the members of the expedition were too busy to worry about it or complain. Lewis and Clark wrote in their journals as much as they could remember about what they had seen on the trip. Others worked to prepare for the journey back to St. Louis. When the long winter was over, it was time to leave.

Six months after leaving Fort Clatsop, Lewis and Clark reached St. Louis. There, they prepared a report for President Jefferson. The report was encouraging in many ways. Lewis and Clark told the President that the land in Oregon was not only rich in furs, but would make good farmland. They presented maps of the Northwest and suggested a trade route along the Columbia River. Although they had not found the Northwest Passage, they did open up the way for more trade and new settlers to come to Oregon. More important, their trip gave the United States a solid claim to the Oregon Country.

Section Review

Write your answers on a sheet of paper.

1. Why did President Jefferson send Lewis and Clark west?
2. What part did Sacajawea play in the expedition?
3. In what ways was the Lewis and Clark expedition important to the United States?
4. Why do you think it was important for Lewis and Clark to record what they saw along the way?

4 Americans and the Fur Trade

The first Americans to follow Lewis and Clark to Oregon were fur traders. They wanted to set up trading posts along the Columbia River. Great Britain had started a large fur-trading business in North America called the North West Company. This company had slowly pushed its way west from eastern Canada into the Pacific Northwest. Americans, however, wanted to keep the fur-trading business along the Columbia River for themselves.

John Jacob Astor

The richest fur merchant in the United States was John Jacob Astor. Astor wanted to be the first person to set up a fur-trading post on the Columbia River. First he formed the Pacific Fur Company. Then in 1810, he sent two expeditions to start a trading post at the mouth of the Columbia River. One group was to go by land. The other group was to go by water. Sending two expeditions turned out to be a wise plan because both groups ran into trouble.

John Jacob Astor

The Tonquin *crossing the bar to enter the Columbia River*

The Group that Came by Sea

Those who came by sea ran into trouble the minute they arrived at the mouth of the Columbia River. Eight men died when their ship, the *Tonquin,* tried to sail over the sandbar to enter the river. Several months later, the *Tonquin* was destroyed, and 27 men were killed by Indians while trading furs on Vancouver Island. Most of the group's trade goods were still on the ship when it was destroyed. In 1811, the few traders who had remained on the Columbia River built Fort Astoria on the river's south bank.

The Overland Group

The group that came by land was led by Astor's partner, Wilson Price Hunt. His group was made up of French Canadians, Scots, and Americans. The guide for the group was Pierre Dorion (pee-**air doh**-ree-uhn). Dorion brought along his Indian wife, Marie, and their two sons.

Hunt's group was not as well prepared as Lewis and Clark had been for the hard journey west. This proved to be a mistake. On the way to Oregon, three people died. The overland group finally reached Fort Astoria in February 1812.

Astoria

In July 1811, a small party of Astorians set out on their first trading expedition up the Columbia River. They were hoping to trade with the Indians for beaver skins. Beaver skins could be sold at a good price in Europe and the United States. The soft fur close to the skin was the most valuable part. It was used to make hats.

For almost two years, the Astorians made a success of the new Pacific Fur Company. But in 1812, the United States and Great Britain went to war. The Americans at Astoria were outnumbered by the British of the North West Company. Fearing that Astoria might be taken by force, the trading post was sold to the North West Company.

In the years that followed the War of 1812, the United States and Great Britain settled many old problems. In 1818, they reached an agreement that was important to Oregon. They decided that the lands west of the Rocky Mountains would be "free and open" to the citizens of both countries for a period of 10 years. This meant that people from both countries were free to live and trade in Oregon until 1828.

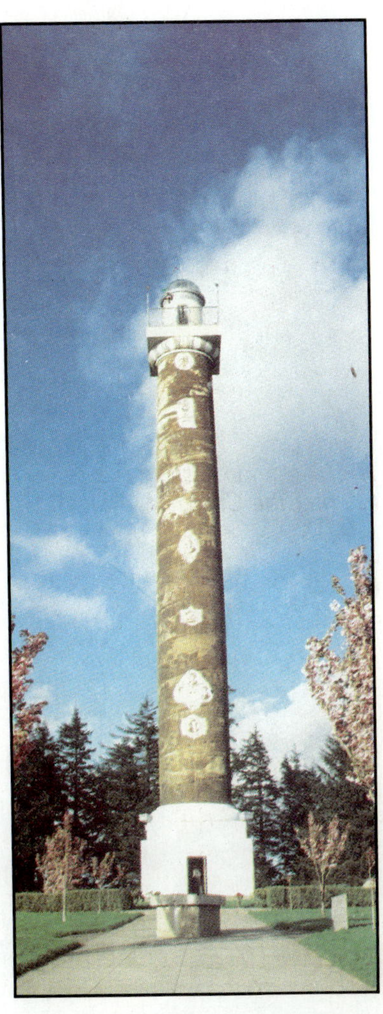

The Astor Column was erected in Astoria in 1926. It shows scenes of Astoria's early history.

Section Review

Write your answers on a sheet of paper.

1. Who was John Jacob Astor? What did he do?
2. Describe the trouble Astor's expeditions had on their way to setting up the trading post at Astoria.
3. Why was it important for fur traders to make friends with the Indians?

FAMOUS OREGONIANS

MARIE DORION

In March of 1811, Marie Dorion, her husband, and two young sons were asked to join the Astor fur-trading party going to Oregon. She was a young Iowan Indian and spoke many Indian languages.

The trading party reached Oregon in February 1812. A year and a half later, the party went out in search of furs. They built a cabin at the point where the Boise and Snake rivers meet.

In January 1814, the party was attacked by a group of Indians. Marie Dorion and her children were the only ones to escape alive. She gathered up her sons and some supplies and headed for the Columbia River.

After traveling 193 kilometers (120 miles), the three became trapped by a snowstorm. Marie Dorion built a small cave from branches and snow. Here the family lived for 53 days until their food ran out.

Forced to leave the cave, they were nearly blinded by the bright sunlight. They were lost for three days before finally reaching a friendly Walla Walla Indian camp. In time, they settled in the Willamette Valley. Marie Dorion's exciting story was well known in her lifetime and is retold in many books today.

5 British Fur Companies

Even though Great Britain and the United States had agreed to share the Oregon Country, two British fur-trading companies almost completely controlled the region from 1818 to 1828. You have read about the North West Company. This was the group that took over John Jacob Astor's trading post at Astoria. For years the North West Company had worked hard but had failed to take power away from another British fur-trading group in eastern Canada. This was the Hudson's Bay Company. In 1821, the North West Company became a part of the Hudson's Bay Company. Most of the workers of the old North West Company stayed to work for the Hudson's Bay Company. The Hudson's Bay Company moved into the Pacific Northwest. For many years, it was the only fur-trading company in the Oregon Country. Every other group that tried to move in was forced out almost as soon as it started business.

The coat of arms of the Hudson's Bay Company

Dr. John McLoughlin

McLoughlin and the Hudson's Bay Company

The leader of the Hudson's Bay Company in the Oregon Country was Dr. John McLoughlin (meh-**klof**-luhn). McLoughlin had studied medicine in eastern Canada before becoming a partner in the North West Company in 1814. When the North West Company became part of the Hudson's Bay Company, McLoughlin stayed on. In 1824, he was sent to the Oregon Country to head the Columbia River Department of the Hudson's Bay Company.

McLoughlin moved the center of the company's business in Oregon to Fort Vancouver. Fort Vancouver was built on the north bank of the Columbia River about 160 kilometers (100 miles) from the river's mouth. McLoughlin sent his traders out in all directions from Fort Vancouver. They paddled up and down the Columbia River and its many tributaries looking for furs. Trading posts were set up as far north as British Columbia in Canada.

Trading and Trapping

The Hudson's Bay Company carefully planned where it would set up each of its trading posts. Each post had to be put in a place where many fur-bearing animals were. The company traded for many kinds of furs. It wanted more than just sea otter skins. It wanted furs from beaver, mink, bear, and other animals. Each trading post also had to be near places where many Indians lived. The Indians trapped the animals and brought the furs to the company trading posts. In return, they received blankets, fishhooks, needles, thread, mirrors, and knives.

At times, company traders would go into the woods to trap the animals themselves. These trapping expeditions were often dangerous. The Indians wanted to be the only ones to bring in the furs. Without furs, the Indians would have nothing to trade at the trading posts. Company trappers had to be very careful. Those who were not careful were often killed by Indians.

This painting is called The Trading Room at a Hudson's Bay Post.

Fort Vancouver and the surrounding countryside

Summer at Fort Vancouver

Summer was the busiest time of year at Fort Vancouver. Ships carrying trade goods from Great Britain arrived in the late spring. The goods had to be taken off the ships, checked, and sent to the trading posts. Clerks worked from morning to midnight adding and subtracting numbers in their account books. Carpenters were kept busy repairing ships. In late summer, other workers packed the furs and loaded them on ships. In the fall, the ships left the Columbia River for their return trip to England or other ports.

The Influence of the Hudson's Bay Company

As time passed, nearly everyone in the Oregon Country fell under the influence of the Hudson's Bay Company. McLoughlin hired many Indians as trappers and guides. He also set up schools for young Indians. To the Indians, whom he ruled with a strong hand, McLoughlin was a "good chief." He was able to keep peace with most of the Indians in the Oregon Country for many years.

Three of Oregon's most important industries—lumbering, farming, and food processing—were started by John McLoughlin and the Hudson's Bay Company. In 1827, McLoughlin hired a group of Kanakas (keh-**nak**-ehs) to cut lumber for the company. The Kanakas were from Hawaii. A year later, a small sawmill was built near Fort Vancouver. Hawaii received the first lumber cut in the Pacific Northwest.

McLoughlin allowed workers who no longer wanted to work in the fur-trading business to set up farms. He loaned the new farmers animals and gave them seed. All the animals raised had to be returned to the company. And the crops that were harvested had to be sold through the company.

McLoughlin also started a small food-processing business. Fish were packed and then shipped to Alaska and Hawaii.

Under McLoughlin's direction, the Hudson's Bay Company in Oregon grew stronger and richer every year.

Section Review

Write your answers on a sheet of paper.

1. How did the Hudson's Bay Company get furs?
2. What three important industries in Oregon were started by John McLoughlin and the Hudson's Bay Company? Describe how each one was started.
3. How do you think Americans felt about the growing influence of the Hudson's Bay Company in the Oregon Country? What could they do about it?

CHAPTER 5 American Settlement

The year is 1843. A wagon train is ready to leave Independence, Missouri. The wagon master yells, "Wagons roll!" The people are excited and happy. After months of getting ready, they are at last on their way to Oregon!

At the end of this chapter, you should be able to:

○ Describe the people who dreamed of starting American settlements in Oregon.

○ Describe how missionaries and pioneers helped settle Oregon.

● Use a grid to find places on a map.

○ Explain how the gold rush affected Oregon.

1 Dreams of Settlement

In 1827, Great Britain and the United States agreed to share the Oregon Country for an unlimited period of time. At this time, there were only a few hundred people living in Oregon who were not Indians. Most of them were French-Canadian or English fur traders.

As you have read, there was also a small group of Hawaiian workers in the Oregon Country. These people were called Kanakas or Owyhees (oh-**why**-eez). The Kanakas had come to Oregon as deckhands on ships. Not only were they good boat handlers, they were also among the best hunters in the world. This made them important helpers in the fur trade. The Owyhee River in southeastern Oregon was named in honor of two Kanakas who were killed nearby.

Fur trader

In later years, many people moving west stopped to rest at Fort Hall, which Wyeth had built on the Snake River.

Within two years, Wyeth returned to the Oregon Country. He set up two trading posts. For awhile it looked as though he might even succeed in setting up a large settlement. But the Hudson's Bay Company was too strong for Wyeth to fight for long. Once again he was forced to leave Oregon and return to Massachusetts.

Yet Wyeth had not really failed. Eight or nine of Wyeth's group stayed in Oregon. They were among the first American settlers in the Oregon Country. Within a few years, thousands of Americans would make their way west to Oregon.

Section Review

Write your answers on a sheet of paper.

1. Why did many Americans want American settlers to move to the Oregon Country in 1827?

2. What part did Nathaniel Wyeth play in the American settlement of the Oregon Country?

3. How did the arrival of non-Indian people to the Pacific Northwest help and hurt the Indians who lived there?

2 Missions and Missionaries

Some of the first American settlers in the Oregon Country were **missionaries.** Missionaries are people who teach their religion to others. The missionaries who went to Oregon wanted to teach the Indians about the Christian religion. They also wanted to help cure the Indians of sicknesses that had been brought by the explorers and traders. They planned to teach the Indians a new way of life that would make them more like other Americans. Jason and Daniel Lee were the first to put these ideas into practice.

missionary
a person who teaches his or her religion to others

Jason and Daniel Lee

Jason and Daniel Lee had come to Oregon with Nathaniel Wyeth in 1834. When Wyeth left Oregon, these two missionaries decided to stay. They built the first religious settlement, or **mission,** in Oregon. It was built on the southern edge of a French-Canadian settlement called French Prairie. French Prairie was about 16 kilometers (10 miles) north of where the city of Salem is today.

mission
a community set up by a religious order

Laying out an Indian mission

Jason Lee

Although there were few Indians living in the Willamette Valley in 1834, the Lees chose to build their mission in this region for two reasons. The Indians who lived in the Willamette Valley did not wander from place to place. This would make it easy for the missionaries to find them. Also, the Lees thought that large numbers of settlers would someday make their homes on the rich land of the Willamette Valley. They planned to serve the settlers by performing marriages and holding church services.

Before the mission building was even finished, the first Indian pupils arrived. In the next four years, Jason Lee taught 52 Indian children how to read, write, and do some arithmetic. He taught the Indians how to grow their own food. He also taught them about the Christian religion.

Lee wrote many letters to missionary groups and to churches in the East. He reported on the work he was doing in Oregon. Many groups sent money to Lee so he could continue his work. Soon more missionaries came to help.

With additional money and missionaries, Lee was able to set up more missions in Oregon. Daniel Lee and his family were sent to the mouth of the Columbia River to build a mission for the Clatsop Indians. A mission at The Dalles served the largest number of Indians.

In 1841, Jason Lee moved his mission to Chemekta (cheh-**meh**-keh-tah). This settlement was later renamed Salem. At this mission, the Indians and missionaries worked a large farm and raised herds of horses and cows. They also ran a small school. In time, they started a mission store. This mission was, at the time, the largest American settlement in the Oregon Country.

The Whitmans

Marcus and Narcissa (nahr-**sis**-uh) Whitman were among the first missionaries to go to Oregon. Like many other missionaries, the Whitmans taught the Indians a new way of life. This new way of life had a very different set of rights and wrongs. When Marcus Whitman forgave an Indian who slapped him in the face, the other Indians did not understand. In the Indian culture, such an insult could not be forgiven. When the Indians used things that belonged to the missionaries and did not return them, the missionaries did not understand. Unlike the Indians, whose things belonged to everyone in the tribe, Americans did not share their belongings as though they had no owner. The Indians and the missionaries worked well together in some ways, but in many ways they could not understand one another.

Dr. John McLoughlin welcomes the Whitmans and the Spaldings to Fort Vancouver in 1836. The women were the first white women to cross the Rocky Mountains.

The Catholic missionary Father DeSmet poses here with several of his Indian converts.

The Catholic Missionaries

The Lees and the Whitmans were Protestants (**praht**-is-tehnts). Protestants are one of a number of groups of people who believe in Christianity. Another group of Christians is the Catholics.

A number of Catholic missionaries from eastern Canada came to the Oregon Country after the Protestant missionaries. The Hudson's Bay Company brought Father Blanchet and Father Demers (deh-**marz**) to perform marriages for their French-Canadian workers. They and other Catholic missionaries traveled to the different trading posts and built some churches. They also kept records of the people living in the Oregon Country.

Missionaries and the Indians

The missionaries had come to Oregon partly to cure sickness among the Indians. Yet 15 years after the first missionaries had arrived, the Indians were suffering from even more sickness than before.

Some Indians began to think that missionaries like the Whitmans were trying to kill them. They thought the missionaries were giving them bad medicine. On November 29, 1847, Cayuse Indians killed the Whitmans and 12 of their helpers. This killing has been called the Whitman Massacre (**mass**-ah-ker).

Though the missionaries helped the Indians in some ways, they also caused problems. On the one hand, they taught the Indians how to farm and how to read and write. But on the other hand, the missionaries wrote a lot of letters to the people back home. These letters brought thousands more settlers to the Oregon Country. The settlers took more and more of the Indians' land. More Indians got sick and died from sicknesses that the settlers brought. Within a few short years, trouble arose between the settlers and the Indians in Oregon.

Section Review

Write your answers on a sheet of paper.

1. Why did the first missionaries go to Oregon?
2. How were Jason and Daniel Lee important to the early settlement of Oregon?
3. Why did the Cayuse Indians kill the Whitmans?
4. How did the missionaries in Oregon help the Indians? cause problems for the Indians?
5. Why did the missionaries and the Indians have such a hard time understanding each other?

NARCISSA WHITMAN

Narcissa Whitman was one of the first women to cross the Rocky Mountains. In the early 1800's, only a few explorers, trappers, and traders had made that journey. But Narcissa Whitman had a dream. She wanted to bring Christianity to the American Indians. In 1836, she and her husband, Marcus, left New York and headed west.

In those days, many areas had no roads. There were few stores in which to buy food and supplies. Many people did not want to cross the Rocky Mountains. But the Whitmans were not afraid of hardships. Finally they arrived in what is now the state of Washington. They set up a mission near present-day Walla Walla.

Narcissa and Marcus Whitman lived among the Cayuse Indians. Narcissa started a school where she taught English and singing. The Whitmans also planted crops and built a mill to grind corn and wheat.

More and more people were encouraged by the Whitmans' example. Settlers began moving into the Oregon Country. Many bought food and fixed their equipment at the mission. The Whitmans helped the Oregon Country become a settled area.

3 The Pioneers

Large numbers of American settlers soon followed the missionaries to the Oregon Country. These new settlers thought of the Oregon Country as a great, unsettled land, or **frontier.** They believed that this land was open to them, even though American Indians had settled there many years earlier. These new settlers were **pioneers** (pie-uh-**neerz**). This is the name given to people who try something first and open the way for others to follow.

frontier
land that is mostly unsettled

pioneer
a person who tries something first and opens the way for others to follow

The first pioneers went to Oregon for many reasons. Some were drawn by the promise of free land. Others were looking for adventure. A few went because they did not want the British to gain control of the region. But most of them went because they hoped that Oregon would offer a better life than the one they were leaving behind.

Pioneers on their way to Oregon

Frémont Marks the Path to Oregon

Before American settlers could settle in Oregon, a route west had to be found. It had to be a route over which wagons could pass. An American named John C. Frémont led a group to Oregon in 1842. Frémont's job was to map the mountains, valleys, and rivers that settlers would have to cross. Frémont's wife, Jesse Benton, helped him. She wrote reports about the locations of trading posts and conditions along the route. John Frémont's work shaped the path to Oregon. He became known as the "pathfinder" of the Far West. Find and trace the route he followed on the map on page 131. This route became the Oregon Trail. In the next few years, almost 10,000 settlers took this route to Oregon.

The Oregon Trail

Many people who took the Oregon Trail left from Independence, Missouri. That is where the first Oregon pioneers set up camp in the winter of 1843. They waited for spring. When the grass turned green, it was time to leave for Oregon. Today this journey might take you only a few hours by plane. But in those days, it would take the pioneers four to six months to reach Oregon.

This picture from the movie The Covered Wagon *shows people praying for a safe journey to Oregon.*

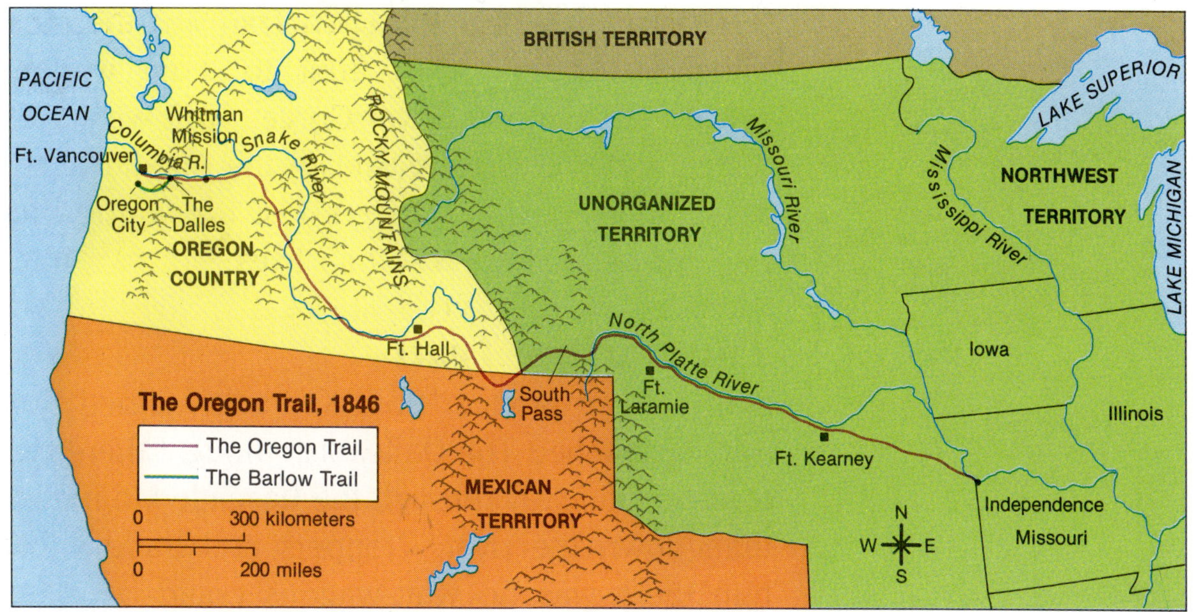

A Day on the Oregon Trail

At six o'clock in the morning, a bugle sounded to start the day's march. Each wagon had a place in line, chosen by drawing numbers. The wagon master was in charge. All the wagons had to be ready to roll when the wagon master gave the signal. If everything went well, the wagon train would travel 32 kilometers (20 miles) a day.

The journey was often hard and tiring. Crossing streams with wagons that weighed as much as 3,170 kilograms (7,000 pounds) slowed the day's march. Each wagon carried tools, fresh water, and enough food for the whole trip. The wagons were also loaded with clothes, books, and some furniture. No one looked forward to crossing a deep river. Each wagon had to be unloaded, floated across the river, and then loaded again on the other side. This often took all day!

Everyone had a special job to do. Children looked for wood or buffalo chips to burn for the night's fire. They also helped herd the cattle that families were taking to Oregon.

This drawing shows a pioneer family on a raft floating down the Columbia River to Fort Vancouver.

The last part of the Oregon Trail was the most dangerous. Rafts were built to carry wagons down the Columbia River Gorge. Swift waters often turned the wagons over in the middle of the river. Some of the pioneers lost everything they had carried. Others lost their lives.

The Barlow Trail

In 1845, a pioneer from Kentucky named Sam Barlow reached The Dalles. He thought there had to be a safer way through the Cascade Mountains than down the river. Trappers and traders told him there was no way wagons could be taken through the mountains by land. But Barlow and a party of 12 wagons set out to find a better route.

Barlow and his group wandered up and down valleys and through thick forests. Many of the paths they found were covered by fallen timber. As time passed, the group's food began to run low, and the cold winter weather started to set in. Some of the pioneers turned their wagons around and headed back to The Dalles.

But Barlow wouldn't give up. He and another member of the group, William Rector, went on foot to Oregon City to get supplies. Behind them the wagons struggled on. Day after day passed with no word from Barlow or Rector. The spirits of those who had stayed behind began to sink.

Finally, a shout was heard through the trees. Sam Barlow and William Rector had returned! They brought food and other supplies from Oregon City. All hopes of bringing the wagons through the mountains were forgotten. The group arrived on foot in Oregon City on December 25, 1845.

The wagons were finally brought over the trail in July and August of the next year. The path through the mountains was cleared and widened. Later, pioneers used this path, called the Barlow Road, to cross through the mountains to the Willamette Valley. This was a much safer route than the one down the Columbia River.

A New Life in a New Land

More than 9,000 American pioneers arrived in the Oregon Country between 1843 and 1849. Most of them came along the Oregon Trail. One such group was led by a black man, George Washington Bush. Bush's group became the first American group to settle north of the Columbia River.

In the Oregon Country, the pioneers found the good land and climate they had been looking for. Would they make a success of their new lives? Getting to Oregon was only half the battle. Now the pioneers had to build a whole new life in a new land.

This sign near Mt. Hood marks the site of the old Barlow Road.

Section Review

Write your answers on a sheet of paper.

1. Who were the Oregon pioneers? Why did they go to Oregon?
2. Who was John C. Frémont? How did John Frémont and Jesse Benton help the pioneers who went to Oregon?
3. What was life like for the pioneers on the Oregon Trail?
4. Who was Sam Barlow? How did he help the pioneers?
5. What problems do you think the pioneers faced once they arrived in Oregon?

SOCIAL STUDIES SKILLS

Using a Grid to Find Places on a Map

grid
a series of squares made by evenly-spaced lines used to locate places on a map

If you were planning a trip to a nature park, you might want to have a map like the one below. This map shows all the special places to see in the park.

To help you find things quickly, the map has a set of lines that go up and down and left and right. These lines, which form squares, make a **grid.** Each square in the grid has both a number and a letter name.

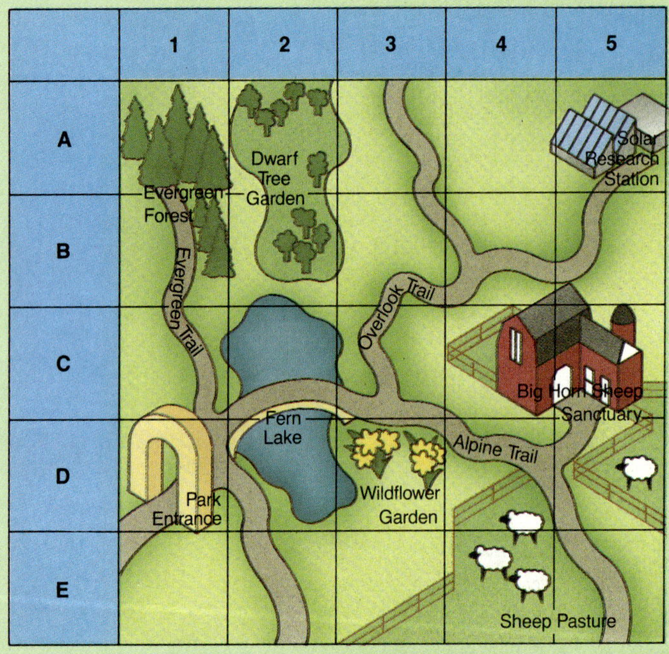

Suppose you wanted to locate the building in square A5. To do this, put your finger on the letter A. Now move your finger across the grid until it is below the number 5. You have located the Solar Research Station. It is in square A5.

Practice Your Skills

1. What is in square D1?
2. What is in square D3?
3. Across which two squares will you find the Dwarf Tree Garden?
4. In which two squares will you find the Big Horn Sheep Sanctuary?

4 Life in the Oregon Country

Most of the early pioneers were farmers. The first thing they had to do was find land to farm. Then each family had to build a house to live in. The homes they built looked very much like the ones they had left behind. Many of Oregon's earliest pioneers came from a region of the United States called the Midwest. The present-day states of Ohio, Indiana, Illinois, Michigan, Wisconsin, and part of Minnesota make up this region. Many settlers also came from Missouri. Early houses in Oregon were built in much the same style as those found in the Midwest and Missouri.

Americans and the Hudson's Bay Company

The end of the Oregon Trail for the earliest pioneers was Fort Vancouver. There the settlers were greeted by Dr. John McLoughlin. McLoughlin gave the settlers the things they would need to build homes and start farms.

The Robert Newell house in Champoeg, Oregon, was built in 1852.

While the Hudson's Bay Company did help the settlers with supplies, it did not help them start new businesses. The company leaders were afraid that American businesses would take trade away from the Hudson's Bay Company.

By the 1840's, there were almost no fur-bearing animals left in Oregon. Most of them had been killed for the fur trade. So the Hudson's Bay Company turned its attention to its other businesses like lumbering and farming. In 1829, the company had set up a sawmill at Oregon City. After the first wagon train arrived, the company sent many of its workers to farm the land north of the Columbia River. The company leaders hoped to make as much money as possible from these businesses.

Even with no help, some American settlers were able to start small businesses. At first, these businesses served only the settlers in the Oregon Country. But then something happened that helped them grow bigger and richer. This was the gold rush.

The Gold Rush

The Blue Bucket Mine was probably the first gold mine discovered west of the Rocky Mountains. In 1845, the Herren family arrived in Oregon. Along the trail, the children had picked up rocks, which they carried in blue buckets. After the family arrived in the Willamette Valley, it was discovered that the rocks were gold. The Herrens tried to find the place where their children had picked up the rocks, but they failed. Other pioneer gold seekers also tried and failed to find the lost Blue Bucket Mine. To this day, it has never been found.

Mining for gold in California during the gold rush

Then in 1848, gold was discovered in California. Suddenly more than 200,000 people rushed to the West Coast from the United States and other countries. By land and by sea they came, hoping to get rich.

The gold seekers had not come to build or to farm. They were too busy looking for gold to raise crops or cut lumber. But the American settlers in Oregon had planted much more food than they needed. They gladly sold the gold seekers the extra food they had raised. They also sold them lumber cut in Oregon.

Some of the newcomers were finding more than $1,000 worth of gold a day. With so many new gold seekers arriving every day, food and housing were hard to get. The gold seekers were willing to pay almost any price for food and housing. Lumber and food prices went sky-high. Many American settlers made a lot of money. The timber industry became Oregon's largest source of income.

The Growth of Towns

Before the gold rush, Oregon City was the only large town in the Oregon Country. During the gold rush, other towns in the Willamette Valley began to grow. Portland, Linnton, Linn City, Milwaukie (mil-**waw**-kee), and St. Helens were among those towns. Each of them wanted to become the center of trade in the Oregon Country. But in the end, Portland won out.

Portland began as a single log cabin in 1844. The cabin and the land around it were claimed by two people from New England. They were Asa Lovejoy and Francis Pettygrove. Lovejoy was from Massachusetts, so he wanted to name the new settlement Boston. But Pettygrove, who was from Maine, wanted to call it Portland. The two men flipped a penny to decide the name. Pettygrove won, so the new settlement was called Portland.

At first Portland grew very slowly. Then the gold rush came. Goods from farms and mills in the Willamette Valley had to be carried to California by ship. Portland's location made it the best port. Large sailing ships could only travel up the Willamette River as far as Portland. Ships could not reach towns farther up the river.

Jacksonville, Oregon, around 1880

Gold was discovered in southern Oregon in 1852. Mining towns sprang up almost overnight as large numbers of gold seekers rushed in to try their luck.

The diggings in and around the town of Jacksonville, Oregon, were by far the richest in the region. During the gold rush days, almost everyone in Jacksonville looked for gold. An old story tells the tale of the local jailer who went out looking for gold. While he was gone, two prisoners in the jail decided to escape. They started digging through the dirt floor of their cell. On the way, they found gold! When the jailer came back to release the two prisoners, he could not understand why they wanted to stay.

After the gold rush, many miners moved away. Many early mining towns became ghost towns. The buildings remained, but the people were gone.

The town of Jacksonville did not become a ghost town. Today, Jacksonville has been rebuilt to look much as it did during the height of the gold rush.

This is the penny that Lovejoy and Pettygrove flipped to name Portland. It can be seen in the Oregon Historical Society in Portland.

Section Review

Write your answers on a sheet of paper.

1. What kind of help did the pioneers get from the Hudson's Bay Company?
2. What kind of help would the Hudson's Bay Company *not* give to the pioneers? Why?
3. How did the gold rush help the pioneers?
4. If you were interested in finding the lost Blue Bucket Mine, what would you use as clues?

CHAPTER 6 Oregon Becomes a State

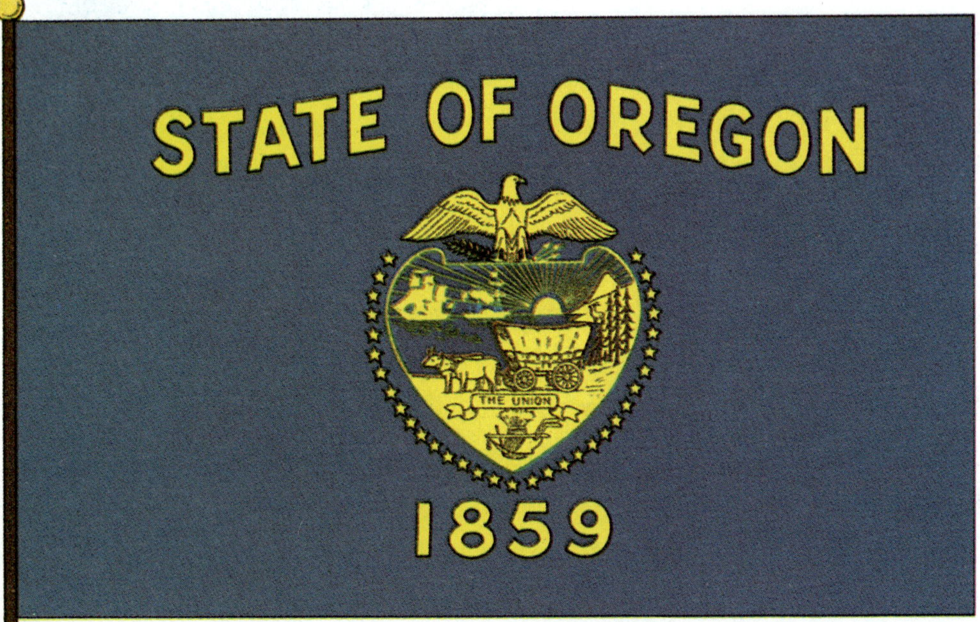

The state flag is the symbol of Oregon statehood. The words and symbols on the flag tell us something about Oregon and its past. You may already be able to explain some of the symbols. Others will become clearer as you read this chapter. It tells the story of how Oregon became a state.

At the end of this chapter, you should be able to:

○ Describe why and how Oregon's provisional government was set up.

● Use latitude and longitude to locate places on a globe.

○ Explain how Oregon became part of the United States.

○ Describe how Oregon became a state.

1 Developing a Government

By the early 1840's, Great Britain and the United States were still arguing about which of them would rule the Oregon Country. As long as no one country ruled the area, there could be no **government.** A government is a group of people who are chosen to make laws and lead a community, state, or country.

government
a group of people who are chosen to make laws and lead a community, state, or country

The Need for a Government

During the 1830's and 1840's, settlers had claimed land on which the Indians had lived and hunted for many years. The settlers thought of the land as their own. When the settlers did not allow the Indians to use it anymore, many Indians became angry. The settlers feared that the Indians would attack them. To protect them from Indian attacks, the settlers needed a government. They also wanted laws to protect their land claims.

Wolves were a problem too. They killed many farm animals. The settlers wanted a government so that hunters could be paid to kill the wolves.

Then in 1841, another problem arose. In that year, a man named Ewing (**yew**-ing) Young died. At the time of his death, Young owned a great deal of property. Young had no family to claim the land he left behind. The settlers could not just take his things for themselves. That could have led to trouble later on when other people without families to take over for them died. The settlers needed a government to decide what to do with Young's money and land and to make laws to cover cases like his.

Forming a Government

provisional government
a kind of government that is set up until a permanent government can be formed

As time passed, the settlers' need for a government grew greater. Some settlers wanted to form a **provisional** (pro-**vih**-shuh-nahl) **government.** A provisional government was one that would have served the settlers until Great Britain and the United States decided which of the two countries would rule the Oregon Country. They hoped that this would lead to Oregon's becoming part of the United States.

Twelve American settlers were chosen to write a report on how the government should be set up. It was decided that they would present their report to other settlers at a meeting to be held on May 2, 1843.

The meeting was held at the settlement of Champoeg (sham-**poo**-ee) on the Willamette River. By May 1, many settlers had gathered to hear the report and to decide if a provisional government should be set up.

Several years after the Champoeg Meeting, these Champoeg pioneers posed for this picture. The ribbon each pioneer is wearing shows the year he or she came to Oregon.

There were two important groups of settlers at this meeting. The first group was largely made up of French Canadians who had once worked as fur trappers for the Hudson's Bay Company but were now farming. Canada was ruled by the British at this time, so the French Canadians were British subjects. The leader of this group was Dr. John McLoughlin. The other group was made up of Americans who had settled in the Willamette Valley as farmers. Their leader was Joseph Meek.

Joseph Meek

During the 1830's, Joe Meek had been a fur trader in the mountains. When the fur trade died out, Joe came down from the mountains and settled in the Willamette Valley. He claimed land and built his house near what is now the city of Hillsboro.

Joseph Meek

Meek never took to farming. He did not like the chores that were a part of farm life. But Joe Meek loved to talk. He could often be found in a neighbor's kitchen eating and telling tales of his fur-trading days in the mountains. Joe liked to stretch the truth a bit, but that was what made his stories so funny. Joe's stories never hurt anyone, and his visits were always welcome. Many farmers considered a free meal a small price to pay for the fun times Joe always brought.

Joe Meek had a serious side too. He was one of the first settlers to talk about setting up a provisional government. At the Champoeg Meeting, he talked his way right into Oregon history.

The Champoeg Meeting

When the meeting began on the morning of May 2, 1843, Joe Meek was very tired. He had been up all night talking with American settlers about the committee's report. From what they had said, Meek was sure that they would vote for a provisional government.

As the voting began, something seemed wrong. Joe Meek thought he was hearing more people say "no" than "yes" to the idea of a provisional government. But neither he nor anyone else was quite sure. Someone thought of the idea of asking everyone voting "yes" to stand together and everybody voting "no" to stand together. Some of the voters did not understand and simply left. Joe Meek was worried. Was the idea of a provisional government going to die?

It was then that Joe Meek took charge. He shouted, "All in favor . . . just follow me!" And they did! There was no official count of the votes, but it was reported that 52 people voted "yes,"

The Champoeg Meeting, May 2, 1843

and 50 people voted "no." Joe Meek had won! The settlers in the Oregon Country would have a provisional government. Oregon was on its way to becoming part of the United States.

Section Review

Write your answers on a sheet of paper.

1. What two countries were struggling for control of the Oregon Country in the 1840's?
2. Why did the American settlers need a government?
3. Who was Joe Meek? What did he do for the settlers in the Oregon Country?
4. What happened at the meeting at Champoeg?
5. Why do you think the settlers wanted the Oregon Country to become a part of the United States?

SOCIAL STUDIES SKILLS

Using Latitude and Longitude

Suppose you were asked to tell where you live. One correct answer would be to name your state. But there is another way to tell someone where a particular place is located.

Mapmakers have created a way of using imaginary lines to help locate places on a map or globe. The equator is an imaginary line that runs east–west around the middle of the globe. Other imaginary east–west lines that are drawn north and south of the equator are called lines of **latitude,** or parallels. Lines of latitude are numbered from 0° to 90°. The lines located north of the equator are labeled **N** for north. The lines located south of the equator are labeled **S** for south. For example, a label for a line of latitude might be 90° N or 90° S.

latitude line
east–west line drawn parallel to the equator on a globe

Another set of imaginary lines is drawn north–south from pole to pole. These north–south lines are called lines of **longitude,** or meridians. The **prime meridian** is a special line of longitude. It is the starting point for measuring all other lines of longitude. Each line of longitude is numbered from 0° to 180°. Lines located west of the prime meridian are labeled **W** for west. Those east of the prime meridian are labeled **E** for east. For example, a label for a line of longitude might be 90° W or 90° E.

longitude line
line drawn from north to south from pole to pole on a globe

prime meridian
special longitude line that is the starting point for measuring all other lines of longitude

When both sets of lines are drawn across a globe or map, they form a pattern called a grid. This imaginary set of lines makes it easy to locate places on the earth.

Look at the largest globe on page 147. On what line of longitude is New Orleans located? Notice that Wausau, Wisconsin, is also located along this line. How do you tell them apart? You must name their latitudes and their longitudes. New Orleans is located at 30° N latitude and 90° W longitude, or 30° N, 90° W. Wausau is located at 45° N latitude and 90° W longitude, or 45° N, 90° W.

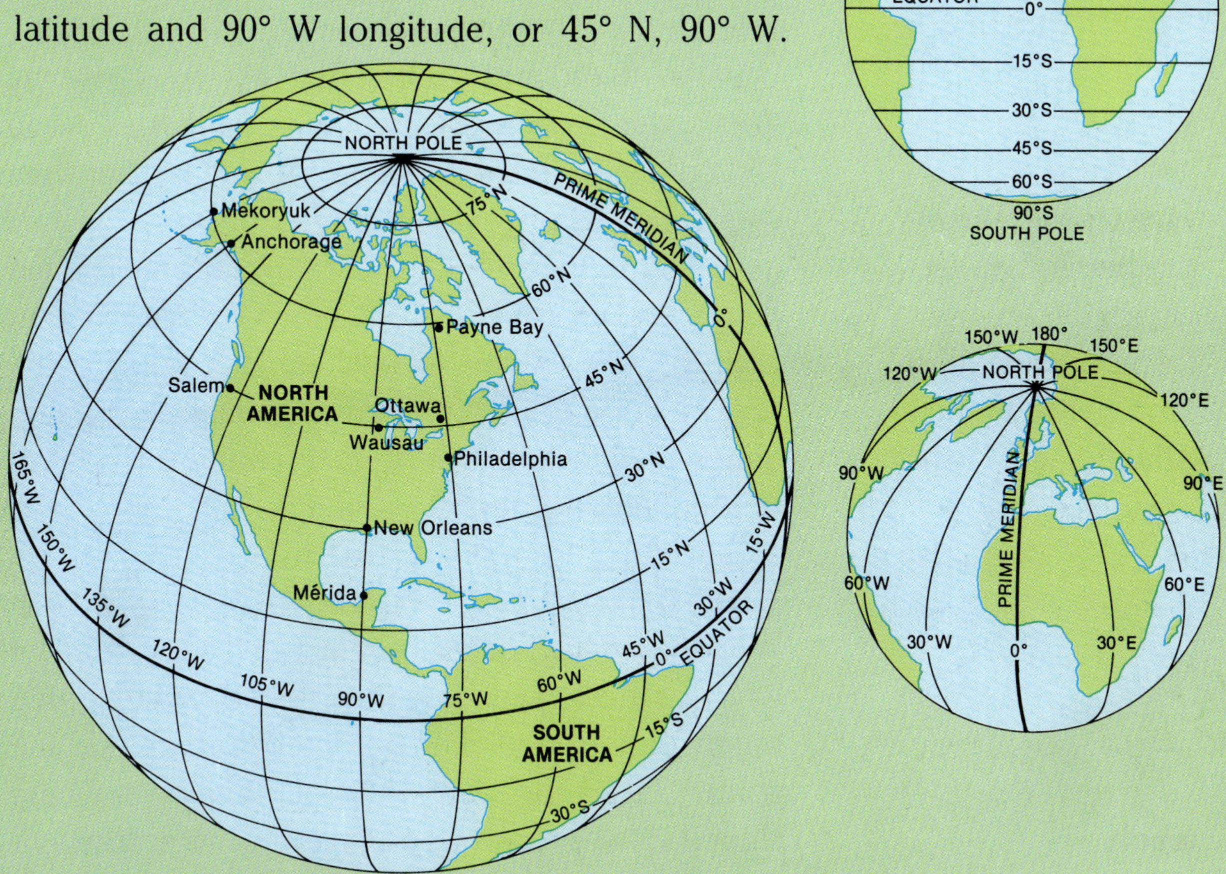

Practice Your Skills

1. What city is approximately 45° N, 75° W?
2. What is the latitude of Salem, Oregon?
3. What is the longitude of Mérida, Mexico?
4. What is the approximate location of Anchorage, Alaska? Payne Bay, Canada?

2 "Fifty-Four Forty or Fight!"

The provisional government of 1843 was only a beginning. As you have read, the American settlers hoped that it would lead to Oregon's becoming part of the United States.

From Coast to Coast

During the 1840's, many people in the United States came to believe that their country should rule all the land between the Atlantic and Pacific oceans. It did not matter that the lands in the West were claimed by other countries. The United States meant to control them. This idea was called **Manifest Destiny.**

Manifest Destiny
the belief that the United States was meant to rule all the land between the Atlantic and Pacific oceans

At this time, both Great Britain and the United States still claimed the Oregon Country. Neither country was willing to give up its claim to the region. For a time, it looked as though the United States and Britain would go to war over control of the Oregon Country.

The Boundary Problem

In the 1840's, Great Britain ruled almost all of what is now Canada. The United States ruled much of the land that bordered Canada on the south. Over the years, Great Britain and the United States had signed several **treaties,** or agreements, to set up boundaries between the lands they controlled. By 1842, the boundary between the United States and Canada, west to the Rocky Mountains, had been agreed upon. But the two countries could not agree upon the boundary between the Rocky Mountains and the Pacific Ocean.

treaty
a formal agreement made between countries and signed by each

The map on this page shows the boundaries that the United States and Great Britain wanted in the Northwest. Americans wanted the northern boundary of the United States to be set at 54°40′ N. This line is between 54° and 55° N. This boundary would give all of the Oregon Country to the United States. Many Americans felt very strongly about this boundary. "Fifty-four Forty or Fight!" became a well-known saying all over the United States. It meant that the United States would go to war with Great Britain, if need be, to get the northern boundary of the United States set at 54°40′.

The British claimed that the northern boundary of the United States should be set at 42° N. This would have made the Oregon Country part of Canada. As more and more American settlers moved into the Willamette Valley, the British decided to give in a little. They suggested that the boundary follow the path of the Columbia River up to 49° N. Then the boundary would follow the forty-ninth parallel east to the Rocky Mountains. Find this boundary on the map.

The United States would not agree to this new boundary. It was not willing to give up so much land. Both sides worked hard to come up with a boundary on which both countries could agree. They finally decided on one in 1846.

The Treaty of 1846

In 1846, Great Britain and the United States agreed to divide the Oregon Country along the 49th parallel. Find this line on the map on page 149. Great Britain would get the land to the north of the line, and the United States would get the land to the south. The British Hudson's Bay Company was allowed to keep its land in the region now owned by the United States. But it no longer had the power it had once had in this region.

In 1842, Marcus Whitman met with Daniel Webster and President Tyler to plead for Oregon's being made a part of the United States.

Becoming a Territory

When news of the treaty reached Oregon, the settlers began to hope that the region would soon be made a **Territory** of the United States. As a Territory, the settlers and their property would be protected by the United States government. Becoming a Territory was also the first step toward becoming a state. They waited for over a year, but nothing happened.

Territory
a part of the country that is under the protection of the United States but does not have the standing of a state

In 1848, two Oregonians decided to go to Washington, D.C., to ask the government to make Oregon a Territory. One of them was Joe Meek. Meek spent his time talking to any member of the government he could find, to explain why Oregon should be made a Territory. He even talked to the President, James K. Polk! President Polk asked **Congress** to make Oregon a Territory. Congress is the part of the United States government that makes many of our country's laws. On August 13, 1848, Congress voted to make Oregon a Territory of the United States.

Congress
the part of the United States government that makes many of our country's laws

Section Review

Write your answers on a sheet of paper.

1. Before 1846, where did Americans want the northern boundary of the United States set? Where did Great Britain want it set?
2. What was decided by the Treaty of 1846?
3. Why did the settlers in Oregon want Oregon to be made a Territory of the United States?
4. Why do you think some Americans threatened to go to war with Great Britain over the boundary in the Northwest?

3 Becoming a State

It did not take long for Oregonians to realize that they would be better off if Oregon was a state instead of a Territory. As long as Oregon was just a Territory, they had no say over how much money the United States government should spend on Oregon or how many soldiers should be sent to protect the settlers. These conditions would change when Oregon became a state. But statehood seemed a long way off. Then, in 1850, an important law was passed.

The Donation Land Act

The Donation Land Act was passed by Congress in 1850. This law had two important parts. The first part allowed every male settler over the age of 18 who had settled in Oregon for the four years before December 1850 to claim 129 hectares (320 acres) of free land. If he married by December 1851, his wife was allowed to claim the same amount of land in her own name. The first part of the law was important to the thousands of people who had settled in Oregon during the 1830's and 1840's. It meant that the United States government would protect their land claims. It also meant that the settlers would not have to pay for the land they had claimed.

The second part of the Donation Land Act said that anyone who settled in Oregon from 1851 to 1855 could also claim free land. They could claim about half as much as the earlier settlers. In order to get the land, the new settlers had to agree to farm it for several years. There was so much land in Oregon in 1850 that people came by the thousands to claim it.

Trouble Between the Settlers and Indians

As more and more people poured into Oregon, trouble between the settlers and the Indians increased. As you have read, Indians killed 14 people at the Whitman mission in 1847. This event shocked the settlers. It touched off a series of wars that lasted for many years.

The Indians fought hard to keep their old ways of life, but that proved impossible. Over the years, the government paid the Indians for some of their land and set aside other land for them. The lands that the government set aside as homelands for American Indians were called **reservations.** Reservation land was often of poor quality. The Indians were forced to live on these reservations for many years. Today many Indians still choose to live on reservations, but they are allowed to live anywhere they choose.

reservation
land set aside as a homeland for American Indians

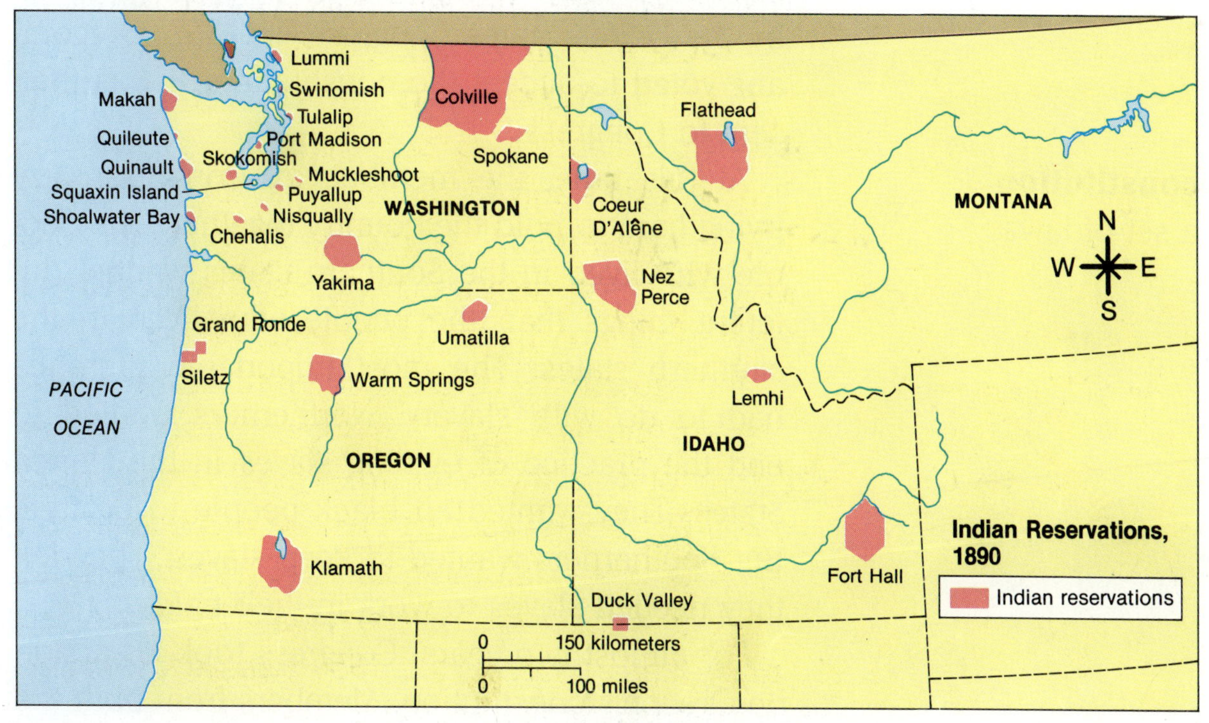

Changes in Oregon's Shape

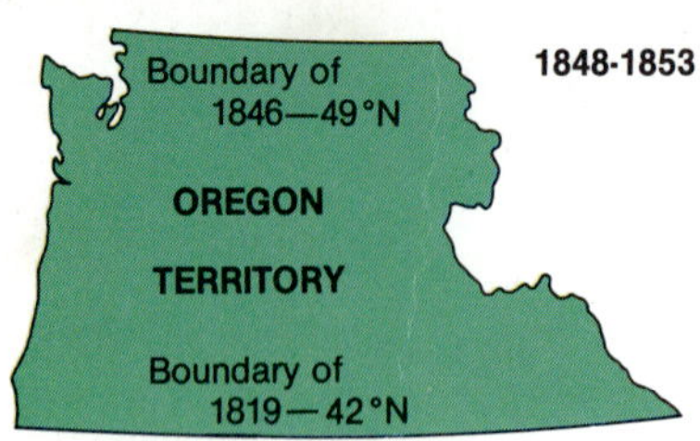

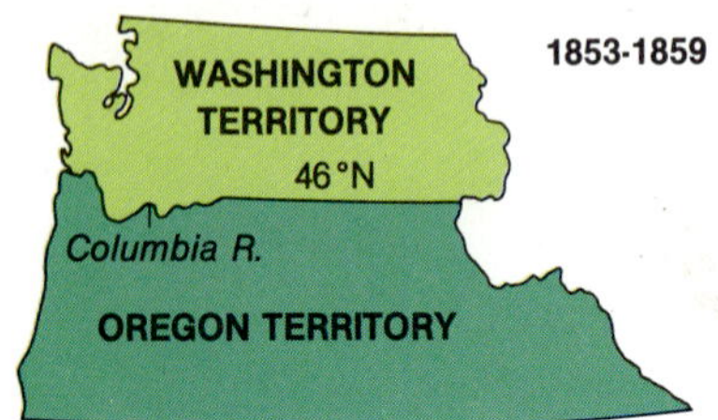

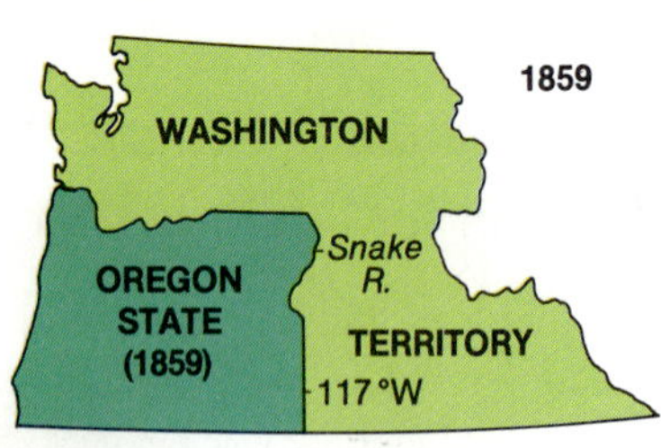

The Shape of Oregon Changes

When Oregon became a Territory in 1848, it stretched from the Rocky Mountains to the Pacific Ocean. What were to become the states of Oregon, Washington, Idaho, and parts of Montana and Wyoming were part of the Oregon Territory.

During the 1850's, the settlers north of the Columbia River asked the United States government to divide the Territory into smaller parts. In 1853, the United States government set up the Washington Territory north of the Columbia River. The land south of the river remained the Oregon Territory. The maps on this page show this change.

The Thirty-Third State

constitution
a set of laws

As soon as the Territory was divided, the settlers in Oregon began to take the steps needed to become a state. The first thing they had to do was write a **constitution,** or set of laws. The constitution had to be approved by the people living in the Oregon Territory. It also had to be approved by the United States Congress. In 1857, Oregonians voted to accept the constitution. It was then sent to Congress.

At this time, the members of Congress were trying hard to hold the country together. The people who lived in the Southern states wanted different things than the people who lived in the Northern states. The most important difference had to do with slavery. Northerners wanted to end the practice of owning slaves in the United States. They wanted all black people to be free. But Southerners wanted to keep slaves. They felt they needed slaves to work in their fields.

For almost two years, Congress took no action on Oregon's constitution. Members from both the

North and the South found things in the constitution that they did not like. For one thing, Oregonians had said that Oregon would be a free state. This meant that no one living in Oregon would be allowed to own slaves. This pleased Northern members of Congress but angered those from the South. On the other hand, the Oregon constitution said that no free blacks would be allowed to settle in Oregon. This pleased the Southerners but angered the Northerners.

Finally, in 1859, Congress voted to accept the Oregon Constitution. On February 14, 1859, President Buchanan signed the Oregon Admissions Act. This law made Oregon the thirty-third state of the United States. It also set the state's present boundaries. You can see these boundaries on the map on page 154.

Oregonians celebrating the news of Oregon's statehood in 1859.

Section Review

Write your answers on a sheet of paper.

1. How did the Donation Land Act of 1850 affect the future settlement of Oregon?
2. How did the government try to solve the problems between the Indians and settlers in Oregon?
3. What happened to the Oregon Territory in 1853?
4. Why did Congress not take any action on the Oregon Constitution for almost two years?
5. When did Oregon become a state?
6. How would being a state affect Oregonians in the future?

Close-up on

Pendleton Round-Up Since 1910, the people of Pendleton, Oregon, have held an event to honor the Old West. It is called the Pendleton Round-Up. People dress in the costumes of the Old West. They act as cowboys, pioneers, settlers, and miners. For four days every September, Pendleton becomes a spirited town of the Old West.

Today more than a thousand Indians attend the round-up. They set up camp by the Umatilla River just as their families did long ago. The Indians take part in many of the round-up events.

At night some of the Indians act in a play about the Old West. The play is called the Happy Canyon Pageant. It tells about how the settlers changed the Indians' lives. After the play, there is a dance. The play and the dance are highlights of the round-up.

OREGON

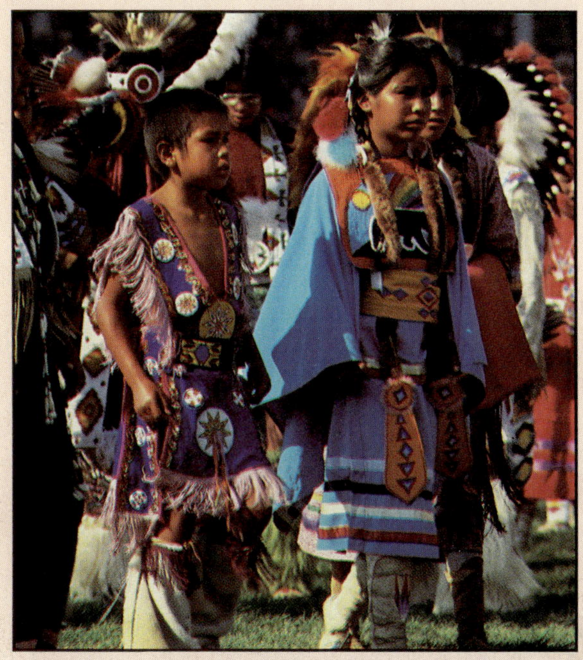

Everyone in the parade dresses in clothing of the Old West. No modern transportation is allowed. People ride in wagons, carts, carriages, and coaches. They also ride horses or go on foot. It is the only parade of its kind in America.

When the Pendleton Round-Up is over, life in this small eastern Oregon town returns to normal. But in a year it will once again return to the days of the Old West.

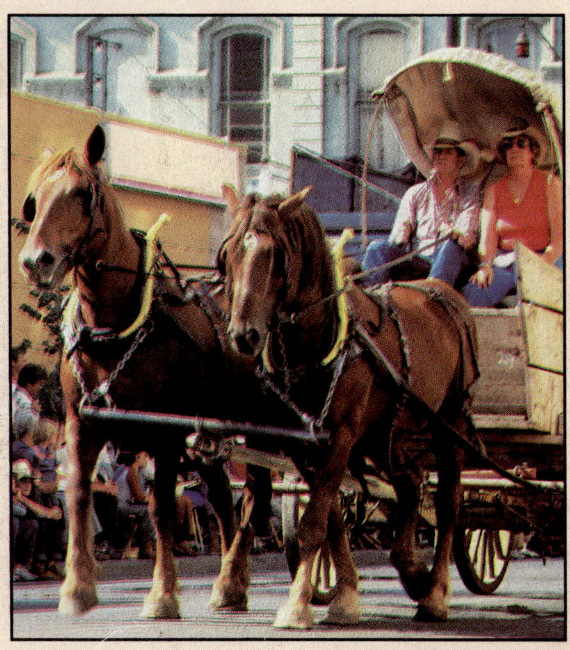

The rodeo is also popular. Cowboys compete in difficult events for points and prize money. Steer roping, bulldogging, and bull riding are among the hardest events to win. Other exciting contests include riding a wild horse, milking a wild cow, and stagecoach racing.

The Westward Ho parade is the largest event of the round-up. Many townspeople and Indians take part in the parade.

UNIT REVIEW

Word Work

Write the sentences below on a sheet of paper. Fill in the blanks with the correct words from the list.

explorer	government
merchant	artifact
reservation	culture
pioneer	missionary

1. A ____ is a person who teaches others about religion.
2. An ____ is a weapon, tool, or other article that was made and used by people who lived long ago.
3. A person who buys and sells goods is called a ____.
4. ____ is the way of life shared by a group of people who have the same past, customs, beliefs, and often language.
5. A person who tries something first and opens the way for others to follow is called a ____.
6. A group of people who make laws and lead a community, state, or country make up a ____.
7. A person who goes to faraway places in search of something is called an ____.
8. Land set aside as a homeland for American Indians is called a ____.

Knowing the Facts

Write your answers on a sheet of paper.

1. How did the Coastal Indians use the resources of their environment to live?
2. What were the earliest explorers looking for in the Pacific Northwest? What did they find that proved to be valuable?
3. Who was Dr. John McLoughlin? How did he help the people of Oregon?
4. How did large numbers of American settlers get to Oregon in the 1840's?
5. How did the California gold rush affect Oregon?
6. Who was Joseph Meek? What part did he play in setting up Oregon's provisional government? in Oregon's becoming a Territory?

Using What You Know

Choose one of the following activities to do. Follow the instructions given here.

1. Make a model of either a Coastal or Plateau Indian village.
2. Draw a picture or make a model of an early sailing ship like the ones used by the explorers of the Pacific Northwest.
3. Pretend you are a settler going west to Oregon. Decide what you will take in your covered wagon. Make a list.
4. Make a poster showing the Oregon state flag. Find out and label the meaning of each symbol shown on the flag.

Skills Practice

Use the altitude diagram on page 101 to answer the following questions. Write your answers on a sheet of paper.

1. How does the temperature change as you go up this mountain?
2. What is the climate like at 3,000 meters (9,843 feet)?
3. What is the plant life like between 2,500 meters (8,203 feet) and 3,000 meters (9,843 feet)?
4. In which zone can cactus and sagebrush be found?

Use the following map to answer the questions below.

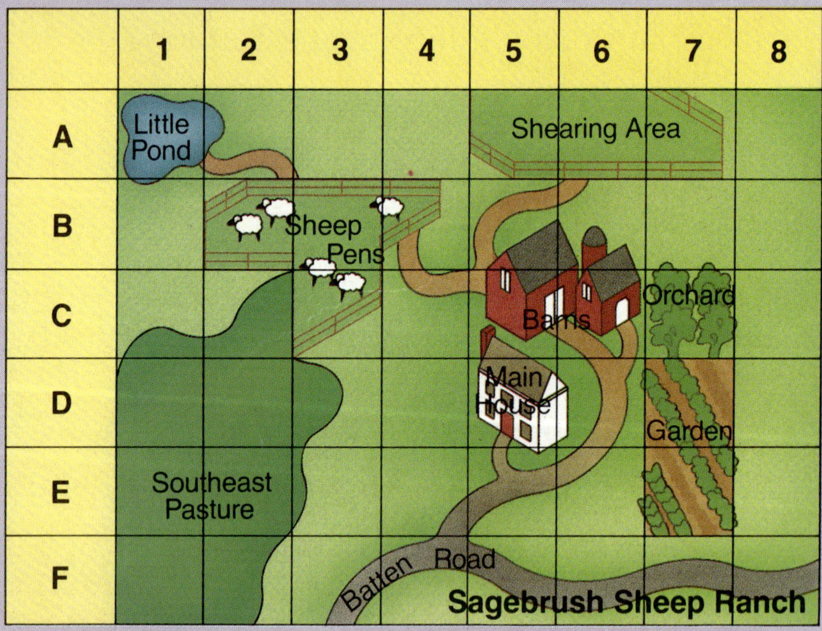

1. In which square is the main house?
2. What would you find in squares C5 and C6?
3. In which squares is the shearing area?

4. Which is bigger—the orchard or the garden?
5. Where is Batten Road located?

Use the following map to answer the questions below on latitude and longitude.

1. What city is approximately 46° N, 124° W?
2. What is the latitude of Florence, Oregon?
3. What is the longitude of Salem, Oregon?
4. Between which two lines of latitude is Medford, Oregon, located?
5. What is the approximate location of Eugene, Oregon?
6. What is the location of the point where the states of Nevada, Idaho, and Oregon meet?

UNIT 3 A Growing State

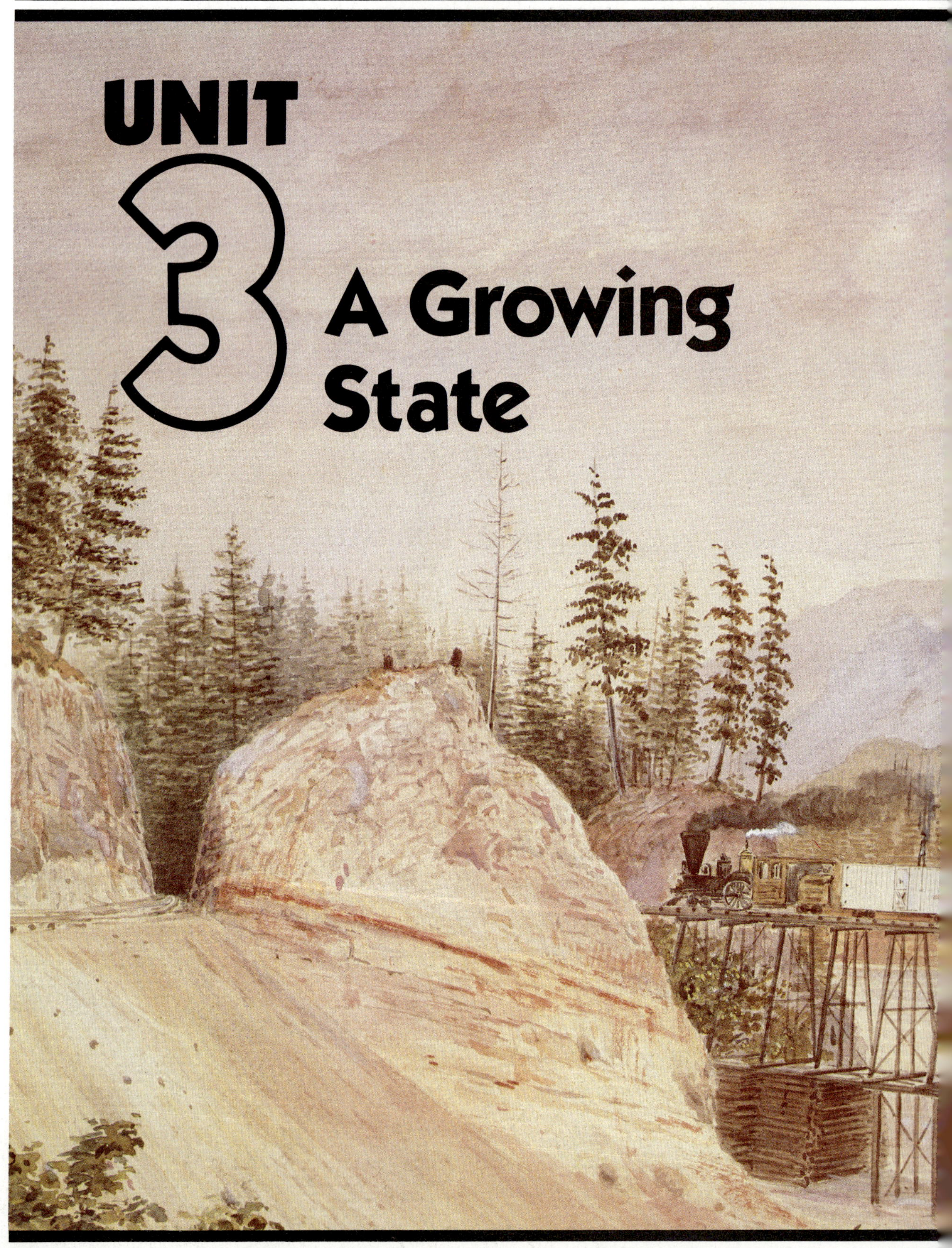

CHAPTER 7 Moving People and Products

The second half of the 1800's brought new sights and sounds to Oregon. Steamboats crowded the rivers. Trains rattled along thousands of miles of railroad track. Farms, sawmills, and canneries rang with the sounds of steam-powered machines. Oregon was growing.

At the end of this chapter, you should be able to:

- ○ Describe how steamboats and railroads helped move people and goods in Oregon in the late 1800's.
- ○ Explain how the railroads helped Oregon's industries grow.
- ○ Describe how the farming, lumbering, and fishing industries in Oregon grew in the late 1800's.
- ● Compare a table and a graph.

1 Steamboats and Railroads

During the 1840's, settlers had come to Oregon by the thousands. But during the 1850's and 1860's, people streamed into Oregon by the tens of thousands! Many of them were headed for the goldfields of southern Oregon and Idaho.

When the first gold seekers arrived in Oregon, there were no roads for them to use. In those days, the fastest and easiest way to the goldfields was along the rivers. The Columbia and Willamette rivers quickly became like the superhighways of today.

Thousands of miners were carried to the goldfields on **steamboats.** These boats have large paddle wheels that are turned by steam power. They can travel up a river as easily as they can travel down one. By the early 1860's, steamboats were carrying almost 40,000 passengers a year on the Columbia River alone.

steamboat
a boat powered by steam

Steamboats also carried almost everything that was grown or made in Oregon to large towns along the rivers. There the goods could be sold or shipped to ports outside of Oregon. On the return trip, steamboats carried equipment and supplies to the Oregon farmers and miners.

Steamboat Captains

With so many passengers and goods to carry, steamboat shipping became a big business. Each steamboat captain tried to get as much business as possible. Some built faster boats. Others built fancy boats with beautiful dining rooms and private bedrooms.

The steamboat Bailey Gatzert *carried passengers on the Columbia River from 1890 to 1926.*

Some of the steamboat captains were even more interesting than their boats. One was Minnie Hill. She was the first woman in Oregon to become a steamboat captain. For many years, she ran a successful business on the Columbia River. Another successful steamboat captain was John C. Ainsworth. Ainsworth was so successful that other captains tried hard to take business away from him. They did this by lowering the prices they charged to carry passengers and goods. To protect his business, Ainsworth set up a company in 1860 called the Oregon Steam Navigation Company. In time, this company controlled all the steamboat traffic and ports along the Columbia River.

Minnie Hill was the first woman in Oregon to be licensed as a steamboat captain.

The Coming of Railroads

Steamboats helped to move people and goods from one region of Oregon to another. But in the 1860's, Oregon was still cut off from much of the rest of the country. There was no fast and easy way to move people and goods between Oregon and the other states.

Railroads helped to solve this problem. In the late 1800's, railroad lines connecting the east and west coasts of the United States were built. These rail lines, called **transcontinental railroads,** were important to Oregon in two ways. They carried thousands of settlers to Oregon who would never have crossed the continent in a covered wagon. And they made it possible to send goods between Oregon and eastern markets. Other rail lines connecting Oregon to California were built. This opened up a rich trade between these two states.

transcontinental railroad
a railroad that crosses a continent from one end to another

The companies that built the railroads were interested in making money. They hoped that the people who lived near the railroads would pay to have their goods shipped by train. But first, many miles of track had to be laid. Much of it had to be laid through areas where few people lived. To lay the track, the railroad companies needed help from the government.

The government helped by giving free land called **land grants** to companies that built railroad lines. The land grants were wide stretches of land that ran along the railroad routes. The Northern Pacific Railroad Company received large land grants in Oregon for building part of its transcontinental railroad across the state.

land grant
free land given by the government to a railroad, school, or other organization

Land grants helped the railroad companies in two ways. First, the railroad companies did not have to pay for the land on which they laid the tracks. And second, they could sell any land they did not use. The people who bought this land started farms or businesses on it. Because the land was so close to the railroad, they moved their goods by train. This helped the railroad companies make more money.

A railroad depot in Salem, Oregon, around 1900

Railroads in Oregon

The promise of land grants encouraged companies to build railroads in Oregon. In 1883, the Northern Pacific Railroad was finished. It connected Portland, Oregon, to St. Paul, Minnesota.

The Southern Pacific Railroad gave Oregon its first rail link to California in 1887. Before this railroad was built, the trip from Portland, Oregon, to Sacramento, California, took seven days by stagecoach. With the railroad, the same trip could be made in only one and a half days.

Section Review

Write your answers on a sheet of paper.

1. How were steamboats important to Oregon?
2. In what ways were the transcontinental railroads important to Oregon?
3. In what ways did government land grants help railroad companies?
4. What do you think happened to the cost of steamboat transportation when one company gained control of all steamboat traffic and ports along Oregon's rivers?

2 The Growth of Industry

The coming of the railroads helped Oregon's industries grow. Oregonians could send by train, goods such as food and lumber to almost all parts of the United States. Many new settlers came to Oregon on the railroads. Oregonians could now sell goods to many more people than was possible before railroads were built in the state. They could make more money. They used some of the money to increase the size of their farms and businesses. They bought new equipment from distant markets and hired more workers. This helped Oregon's industries grow.

Progress in Farming

As more and more people moved into Oregon, farming became a big business. Many of the newcomers settled in the cities. To feed these people, farmers increased their crop and animal production. Many new farms were started. For the first time, thousands of hectares (acres) of land in eastern Oregon were used for farming.

The railroads made it possible for large farms to develop in eastern Oregon. During the 1870's, train tracks had been laid along the Columbia River from Portland to the eastern regions of the state. Farmers in eastern Oregon could send their farm goods to Portland by train. Most of the farm goods raised in Oregon during the late 1800's went to feed the people in the state. Fewer farm goods were sold to people in other states.

Large wheat farms were started near the Columbia River. Machines helped farmers harvest the wheat. Without machines, farmers in eastern Oregon could not have worked such large farms.

Harvesting wheat with a steam tractor

ranching
the raising of large herds of animals such as cattle, sheep, or horses

Ranching also became a big business in eastern Oregon. Ranching is the raising of large herds of animals such as cattle, sheep, or horses. Ranchers like Peter French and Ben Snipes started some of the largest ranches in the country. It was said that Ben Snipes alone owned about 100,000 horses.

During the late 1800's, Oregon ranchers raised thousands of sheep. This caused the amount of wool produced in Oregon to double in only five years. Buyers from all over the world arrived on the trains every year to buy Oregon sheep and wool.

But the 1800's were also hard years for farmers and ranchers in Oregon. In 1884–1885, the worst snowstorm in Pacific Northwest history destroyed whole herds of animals. By the late 1880's, the lumber industry had replaced farming as the single, largest source of income in the state.

Growth of the Lumber Industry

Like farming, the lumber industry in Oregon grew to meet the needs of the new settlers. New houses and places of business had to be built. The railroads carried millions of logs to the sawmills every year. Most of Oregon's lumber was sold to people who lived in the state. Some was sold to people in other countries. And large amounts were sold to people who lived in other parts of the United States.

California was one of the Pacific Northwest's best lumber customers. In 1889, ships carried over 300 million board feet of lumber to California's port cities. Trains carried the lumber to other parts of the state.

Large amounts of Oregon lumber were sold to people who lived east of the Rocky Mountains. The lumber was loaded onto trains at Portland. The trains carried the lumber to cities like Denver, Colorado, and Omaha, Nebraska. By selling to more people, Oregon's lumber industry grew.

A logging train in Oregon in the 1890's

Workers canning salmon

The Fishing Industry

Like lumbering and farming, Oregon's fishing industry grew in the late 1800's. In the 1860's, large canneries were built along the Columbia River. Cannery workers prepare salmon and other fish for shipment to faraway places. The fish were packed in tin cans to keep them from spoiling. By the 1870's, the salmon industry alone was bringing millions of dollars a year to Oregon.

Section Review

Write your answers on a sheet of paper.

1. How did the coming of the railroads help Oregon's industries grow?
2. What progress was made in farming in the late 1800's?
3. In which regions of the country was lumber from Oregon sold in the late 1800's? How was the lumber transported to each region?
4. Why do you think farming, lumbering, and fishing became Oregon's chief industries in the late 1800's?

PETER FRENCH

At the age of 23, Peter French knew more about cattle ranching than most. In 1872, the California cattle rancher French worked for gave him a herd of cattle. French drove the herd north and built a ranch in the Donner-Blitzen River valley in Oregon.

For 25 years he worked hard and made his ranch one of the best around. He hired good people and treated them well. He worked as hard as they did, and they all liked Peter French.

But not everyone liked the owner of the P Ranch. Indians who were angry over the loss of their land attacked French and his cowhands. Farmers put up fences to keep French's cattle away from their crops.

Peter French fought a running battle with the Indians and the farmers. For a long time his toughness and his skill with a gun protected his large ranch.

But one day, while Peter French was riding on his ranch, a farmer shot and killed him. Cowhands and ranchers were filled with sadness at the loss of their hard-working friend.

Today the P Ranch is a protected place for wild birds. But some of French's buildings are still there.

SOCIAL STUDIES SKILLS

Comparing a Table and Graph

Suppose you wanted to put together some facts about Oregon's lumber production. There are a number of ways you can display information. But some ways are better than others to show facts and figures.

table
a list of facts displayed in columns with titles

You could use a **table.** On the table, you could list Oregon's lumber production in any given year. Look at the table below. It shows exactly how many board feet of lumber were produced in Oregon in five years. By reading the figures carefully, you can see that Oregon's lumber production increased over time.

bar graph
a diagram using bars to stand for numbers

You could also show this information by drawing a diagram called a **bar graph.** On a bar graph, bars stand for numbers or amounts. Look at the bar graph on the next page. The years are listed on the left side of the graph. Numbers representing millions of board feet of lumber are listed along the bottom of the graph. Each bar shows how many board feet of lumber were produced in Oregon in a given year.

Oregon's Lumber Production
(in board feet)

Year	Board feet
1859	41,169,000
1869	75,193,000
1879	177,171,000
1889	444,565,000
1899	734,181,000

A bar graph is useful because without even reading the numbers, you can tell that Oregon produced more than twice as much lumber in 1879 as it did in 1869. You can see this because the bar that stands for 1879 is more than twice as long as the bar that stands for 1869. So when you want to list facts, you can use a table. When you want to compare facts, a bar graph may be more useful because it is easier to read and understand quickly.

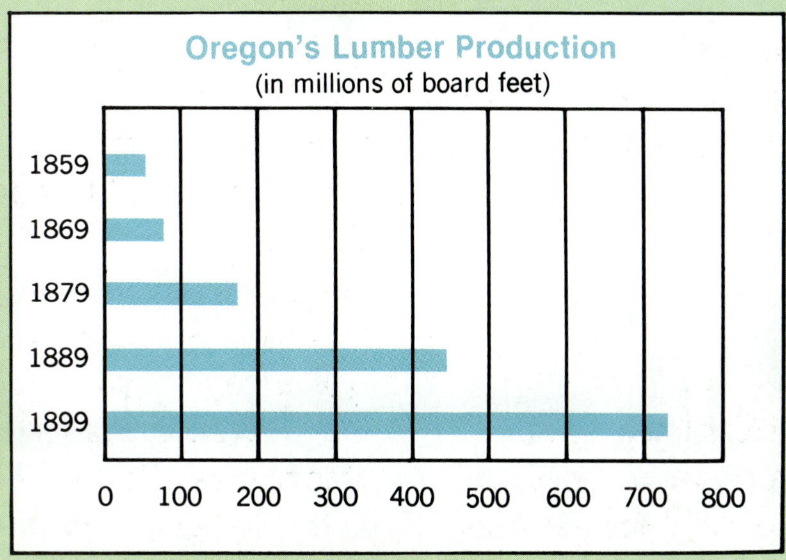

Practice Your Skills

1. Exactly how many board feet of lumber were produced in Oregon in 1859? Did you use the table or the bar graph to find this information?
2. In what year did Oregon produce the most lumber? Was it faster to use the table or the bar graph to find out? Why?
3. How many more board feet of lumber were produced in 1899 than in 1889? Was the table or graph more useful in figuring this amount? Why?

CHAPTER 8 People and Cities

A street scene of Albany, Oregon, in 1910

During the late 1800's, many people moved to Oregon. Some went by train, and others arrived on ships. Many of the newcomers brought different cultures to the state. Together with the earlier settlers, they built the Oregon we know today.

At the end of this chapter, you should be able to:

- ○ Identify the cultural groups that settled in Oregon in the late 1800's.
- ● Read a line graph.
- ○ Describe the growth of Oregon's cities.
- ○ Describe how schools, libraries, newspapers, and the arts developed in Oregon in the 1800's.
- ● Read a population density map.

1 Oregon's People

The **population** of a place includes all the people who live there. When Oregon became a state in 1859, its population was very small. As gold was discovered and the railroads were built, Oregon began to attract thousands of new settlers.

population
all of the people who live in a particular place

Most of the settlers who came to Oregon in the late 1800's came from other regions of the United States. They came on the railroads. Like the settlers who had arrived in the 1840's and 1850's, many were from the Midwest. As you have read, a lot of these people took jobs in Oregon's growing industries.

Many people from other countries also settled in Oregon in the late 1800's. People who come from another country to live in a new land are called **immigrants.**

immigrant
a person who comes from another country to live in a new land

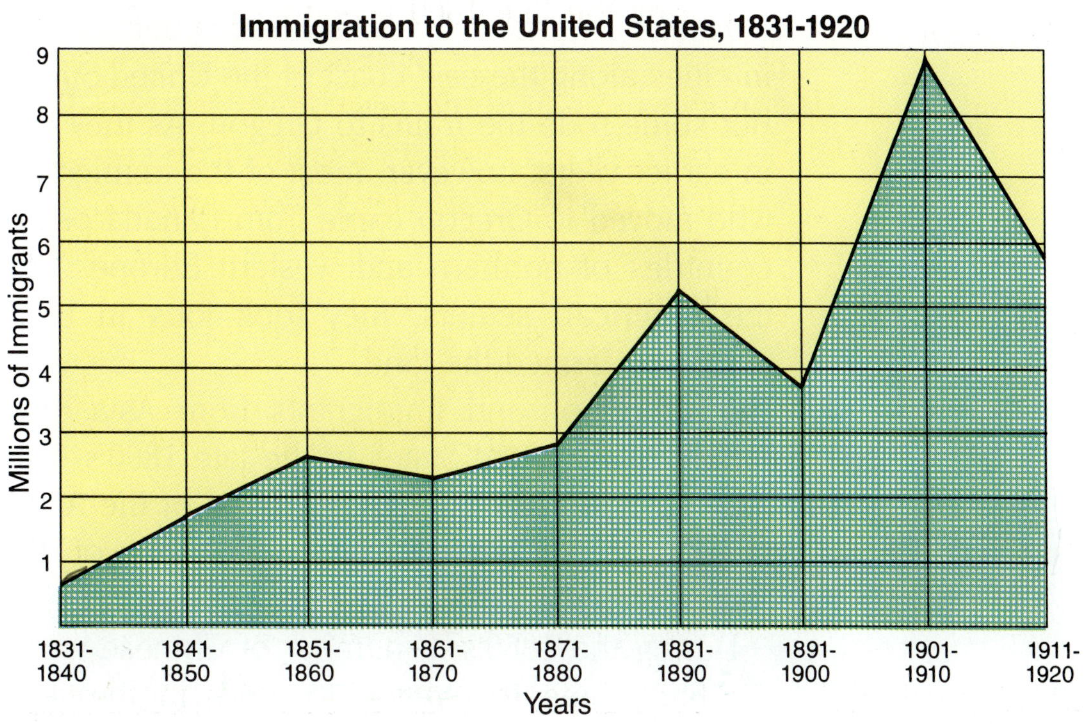

The Immigrants

Most of the immigrants who settled in Oregon in the late 1800's came from countries in Europe. In fact, many of the American settlers who went to Oregon from the Midwest had been European immigrants in the early 1800's. They had left their homelands in Europe because they believed the United States offered them a chance for a better life.

The immigrants who came to the United States in the late 1800's came for much the same reason. But the new immigrants were different from the earlier immigrants. Most of the earlier immigrants had come to the United States from countries in northern and western Europe. These countries include Great Britain, Ireland, Germany, Norway, and Sweden. In the late 1800's, large numbers of immigrants came to the United States from countries in southern and eastern Europe. These countries include Italy, Russia, Poland, and Greece.

Most of the new European immigrants settled in cities along the east coast of the United States. But some rode the trains to Oregon. As they had in earlier years, however, most of the immigrants who moved to Oregon came from Canada or the countries of northern and western Europe. Like the American settlers, they took jobs in businesses or farmed the land.

Several thousand immigrants from Asia also came to the United States in the late 1800's. Unlike the European immigrants, most of the Asian immigrants settled on the west coast of the United States.

During the 1860's, a number of Chinese workers had come to Oregon to work in the gold

European immigrants tagged with free railroad passes wait to travel to their new homes.

mines. In later years, many were brought in to help build the railroads. By the late 1800's, a lot of Chinese immigrants had settled in and around the city of Portland. Hundreds worked in the salmon canneries. Others worked at woodcutting and farm jobs. A few merchants started shops and set up businesses.

After 1886, Japanese immigrants were allowed to enter the United States. By the 1890's, several hundred had settled in Oregon. Some started their own farms around the present-day cities of Gresham and Hood River. But most of the Japanese settled in Portland. There they started businesses or took jobs working for others.

The immigrants were not always made to feel welcome in the communities where they settled. Some people feared that they would take jobs away from American workers. Others disliked the immigrants because they were different. The immigrants were sometimes treated badly, and laws were passed that were unfair to them.

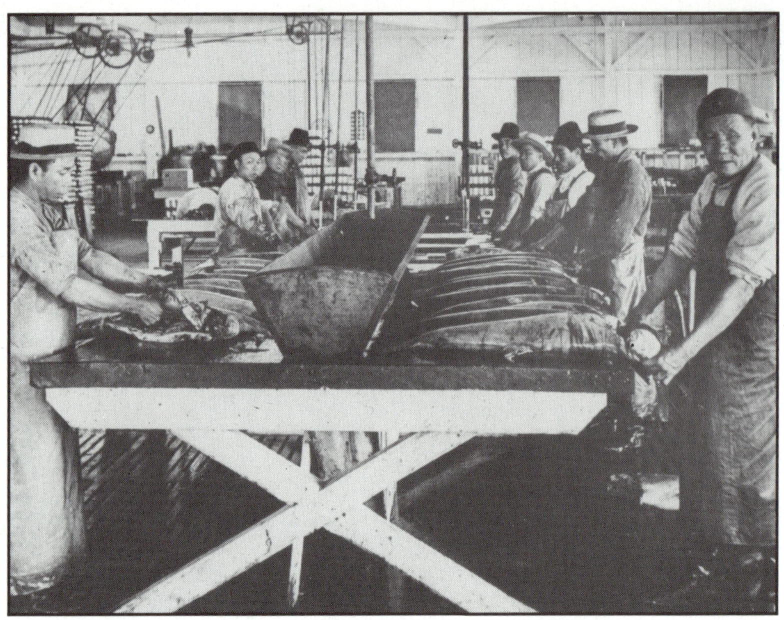

This photograph taken in 1904 shows Chinese workers preparing salmon in one of Astoria's canneries.

Despite these laws, many immigrants stayed in America. They worked hard to build new lives for themselves and their children. Most of them learned English and adopted many "American" customs. But they also held on to some of their old ways of life. In time, some of their customs and traditions became part of the American culture. Oregon today is a rich and varied place because of the cultures brought to the state by people from other countries.

Section Review

Write your answers on a sheet of paper.

1. What groups of people settled in Oregon in the late 1800's?
2. What contributions did these newcomers make to the state?
3. Asian immigrants were often treated worse than the European immigrants. Why do you think this was so?

SOCIAL STUDIES SKILLS

Reading a Line Graph

Over the years, Oregon's population has grown larger. What kind of graph would you use to show this information? A **line graph** is a way to show how things change over a period of time.

line graph
a graph that uses lines to show information and how that information changes

This line graph shows how Oregon's population changed from 1860 to 1920. The numbers running up the left side of the graph represent the number of people who were living in Oregon. The years between 1860 and 1920 have been spaced across the bottom of the graph.

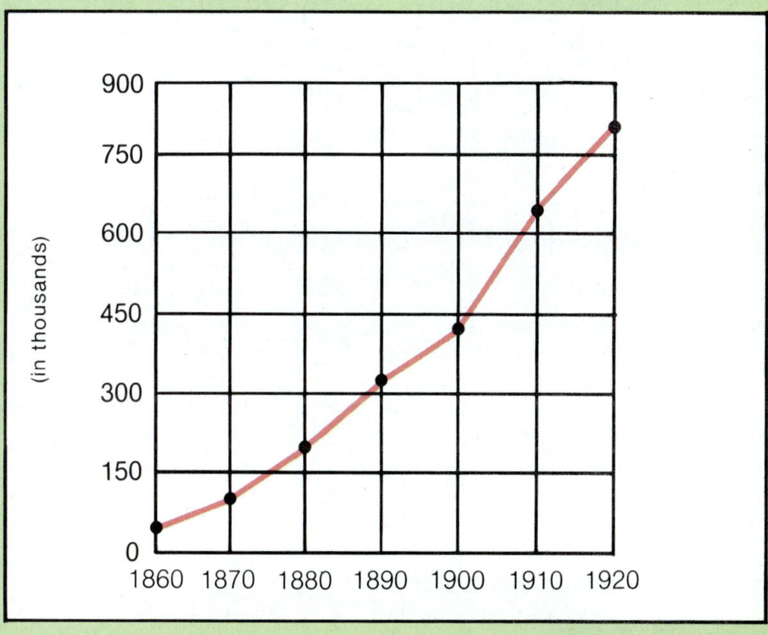

On the line above each year, there is a dot next to the population figure for that year. If you connect these dots with a line, you can see how Oregon's population changed from 1860 to 1920.

Practice Your Skills

1. What was the population of Oregon in 1860?
2. In what year was the population of Oregon the largest? What was the population in that year?
3. Between what two years did Oregon's population grow the most?

2 The Growth of Cities

Before the coming of the railroads, very few people in Oregon lived in towns. Most people lived in **rural,** or farming areas. As you have read, the railroads helped industries grow. As Oregon's industries grew, so did its cities.

rural
away from cities and close to farms

Why Cities Grow

Most cities begin as tiny settlements where a few small businesses are started. These businesses serve the people who live in or near the settlement.

Transportation, or ways of moving people and things from place to place, is important to people who live in a growing settlement. Farmers and business owners need to move their goods to markets. Because of this need, most of Oregon's towns and cities were started along transportation routes.

transportation
ways of moving people and things from place to place

The oldest cities started along rivers. For many years, the rivers were the only easy way to move goods from place to place. They also provided water power that ran the machines in early mills.

Oregon City, Oregon's first large town, was built on the east side of the Willamette River.

Then the railroads were built. As you have read, the railroads made it possible to transport goods to more distant markets. This helped businesses grow. As businesses grew, so did the cities. More people moved to the cities to work in businesses. And new businesses were started to meet the needs of people in the cities. Cities connected by railroad lines grew larger.

Wagon roads were also built in Oregon in the late 1800's. They connected the rural parts of a region to its nearest city. Most of the roads were short. Some helped cities grow. In the 1850's, a road was built through the West Hills of Portland. This road connected Portland to the farming regions of the Tualatin Valley west of the city. Farmers brought their goods in wagons over the road to Portland. This road helped Portland grow larger than other nearby cities like Milwaukie and Oregon City, which were located on the east side of the Willamette River. Portland also grew larger than these cities because it was the farthest point that ocean-going ships could travel to up the Willamette River year round.

These horse teams, gathered on the main street of Rufus, Oregon, in 1880, are loaded with sacks of wheat.

The Growth of Portland

As you have read, Francis Pettygrove named the city of Portland in 1845. In that same year, he started Portland's first business. It was a warehouse for storing goods. The following year, Pettygrove opened Portland's second business, a store.

From this small beginning, Portland grew into Oregon's largest city and leading center of trade and industry. Why did Portland attract more people and businesses than other towns in Oregon? The answer is transportation.

As you have read, transportation routes help cities grow. Portland's location near the mouth of the Willamette River made it the best port in the state. Then in the 1850's, the road connecting Portland to the Tualatin Valley was built. Finally, by the late 1800's, Portland was connected to markets all over the country by the railroads. These three forms of transportation—shipping, roads, and railroads—brought more businesses and people to Portland than to any other city in the state.

During May and early June, the Willamette River regularly overflowed its banks. In 1894, the waters flooded several blocks of downtown Portland.

New businesses and organizations were started to serve the growing population of the city. Churches and schools were built, and newspapers were printed. Police and fire departments were formed to protect the people and their property. An amusement park was even built!

As more and more people moved to Portland, it began to get crowded. Almost everyone lived on the west side of the Willamette River. Improvements in transportation helped the people spread out. For many years, there was no bridge across the Willamette River. People wishing to cross the river had to take a boat. Then in 1887, the first bridge opened. It was built of wood and was named the Morrison Bridge. This bridge and the others that followed helped the east side of the city grow and develop.

Streetcars also helped the city grow larger in size. A streetcar is a large car or coach that runs on rails. It can hold many people. The first streetcars were pulled by horses. Soon horse power was replaced by steam power. Finally, in the late 1800's, electric streetcars replaced the steam-powered cars. Streetcars made it possible for people to live farther from the center of the city. They could ride streetcars to their jobs. Houses were built along the streetcar lines. As the streetcar lines got longer, people could move farther away and still have transportation into the city.

streetcar
a large car or coach that runs on rails

Today buses move large numbers of Portlanders from place to place. The first buses were put into service in the 1920's. A new electric railway is currently being built to connect Portland to nearby communities. With buses, cars, and the new railway, people can spread out even more and still have transportation into the city.

Other Cities Grow

Like Portland, other towns and cities in Oregon grew in the late 1800's. New businesses were started to serve the growing population in all regions of the state.

The city of Salem is near the center of the Willamette Valley. It is the capital of Oregon. Many people who work for the state government live and work in Salem. As more people moved to the state in the late 1800's, the government became larger. The growth of the government helped Salem grow.

Salem was connected to other parts of the state by good transportation routes. Goods could be shipped in and out of Salem along the Willamette River or on the railroads. Unlike Portland, however, large ocean-going ships could not reach Salem. Goods going to distant markets had to be carried to Portland on boats or trains.

The city of Eugene lies about 100 kilometers (62 miles) south of Salem on the Willamette River. In the 1870's, two things happened that helped Eugene grow. First in 1871, the railroad line being built down the Willamette Valley from Portland to California reached Eugene. As it did in other cities, the railroad helped industries in Eugene grow. The city grew along with the growth of the lumber industry at the southern end of the valley.

university
a school that offers the highest level of education

The second thing that helped Eugene grow was the founding of Oregon's first state **university** in 1876. A university is a school that offers the highest level of education. Over the years, more and more people went to Eugene to study at the university. Businesses grew to meet the needs of the students and teachers who lived in the city.

Eugene, Oregon, 1916

South of Eugene in the Klamath Mountain region is the city of Medford. The city lies at the eastern end of the Rogue River valley. Medford grew along with the business of growing fruit in large orchards.

East of the Cascade Mountains, the town of Pendleton grew as large farms and ranches developed in the region. Farm goods from many parts of eastern Oregon could be carried to Pendleton and from there to Portland on the trains. The manufacturing of woolen goods also became an important industry in Pendleton. By 1900, Pendleton had become the chief market for wool in the United States.

Section Review

Write your answers on a sheet of paper.

1. Where were Oregon's first cities built? Why?
2. What transportation routes helped the city of Portland grow into Oregon's leading center of trade and industry?
3. What do you think causes a city to stop growing or to lose some of its population?

3 Building a Better Life

Many people moved to Oregon in the 1800's because they hoped to build a better life for themselves and their families. They hoped to make enough money to live comfortably. But a "better life" meant much more than that to most people. It meant learning more about the world around them. Schools, libraries, newspapers, and the arts became important parts of life in every part of Oregon.

Schools

Two kinds of schools were started in Oregon in the 1800's. They were public schools and private schools. Public schools are supported by **taxes,** or money that people must give to the government to pay for community needs. The government then gives some of this money to the schools to buy books, hire teachers, and take care of the buildings. Private schools do not receive any tax money.

tax
money that people must give to the government to pay for community needs

In 1856, Oregon got its first public school building. It was called Central School, and it was located in Portland. At first, only white children were allowed to attend this school. Then black parents signed a petition asking that their children also be admitted. In 1871, black children were admitted to all public schools in the city.

Private schools were also started in Oregon in the late 1800's. Some, like St. Mary's Academy in Portland, and Spencer Hall in Milwaukie, were started by religious groups. Others were started by people who simply had an interest in education. One such school was started by a remarkable woman named Tabitha Brown.

Tabitha Brown

These children attended school in Astoria, Oregon, in the early 1900's.

In 1846, after a long and dangerous journey, John and Tabitha Brown arrived in Oregon. They thought that they had no money until Tabitha found a small coin, worth about six cents, in the finger of her glove. She used the coin to buy large needles. She traded some old clothes to Indians for animal skins. Then she made the skins into gloves, which she sold. In a few months, she had made about 30 dollars.

With this money, Tabitha started a small school for orphans in a town now known as Forest Grove. For many years, Tabitha worked day and night to make this school a success. Once known as the Tualatin Academy, this school is now Pacific University.

By 1870, there were full- or part-time schools in nearly every Oregon settlement. In that same year, it was reported that only about three out of every 100 Oregonians 10 years of age or older could not read or write.

Libraries and Newspapers

People who are interested in learning about the world around them often read books and newspapers. As early as 1864, a library association was formed to collect books and raise money for a reading room in Portland. In 1911, the government began a library system for most of Oregon. With libraries, the people of Oregon could read more books and learn more things.

Newspapers also helped Oregon's citizens learn more about what was going on in the world around them. As early as 1846, settlers in Oregon City could buy a newspaper that came out once a week. Two other weekly papers—one in Portland and one in Salem—were started in 1850.

Early newspapers were different from the newspapers we read today. They were much smaller and had no headlines or pictures.

Selling newspapers on a street corner

This undated photograph shows the Harney County Sagebrush Symphony Orchestra from Burns, Oregon.

Music

Many of Oregon's newcomers brought with them a great love of music. They started musical groups in almost every part of the state.

In 1866, the Philharmonic Society was started. This group invited orchestras from all over the world to perform in Oregon. As many as 600 people at a time could hear concerts in Portland's Willamette Theater, which was built in 1858. The New Market Theater was built a few years later. Operas were often performed in this theatre.

In 1895, the Oregon Symphony Orchestra was formed. Later, a teacher named Mary Dodge trained enough young musicians to form the Oregon Youth Symphony. Then as now, Oregonians could hear some of the best music in the world right in their own state.

This oil painting of the Skidmore Fountain in Portland was done by Harry Wentz, one of Oregon's most well-known artists, in the early 1900's.

The Arts

The early settlers in Oregon had little time or money to enjoy art. But by the late 1800's, many Oregonians had become interested in collecting and viewing art. They raised money to buy pieces of art and start **museums.** A museum is a room or building where art, historical, or scientific objects are preserved and put on display. Museums made it possible for many Oregonians to see and enjoy art.

Some of the museums also taught special art classes. One of the first and best art schools in Oregon was part of the Portland Art Museum. By 1905, the people of Portland had raised enough money to build a building large enough for the museum's artworks and art school.

museum
a room or building where art, historical, or scientific objects are preserved and put on display

Artists contributed to the beauty of Oregon's cities. They designed and made many fountains and statues. Several of these can still be seen today in city parks around the state.

Section Review

Write your answers on a sheet of paper.

1. What two kinds of schools were started in Oregon in the late 1800's?
2. Who was Tabitha Brown? What did she do to improve education in Oregon?
3. Why did Oregonians start libraries and newspapers?
4. What musical groups were formed in Oregon in the late 1800's?
5. Where might you go to see some of Oregon's early art?

Reading a Population Density Map

You can find out how thickly settled an area is by reading a **population density** map. Population density is how closely together people live, or how thickly settled an area is. This population density map shows how many people live in each square kilometer (or mile) of Oregon.

population density the number of people living in each square kilometer or mile of an area

In cities and towns where people live very near their neighbors, the population density is high. In the countryside, people live far apart. These areas have low population density.

Look at the map key. It explains what each color on the map means.

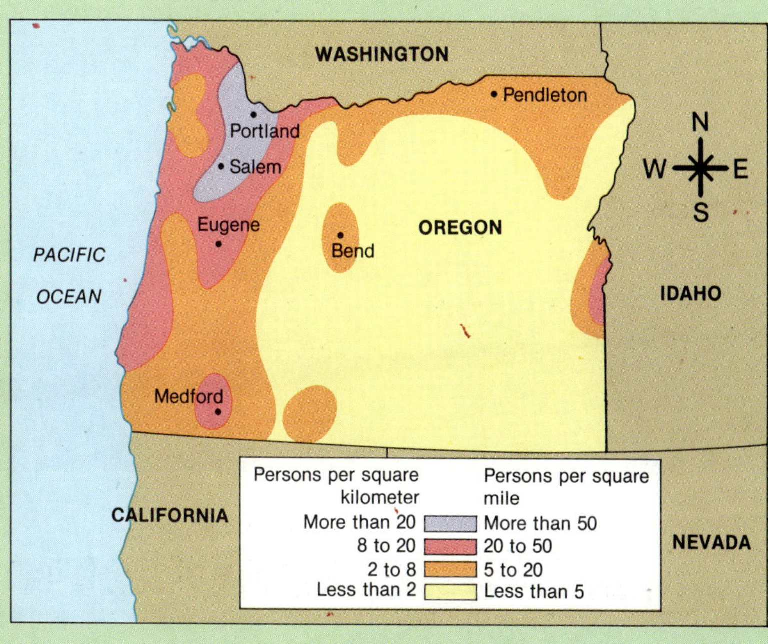

Practice Your Skills

1. How many people are there per square kilometer (or mile) in southeastern Oregon?
2. Which is more thickly settled, western or eastern Oregon?
3. What is the population density in the areas around Portland? Salem? Bend? Medford?
4. Does most of Oregon have a high or low population density?

CHAPTER 9 Problems and Solutions

These people gathered in Portland, Oregon, in 1905 to help women win the right to vote.

Like any place that grows quickly, Oregon had its share of "growing pains." Farmers ran into problems with the railroads. Workers became concerned with improving conditions on the job. In the late 1800's, farmers, laborers, business people, and government leaders became interested in improving conditions in Oregon.

At the end of this chapter you should be able to:

- ○ Describe the problems between farmers and the railroad companies.
- ○ Explain the purpose of the Grange and the Populist Party.
- ○ Describe the Progressive Movement and its effects on Oregon.

1 Farmers and Workers

The spread of railroads across the state pleased Oregon's farmers. Railroads helped farmers bring more of their crops to markets outside Oregon. By selling more crops, Oregon's farmers were able to expand their farms and make more money. Some of this money could be used to buy new farm machinery.

In the late 1800's however, Oregon's farmers began to have problems with the railroads. The companies that owned the railroads began to charge higher and higher prices. Soon many farmers were unable to pay the high prices the railroads demanded. If that happened, the farmer's crops would spoil and could not be sold without the railroads to take them to market quickly. The farmer would lose money and would not be able to keep his farm going.

Many farmers lost their farms this way. Those who remained in business began to blame the railroads for charging unfair prices. Soon farmers all over Oregon began to work together. Their goal was to force the railroad owners to lower their rates.

The Oregon State Grange

Beginning in 1872, Oregon farmers formed groups to fight for lower railroad rates. One of the largest groups became the Oregon State Grange. The Grange came to Oregon in 1873. Grange members wanted to see laws passed that would **regulate,** or limit, the amount that railroads could charge.

regulate
to control, or set limits

This train called the "Potato Special" is shown carrying Oregon farm goods to market in 1910.

The Grange did not succeed in getting a law passed to lower railroad rates. Yet it was one of the first groups in America to fight for lower railroad rates. It was also one of the first groups to give full membership rights to women. The Grange became well known across the United States.

The Grange was successful in another way. Before the Grange was formed, most farming families rarely had a chance to meet with friends and neighbors. Farms in eastern Oregon were often so large that it took a long time to travel from one to another for a visit. After the Grange was started, farmers and their families had a chance to meet often at Grange meetings. Friendships formed through the Grange. They became an important part of farming life in Oregon.

Labor Unions

During the 1880's and 1890's, small business owners and workers joined the farmers in voicing their views about conditions in Oregon. The groups they formed wanted to improve safety in the workplace. They also wanted to see that workers received fair **wages,** or pay, for their work. Groups that fight for the rights of workers are called **labor unions.**

wage
the amount of money a worker is paid for his or her labor

labor union
a group of workers that tries to improve its members' wages and working conditions

In Oregon, labor unions also helped farmers. Farmers wanted to be able to borrow money from the government to keep their farms going. The labor unions supported this idea.

At least one union from those early days still exists. It is the American Federation of Labor, which came to Oregon in 1887. Today the AFL represents millions of American workers.

The first unions were made up of workers with only one trade. This picture of Portland's tailors' union was taken in 1902.

The Populist Party

In 1891, a group of American farmers started a new group to fight for farmers' and workers' rights. It was called the Populist, or People's Party.

The Populist Party favored government control of the railroads. Populists in Oregon, including women such as Sophronia Lewelling, wanted the United States government to build a railroad along the north bank of the Columbia River. This railroad would compete with the privately owned railroads and, hopefully, force railroad rates to drop.

Populists also wanted the government to lend farmers money if they needed it to stay in business. Along with these things, they also wanted free books for Oregon's schools and free housing for people who had lost their jobs.

Few Populists were chosen for office in Oregon. But the Populist Party kept alive the idea of making things better by working to change the laws of the land.

Section Review

Write your answers on a sheet of paper.

1. What problems did Oregon's farmers have with the railroads?
2. How did the Oregon State Grange help farmers?
3. What were the goals of the Populist Party?
4. What do you think the labor unions could have done to get better wages and working conditions for their members?

2 The People Gain a Greater Voice

The Grange, the labor unions, and the Populists fought for better working conditions and greater rights for farmers and workers in Oregon. In the 1890's, another group joined this cause. This group was called the Progressives. The Progressives fought for ways to give the people a greater voice in their government.

Before 1900, the people in Oregon were supposed to be able to control the government by voting for leaders who represented their interests. But during the late 1800's, railroad companies and other big businesses had a lot of power. At times they were able to pressure governmental leaders into passing laws that favored their interests. Some of these laws hurt the people.

The Progressives wanted there to be ways for the people to speak out directly to get more control. In the early 1900's, they were successful in making important changes in Oregon's state government. These changes were brought about through the leadership of William S. U'Ren (you-**rehn**).

William S. U'Ren led Oregon's Progressives in working for ways to give the people a greater voice in their state government.

The "Oregon System"

William U'Ren came to Oregon from Wisconsin in the late 1800's. He made his home in the town of Milwaukie, near Portland. There he opened a law office and soon became active in Oregon government.

U'Ren led the Progressives in working for two important changes in Oregon's government. The first was the **initiative.** The initiative is a way for the people to start, or initiate, a law on their own. To initiate a state law, a certain number of people must sign a **petition.** A petition is a sheet of paper signed by people who support a specific course of action. If enough people sign the petition, the initiative is placed on the state **ballot,** or voting sheet.

The second change U'Ren worked for was the **referendum.** The referendum gives the people a chance to accept or reject a law. If a lot of people do not like a law, they can ask for a referendum vote. To do this, a petition is also needed.

The initiative and referendum were made part of the Oregon Constitution in 1902. By using the initiative, Oregon voters were able to pass other laws that gave them a greater voice in the government. In 1908, the **recall** was adopted. The recall gives the people a chance to vote a leader out of office in a special election. Like the initiative and referendum, the recall gave the people of Oregon more direct control over their laws and leaders.

All of the laws that were passed to give the people of Oregon a greater voice in their government came to be called the Oregon System. The Oregon System soon became well known all over the country. Parts of it were adopted in many other states.

initiative
a way for the people to start, or initiate, a law on their own

petition
a sheet of paper signed by people who support a specific course of action

ballot
a voting sheet from which voters make a selection

referendum
a process that gives the people a chance to accept or reject a law

recall
a process that gives the people a chance to vote a leader out of office in a special election

Saving Natural Resources

The Progressives were also concerned about protecting Oregon's most valuable natural resource—trees. As the railroads opened up more markets for Oregon's lumber, more trees were being cut down every year. The Progressives were the first to realize that Oregon's trees would not last long if they were not protected.

In 1891, Progressives all over the United States helped pass the Forest Reserve Act. This act gave the President the power to set aside large areas of forest land for public use. During President Theodore Roosevelt's term of office (1901–1909), more than 60.7 hectares (150 million acres) of forest land in the United States were set aside. This amounts to an area almost as large as the present-day states of Arizona and New Mexico. In 1905, the Forest Service was created to manage these lands. Today more than half the forest lands in the northwestern United States are part of the United States National Forests.

Planting trees to replace the ones that have been cut down assures Oregon of a continuing supply of timber.

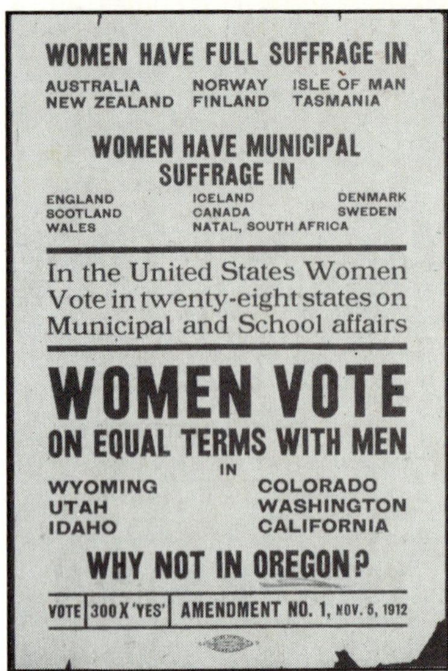

President Roosevelt also had a plan that would protect and preserve all of America's land. People in every part of the country began to realize that all of our natural resources should be protected. President Roosevelt's program led to the founding of the national parks and forest systems we enjoy today. At about this same time, Oregon's Governor Oswald West persuaded Oregon's lawmakers to set aside the state's beaches for public use.

Women's Rights

suffrage
the right to vote

The Progressives also worked for greater rights for women. As part of their plan to give the people a greater voice in government, they supported women's **suffrage,** or the right to vote. Through the efforts of leaders like Abigail Scott Duniway, Oregon's women won this right in 1912. From that time on, the women of Oregon have had a voice in their government.

Section Review

Write your answers on a sheet of paper.

1. Who was William S. U'Ren? How did he help Oregon?
2. How did the initiative, referendum, and recall give the people of Oregon a greater voice in their government?
3. In what ways did the Progressives help to protect America's land and resources?
4. When did women gain a voice in Oregon's government?
5. Suppose you wanted to initiate, or start, a new law. What would you do?

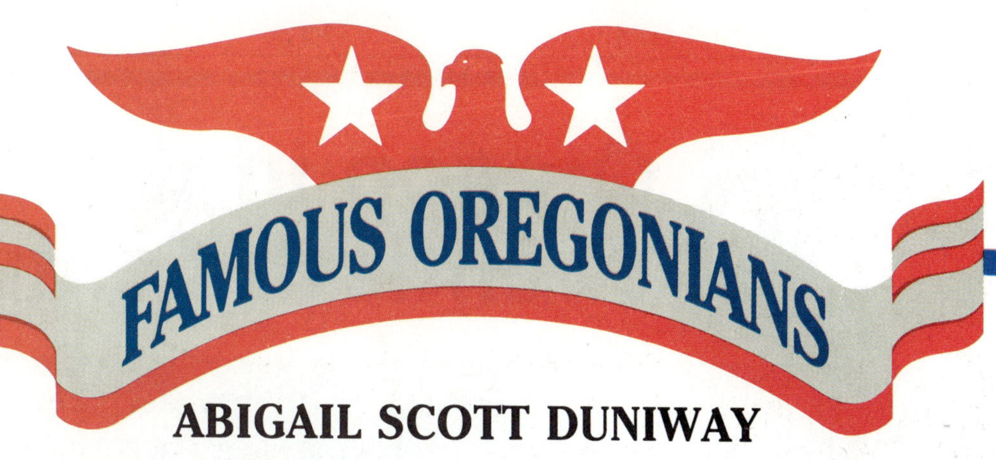

ABIGAIL SCOTT DUNIWAY

Abigail Scott Duniway was one of Oregon's earliest fighters for women's rights. Her battle for women's rights began in 1862. In that year, her husband, Ben, made a bad business deal. The Duniways were forced to pay for it with their land. It was then that Abigail learned how unfairly the law treated women.

At that time, women could not own land, but they were held responsible if their husbands made bad land deals. Women were also not allowed to borrow money. But, again, they were held responsible for their husbands' debts.

Abigail Duniway knew that until women were given the right to vote, they would never be treated fairly by the law. She began *the New Northwest,* a newspaper for and about women's rights. She also traveled all over Oregon speaking out in favor of women's suffrage.

Though many people were against giving women the vote, Abigail kept going. In 1912, after years of setbacks, Abigail Duniway saw her dream come true. Women's suffrage became an Oregon law. Abigail Duniway became the first woman in the state to sign up to vote.

CHAPTER 10 Oregon in the Twentieth Century

This painting by the American artist Thomas Hart Benton shows the growth of our country in the twentieth century.

During the twentieth century, Oregon's history was shaped by events that affected Americans all across the country. Things that were happening in other parts of the country and the world brought changes to Oregon.

At the end of this chapter, you should be able to:

○ Explain why and how Oregon's population grew.

● Read a double bar graph.

○ Describe the changes that occurred in Oregon during the time between the two world wars.

● Read a time line.

○ Describe the contributions Oregonians made to the war efforts of the twentieth century.

○ Describe how Oregon developed after World War II.

1 World War I

World War I started in Europe in 1914. It began when the country of Austria-Hungary started fighting with its neighbor Serbia. You would not be able to find these two countries as they once existed, on a present-day map of Europe. World War I changed the boundaries of many European countries. It also brought changes to Oregon and the United States as a whole.

Soon after Austria-Hungary and Serbia went to war, many other European countries joined the fighting. Germany, Turkey, and Bulgaria fought on the side of Austria-Hungary. Together these four countries were called the Central Powers. Russia, France, Great Britain, and many other countries joined Serbia in fighting the Central Powers. These countries were called the Allied Powers, or the Allies.

The United States Enters the War

At first the United States tried to stay out of World War I, but this proved impossible. German submarines began attacking American ships. Then in 1917, the United States government learned that Germany was trying to get Mexico to help Germany in an attack on the United States. Mexico did not agree to help the Germans, but the United States government realized that it had to do something to protect its land and people. On April 6, 1917, the United States entered World War I on the side of the Allies. Like Americans in other states, Oregonians helped the Allies win the war.

A Liberty Bond rally in front of the Portland Liberty Temple in 1918.

Oregonians Help Their Country

Many people in Oregon joined the war effort. Oregonians helped fight for their country. Many volunteered to join the armed services. Oregon had among the highest number of volunteers fighting in the war. These soldiers and sailors served in all the places in which the war was being fought.

Oregonians at home also came to their country's aid. Many bought Victory Bonds and Liberty Bonds. These bonds made it possible for the United States government to buy food and war materials for American soldiers in Europe. The government also raised money by increasing some taxes and passing new tax laws. Income taxes and taxes on liquor and tobacco were raised. A "nuisance tax" was passed. It taxed things such as theater tickets and club dues. Even the cost of mailing letters and packages was increased to help pay the costs of the war.

Oregon's rich resources also helped the war effort. The state's wood products, wheat, and beef were sent to the Allies in Europe. During the war, the government was willing to pay high prices for farm goods. Because of this, farmers in Oregon could raise more food and hire more help. Many people went to the state to work on farms at this time.

People at home had "wheatless" and "meatless" days. Oregonians ate no bread or meat on those days. This meant that more wheat and meat could be sent to the soldiers. Extra gasoline was also needed to ship soldiers and supplies to Europe. So like Americans all over the country, the people of Oregon had "gasless Sundays."

Oregon's factories were very busy during the war. The war caused businesses to boom. Shipyards along the Willamette and Columbia rivers built many ocean-going ships. Oregonians had to build ships faster than the Germans could sink them. These ships were used to send soldiers, food, and supplies to Europe.

This picture shows the launching of the ship City of Astoria *in Astoria, Oregon, on October 28, 1916. Oregonians built many ships during World War I to help in the war effort.*

These members of the National League for Woman's Service are shown pitting and canning cherries as part of the war effort in 1918.

Thousands of women in Oregon went to work in factories. They replaced workers who had gone to war. People also moved to Oregon during World War I to work in defense industries. Many defense workers chose to stay in Oregon after the war.

Feelings About the War

Although almost all Oregonians were in favor of the war, a small number were not. Some of these people, called **pacifists,** believed that all problems between countries should be settled by peaceful means rather than by war. Pacifists were not accepted by most Oregonians during World War I. For example, the mayor and the newspapers in Portland wanted a pacifist librarian to be fired from her job. She had refused to buy war bonds. Although she was not fired, she chose to quit her job and leave the state.

pacifist
a person who believes that all problems between countries should be settled by peaceful means rather than by war

This victory parade to celebrate the end of World War I took place in Salem, Oregon, on November 11, 1918.

A large number of Oregonians who were in favor of the war developed strong feelings against anything German. In some places, German street names like Rhine and Bismarck were changed. And in a few cases, German immigrants were treated poorly.

The War Ends

World War I ended on November 11, 1918. The Central Powers had been defeated. The people of Oregon who had served their country during the war served it well. Memorials were built in many parts of the state to honor Oregonians who had died in battle.

Section Review

Write your answers on a sheet of paper.

1. When did the United States enter World War I?

2. How did Oregonians help the government pay the costs of the war?

3. What things were sent from Oregon to help the war effort?

4. How did World War I change Oregon?

MARY FRANCES ISOM

Mary Frances Isom, born in 1865, loved books and spent her whole life working with them. Mary Isom knew the value of reading. She also knew that books were not available to all those who wanted and needed them.

Isom went to college to become a librarian. After her studies were finished, she moved from New York to Portland, Oregon. There she began working in a private library. When it became public in 1902, she became the head librarian.

But many people who lived far away could not visit this public library. In 1903, a law was passed ordering the library to come up with a plan for bringing books to all of the people in Multnomah County. So Mary Isom set up three library branches and 11 reading rooms around the county.

But that was not all she did. During World War I Mary Isom made sure that soldiers in camps and hospitals had books. She even went to France and helped build hospital libraries there.

Mary Isom spent her whole life helping people get the books they needed. When you go to your library, you have people like Mary Isom to thank.

Reading a Double Bar Graph

A **double bar graph** compares two sets of the same kind of information. This graph compares the number of people living in three states during 1910 and 1920. The red bars show the numbers for 1910. The blue bars show those for 1920. The numbers across the top of the graph stand for thousands of people.

double bar graph a graph that compares two sets of the same kind of information

Find the red bar for Oregon. Move your finger right, to the end of the bar. Now move your finger straight up to the number at the top. Do the same for the blue bar. Compare the two numbers. There were over 100,000 more people living in Oregon in 1920 than in 1910.

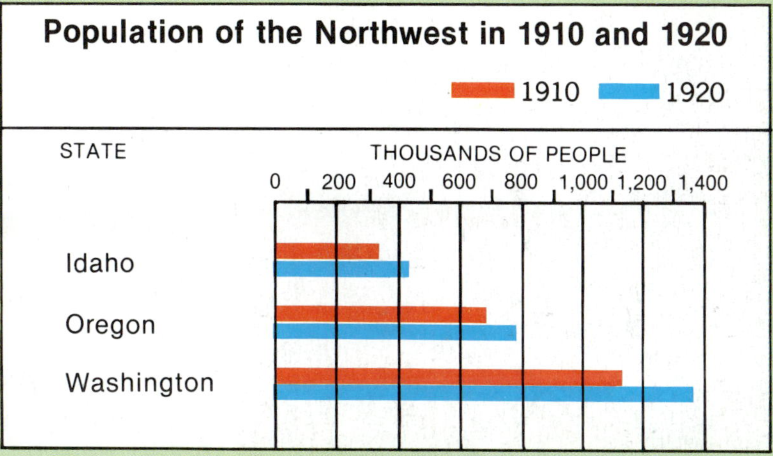

Practice Your Skills

1. What was the population of Idaho in 1910? Was it larger or smaller in 1920?
2. Which state had the largest population in 1910?
3. Which state had a population of almost 700,000 people in 1910? What was this state's population in 1920?
4. Which state's population grew the most? By how much did it grow?

2 The 1920's and 1930's

The 1920's were called the Roaring Twenties. It was a time that "roared" with new ideas and change. New machines and ways of making goods helped Oregon grow in many ways.

Automobiles Bring Change

New inventions and machinery affected the lives of Oregonians in the 1920's. The automobile created many changes. It brought country people to the cities of Oregon. Farmers would drive to big stores in the cities to buy clothing and other goods. Small stores in towns suffered as a result. Many closed down. So did some small theaters and churches.

With the automobile came the need for new roads. Oregonians were the first to pay a gasoline tax. The tax money was used to build new roads and highways. Highways helped Oregon's tourist industry grow. Many people would drive down the Columbia River Highway to see Oregon's beautiful ocean beaches. The government started building parks in all parts of the state.

Early automobile travelers on the Columbia River Highway

New Ideas for Industry

The 1920's also affected Oregon's two most important businesses—farming and lumbering.

New farming methods made it possible to raise more kinds of crops. New machinery, such as the tractor, cut the time needed to plant and harvest crops. So the amount of farm goods that was raised went up. But fancy equipment also cost a lot of money. Many small farmers could not buy this new machinery. Without it they could not compete, and many of them lost their farms during this time.

New ideas made great changes in Oregon's lumbering industry in the 1920's and 1930's. Chain saws made it possible to cut down trees faster. Power equipment, trucks, and new roads made it easier to move logs through the forest.

With these changes, the people of Oregon became more concerned with protecting the state's forest resources. During the 1920's, laws were passed to help protect forests from fires. The government also gave Oregon small trees to replace trees that were cut down.

Diesel-powered equipment made it easier to move logs out of the forests in the 1920's.

Like people all over the country, Oregonians had trouble finding jobs during the Great Depression in the 1930's.

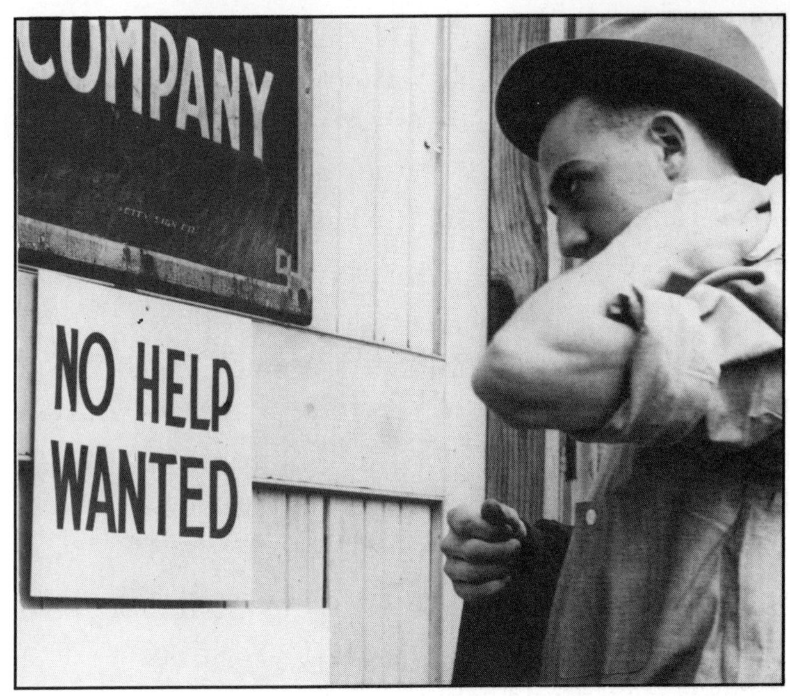

The Great Depression

The good times that most Oregonians had enjoyed during the 1920's ended in the 1930's. During the 1930's, the United States and many countries around the world went through hard times. These years of hard times were known as the Great Depression. Industries and shops closed. Many banks also closed, and people lost their savings. Thousands of people were out of work. Many had no money for food. People stood in long lines to get free bread or a bowl of soup paid for by the government.

Thousands of people came to Oregon during this time. They were mostly from the northern Great Plains region of the United States. Most of them were looking for farm jobs. Farming was what they knew best. Oregonians did not welcome these newcomers. These people competed for the few jobs left in the state. Some Oregonians also did not want to pay higher taxes to take care of these people.

New Deal Projects

When Franklin D. Roosevelt became President in 1933, things began to change. Most of the people in Oregon had voted for him. Roosevelt worked out several plans to help people all over the United States. Together these plans were called the "New Deal."

One New Deal program was the Civilian Conservation Corps. It was for men between the ages of 18 and 25. These men lived in work camps run by the government. They planted trees, built dams, and improved the parks in Oregon. Some ran recreation programs in the towns of the state.

Another New Deal program was the Works Progress Administration. It was known as the WPA. Timberline Lodge on Mount Hood was a WPA project. It is a large hotel made of wood. Oregon Ponderosa pine logs were used for the beams in the main lobby. Stairway posts were made from old telephone poles. Railroad tracks were used to hold logs in three huge fireplaces. Scraps of cloth from Civilian Conservation Corps uniforms were made into braided rugs. Much of the art and furnishings in the lodge were done by women hired through the WPA.

President Franklin D. Roosevelt dedicated Timberline Lodge on Mt. Hood on September 28, 1937.

mural
a large picture painted directly on a wall or ceiling

The WPA also created projects for writers and artists who were out of work. The *American Guide Series* for all the states was written. Artists were given jobs painting **murals** in public buildings. A mural is a large picture painted directly on a wall or ceiling. Edward Quigley was one of Oregon's WPA artists. His mural in Irvington School in Portland shows early settlers coming to Oregon.

The Public Works Administration (PWA) was another New Deal program set up to help people without jobs. The government paid these people to build bridges, schools, and other public buildings. Oregon's post offices and sewage systems were improved through this program.

The Bonneville Dam Project

Bonneville Dam on the Columbia River between Portland and The Dalles was another PWA project. Completed in 1938, it provided low-cost electrical power to farms and industries.

This picture of Bonneville Dam was taken in 1940, two years after the dam was completed.

Not all Oregonians were happy about the dam project. The fishing industry feared that the dam would hurt the salmon runs. Private electric companies disliked government-owned power plants. Coal miners were afraid of losing their jobs if hydroelectric power instead of coal was used in the making of electricity.

But in the long run, the dam was good for Oregon. Cheap electric power helped the state's industries grow. Oregon could now make more kinds of goods. It also improved rural life in the state. Farmers could have refrigerators and electric milking machines. Oregon's dry lands could be irrigated for farming.

Throughout the 1930's, the New Deal projects helped the people of Oregon. But they did not end the Great Depression. The Depression ended in the early 1940's when the United States found itself once again involved in a terrible world war. This was World War II.

Section Review

Write your answers on a sheet of paper.

1. How did the automobile affect life in Oregon in the 1920's?
2. What changes affected the lumbering industry in Oregon in the 1920's?
3. Name two projects in Oregon that resulted from the New Deal.
4. How did the Bonneville Dam help Oregon?
5. Do you think new inventions are always helpful? Why or why not?

SOCIAL STUDIES SKILLS

Reading a Time Line

time line
a way of listing important dates or events in the order in which they happened

A **time line** is a way of listing the dates of important events in the order in which they happened.

The time line below covers almost 100 years of Oregon's history. The earliest date, the one that happened longest ago, appears at the left. The most recent date appears at the right. You read a time line from left to right.

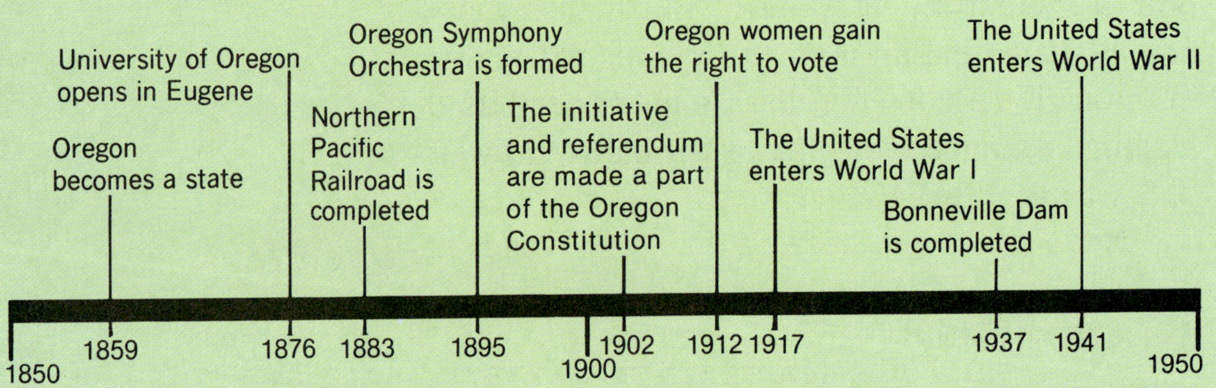

Practice Your Skills

1. What happened in 1859?
2. In what year was the Bonneville Dam completed?
3. What is the most recent event on the time line?
4. How many years are there between the year the United States entered World War I and the year the United States entered World War II?

3 World War II

People had hoped that the First World War would end all wars. But it did not. In the 1930's, the countries of Germany, Italy, and Japan began attacking other countries. These three countries were called the Axis Powers. At first countries like Great Britain, France, and the United States tried to stop the Axis Powers by peaceful means. But this did not work. In 1939, Germany attacked the country of Poland. This was the beginning of World War II.

The countries that fought against the Axis Powers were called the Allies. They included Great Britain, France, the Soviet Union, and many smaller countries. As it had in World War I, the United States at first tried to stay out of the war. But on December 7, 1941, Japanese planes bombed American ships at Pearl Harbor, Hawaii. The next day, the United States declared war on the Axis Powers and became one of the Allies.

Oregon Helps

The people of Oregon once again helped the United States win a world war. Many Oregonians served in the army, navy, air force, and marines. They fought in Europe and on islands in the Pacific Ocean.

On the home front, farmers in Oregon and other states worked hard to feed the armed forces. Families were willing to cut back on such things as meat, sugar, gasoline, and tires, which were carefully divided among them. Each family was allowed only a certain amount of each item. This system was called **rationing.** It was used in every part of the country.

ration
to limit the amount of food or other goods that are in short supply

4 A New Era Begins

In the years following World War II, Oregonians worked hard to make their state a better place in which to live. Laws were passed to protect the rights and improve the lives of all people in the state. Oregonians also worked to protect the state's natural resources and beauty.

The New Oregonians

Many of the people who went to Oregon during World War II made it their home. But after the war, fewer workers were needed to build ships or make war materials. Black Americans had trouble finding new jobs. Many continued to live in the low-cost housing in Vanport. But in 1948, Vanport was washed away when a small dam on the Columbia River broke. Many blacks left the Portland region because they could not get low-cost housing in or around the city.

On Memorial Day 1948, the Columbia River flooded Vanport, Oregon.

Wartime conditions had strengthened black groups. The National Association for the Advancement of Colored People (NAACP) became stronger. New groups to help blacks were formed. One of them was the Urban League. In the 1950's and 1960's, many black Oregonians joined the **civil rights** movement. Civil rights are the rights given to each person by the Constitution.

civil rights
rights given to each person by the Constitution

After the war, Oregon's government passed laws to protect the civil rights of blacks and other minority groups living in the state. The National Guard was opened to all groups. A state fair-employment-practices law was passed. Laws were also passed to **desegregate** public housing. To desegregate is to do away with the separation of people on the basis of race.

desegregate
to do away with the separation of people on the basis of race

Several programs were started for the state's growing number of Spanish-speaking people. **Bilingual** cultural centers were started. Bilingual means in two languages. The first center in Oregon was founded in 1969 near the town of Woodburn. It offered bilingual books, radio programs, and a newspaper. Today Spanish-speaking people are the state's largest minority group.

bilingual
in two languages

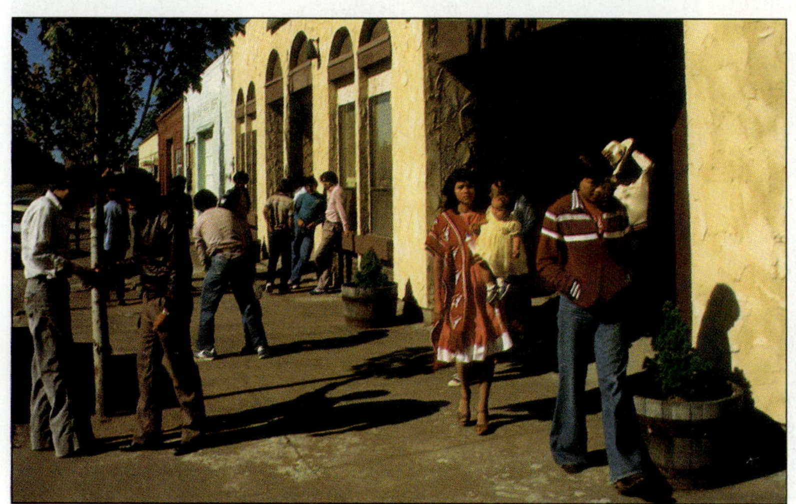

This street scene of Dayton, Oregon shows Spanish-speaking Americans who live in the area.

American Indians

American Indians faced many changes in the 1900's. In the 1880's, the government divided up the reservation lands. It gave the head of each Indian family 65 hectares (160 acres) to farm. The government wanted Indians to live as other Americans did. This did not work.

The government's view of Indians changed in the 1930's. The Wheeler-Howard Indian Reorganization Act was passed in 1934. This law helped Indians to regroup into tribes. The government also promised to protect the rights of Indians. The Indians could have a limited say in reservation governments. They could get aid from the United States to start businesses. The government also bought land to give to the Indians.

In 1960, three tribes on the Warm Springs Reservation in Oregon bought a vacation resort. They used part of the money the government had given them in the 1950's for the loss of their fishing grounds. The fishing grounds were at the site of the Celilo Falls Dam. They also built two factories. These Indians are among the most successful in the United States.

The Warm Springs Indian Tribal Council poses outside the electronics assembly plant on their reservation.

Asian Americans

Feelings against Japanese people living in the United States lessened after World War II. Laws keeping Japanese immigrants from owning land or becoming citizens were changed. In Oregon, they were treated in the same way as other Oregonians. Through the years, they have worked to build better lives for themselves and their families.

In the 1970's, large numbers of immigrants came to Oregon from countries in Southeast Asia. Many came because their homes had been ruined by war. Most of them were from the country of Vietnam.

This picture of Senator Wayne Morse was taken around the year 1950.

Wayne Morse

Oregon moved ahead after World War II with the help of good leaders. Senator Wayne Morse was Oregon's best-known leader at this time. He worked to help the people of Oregon. Most Oregonians liked Wayne Morse because he tried to understand what they wanted.

Morse worked for civil rights and better conditions for workers. He wanted the government to give more aid to schools and students. He also worked to protect Oregon's natural resources and pushed for the building of new power plants.

Senator Morse was not afraid to stand up for what he believed. In the 1960's, he became well known all over the country for his views on the Vietnam War. He was one of a few senators who first thought that the war was wrong. Morse believed in the rule of law. He thought that the war was against the law. In time, many people in the United States came to agree with him.

Industrial Growth and Resources

Throughout its history, Oregon's good transportation routes were important to the growth of industries in the state. But in the 1900's, low-cost electrical power also became important. Dams provided hydroelectric power. They also helped to provide water for irrigation and recreation. The dams have helped to stop floods too.

Nuclear energy has also been used as a source of power in Oregon. But Oregonians have been worried about nuclear plant safety. In 1978, the Trojan Nuclear Power Plant in Rainier, Oregon, was closed for safety reasons. The people wanted it to be strengthened against earthquakes. This was done, and the plant was reopened.

SAVAGE RAPIDS IRRIGATION DAM
WATER FOR 16,000 ACRES OF RICH LAND
SURROUNDING THE CITY OF GRANTS PASS
PEARS, APPLES GRAPES, ALFALFA
CHEAP LAND. SETTLERS WANTED
CHAMBER OF COMMERCE

Nuclear energy is used to make electricity at the Trojan Nuclear Power Plant in Rainier, Oregon.

Oregon has used its resources wisely. It has not only used its rivers to provide cheap sources of power, but it has tried to protect its fish as well. It has found ways to save its forests. Laws have been passed to protect the beauty of the state's land and waters. Oregon has provided its future citizens with a good place to live.

Section Review

Write your answers on a sheet of paper.

1. Why did many blacks leave the Portland area in 1948?

2. How did the lives of blacks, Spanish-speaking people, and Asian Americans in Oregon improve after World War II?

3. How did American Indians on the Warm Springs Reservation improve their lives in the 1960's?

4. What did Senator Wayne Morse do for Oregon?

5. How has Oregon prepared for its future?

Close-up on

Portland Rose Festival The Portland Rose Festival is the biggest celebration held in Oregon. Every June, beautiful roses are honored in shows and parades. Rose Festival banners hang from the streetlamps. People help pay for the festival by buying and wearing rose pins. This shows their pride in the event.

The Portland rose show is one of the finest in the world. Rose growers enter their flowers against thousands of blooms. It is a great honor to win ribbons or silver prizes in the rose show.

The festival parade is the second largest floral parade in America. It is viewed on television by thousands of people. Expert float builders work all year for this event. Some floats are covered with over 50,000 flowers. Many floats cost as much as $18,000 to make. One of the floats is made for a very special person. This person is the Queen of the magic land of Rosaria. She and her court are chosen from among the many high school students in the city.

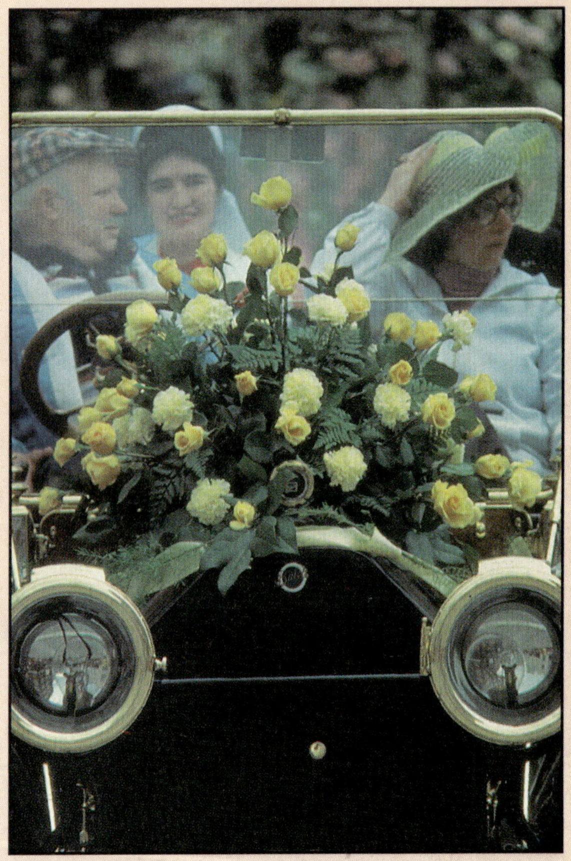

The festival has something for almost everyone to enjoy. Adults can take part in bike, boat, and ski races. Ice-skating and tennis competitions are held too. Children have their own parade. They enter floats and dress up in costumes. The Li'l Britches Rodeo is put on by kids for kids. One of the favorite events is the milk-carton boat race. Young people build large boats out of milk cartons. They ride in the boats and race for prizes.

Portland's Rose Festival is a fun way to start the summer. It is also a great way to honor one of Oregon's most beautiful flowers—the rose.

UNIT REVIEW

Word Work

Write the sentences below on a sheet of paper. Fill in the blanks with the correct words from the list.

ranching	initiative	segregate
population	suffrage	mural
immigrant	ballot	migrant worker
museum		

1. A person who comes from another country to live in a new land is called an ____.
2. To ____ is to separate people of one race from those of another.
3. A ____ is a voting sheet from which voters select a candidate.
4. A person who goes from one region to another to earn a living is called a ____.
5. A large picture painted directly on a wall or ceiling is called a ____.
6. ____ is the raising of large herds of animals.
7. Abigail Scott Duniway worked for women's ____, or the right to vote.
8. All of the people who live in a particular place make up its ____.
9. The ____ is a way for the people to start a law on their own.
10. A ____ is a building where art, historical, or scientific objects are preserved and put on display.

Knowing the Facts

Write your answers on a sheet of paper.

1. How did the coming of the railroads help Oregon's industries grow?
2. What things helped the growth of Portland? Salem? Eugene?
3. Explain how the initiative, referendum, and recall gave Oregonians a greater voice in their government.
4. How did Oregonians help the United States win two world wars?
5. Why did many black Americans and Spanish-speaking people go to Oregon during World War II?

Using What You Know

Choose one of the following activities to do. Follow the instructions given here.

1. Make a model or draw a picture of a steamboat or an early train.
2. Interview someone who lived in Oregon during World War II. Record the questions and answers on a tape recorder or write a report on what you find out.
3. Write a news story about one event in Oregon history from 1860 to the present.
4. Find out what route your family or your ancestors took to Oregon. Make a map showing the route.
5. Make a double bar graph showing the population of Oregon, Washington, and Idaho in 1970 and 1980.

Skills Practice

Use the line graph below to answer the questions. Write your answers on a sheet of paper.

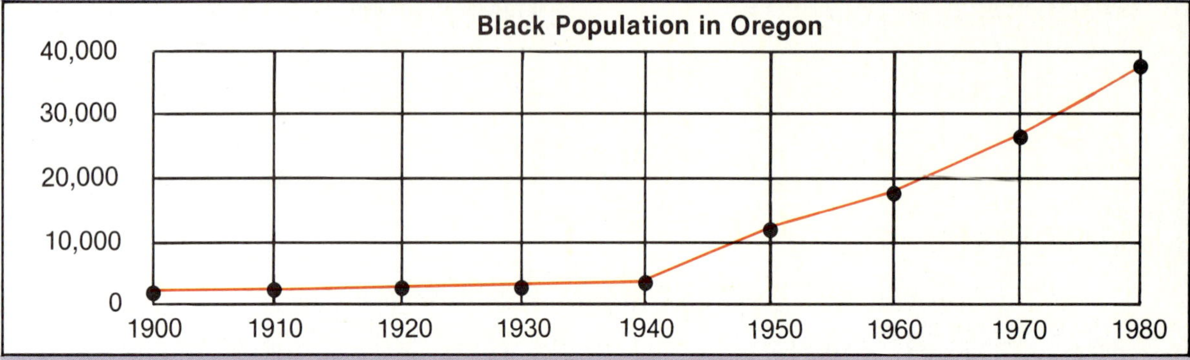

1. What was the first year in which Oregon had a black population greater than 10,000?
2. In what year was Oregon's black population the greatest? What was the black population of the state in that year?

Use the graph below to answer the questions.

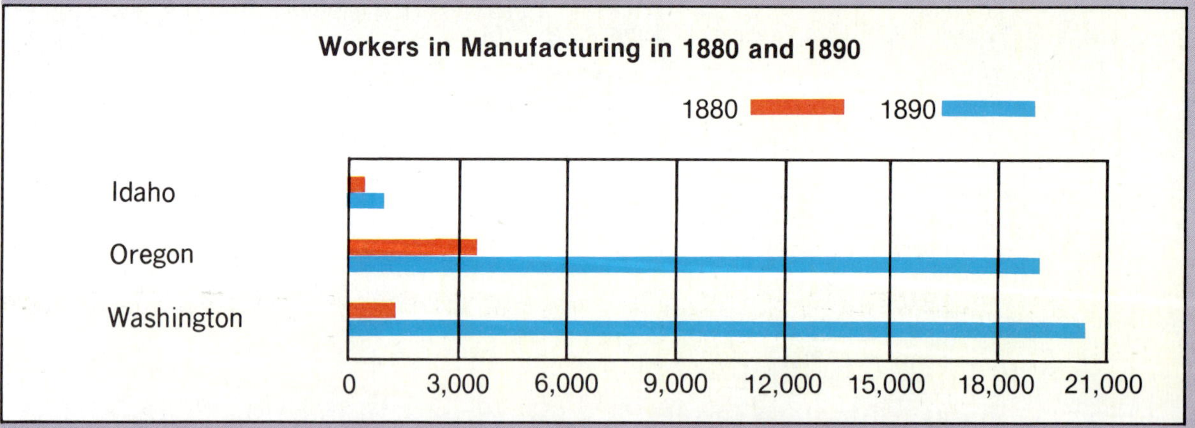

1. About how many people held manufacturing jobs in Oregon in 1880? in 1890?
2. Which state had the greatest increase in the number of people working in manufacturing? By how much did the number increase?

Use the population density map on page 193 to answer the questions below.

1. What is the population density in the area around Pendleton?
2. Which is more thickly settled—southeastern Oregon or southwestern Oregon?

Use the table and bar graph on pages 174 and 175 to answer the questions below.

1. In what year did Oregon produce 444,565,000 board feet of lumber? Did you use the table or the bar graph to find this information?
2. In what year did Oregon produce the least lumber? Was it faster to use the table or the bar graph to find out? Why?

Use the following time line to answer the questions below.

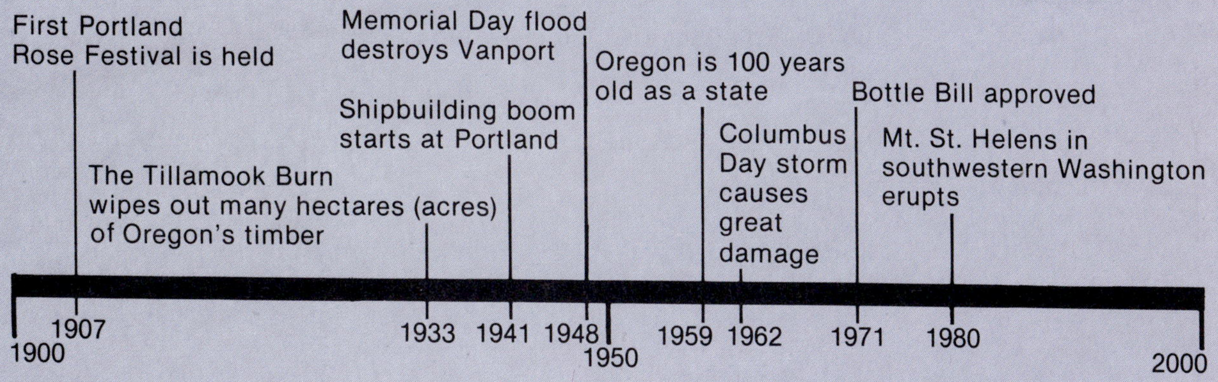

1. What happened in 1948?
2. What is the most recent event on the time line?
3. In what year was the first Portland Rose Festival held?

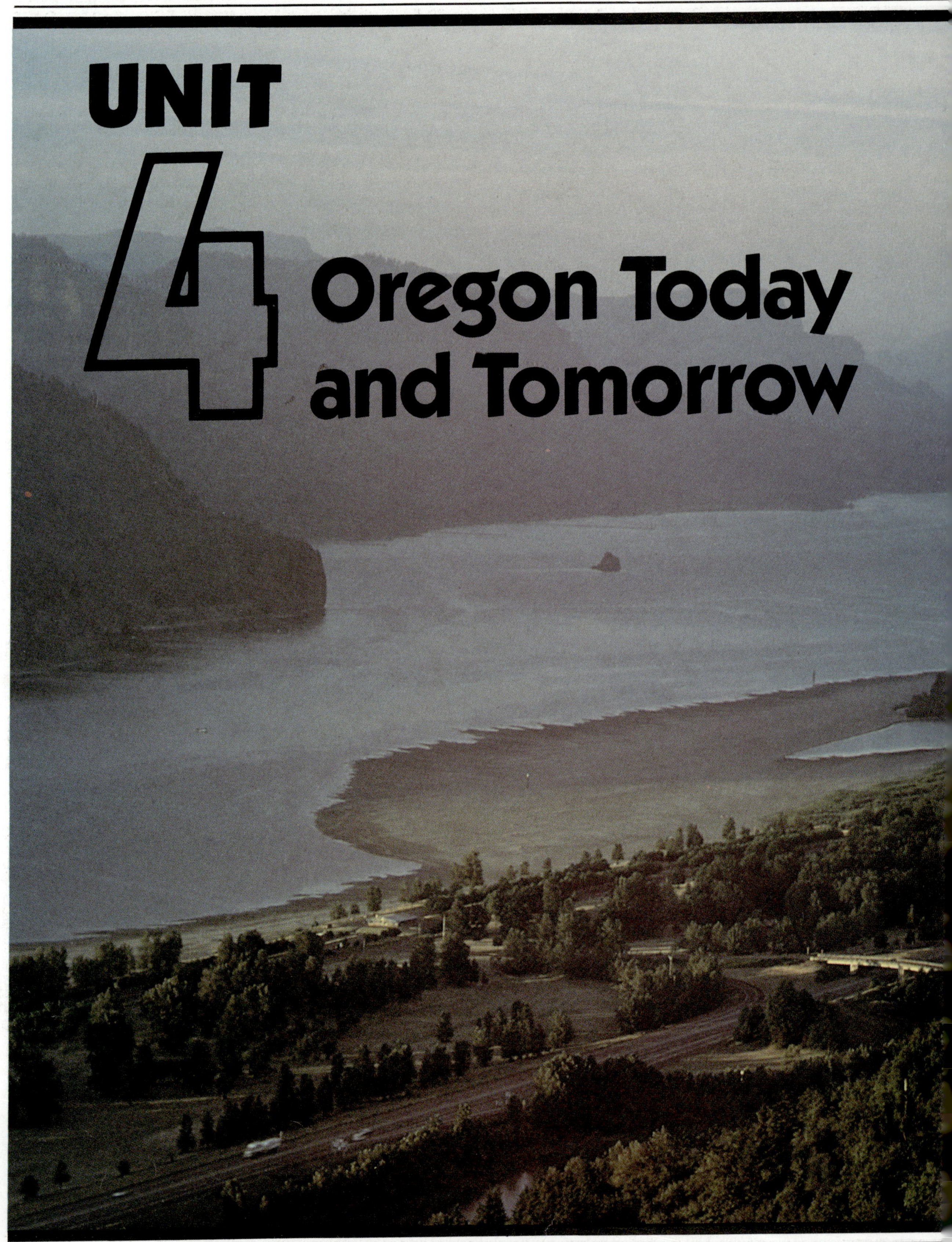

UNIT 4 Oregon Today and Tomorrow

CHAPTER 11 Government

The state capitol in Salem, Oregon

Groups of people living or working together need rules and laws to help keep them safe. They need a government to make and explain the laws. They also need a government to make sure the laws are obeyed. The people who make laws for Oregon form its state government.

At the end of this chapter, you should be able to:

○ Explain the rights and responsibilities of citizens.
○ Describe the duties of local government.
○ Explain how Oregon's state government is organized.
○ Describe the role Oregon plays in our country.
● Read a time zone map.

1 Rights and Responsibilities

Over the years, many different people have moved to Oregon. They needed help in getting along together. They needed a way to set up fire departments, police stations, and schools. Their cities had to be planned. Workers had to be protected in the work place. So laws were made, and people were given certain rights.

People's Rights

Today you have many rights that allow you to live the way you do. Some rights are given to you by law. For example, you have the right to vote when you are 18 years old. You have the right to a fair trial. You may go to any church you like or none at all. You have the freedom to read any kind of book or newspaper. You have many freedoms that people in some other countries do not have.

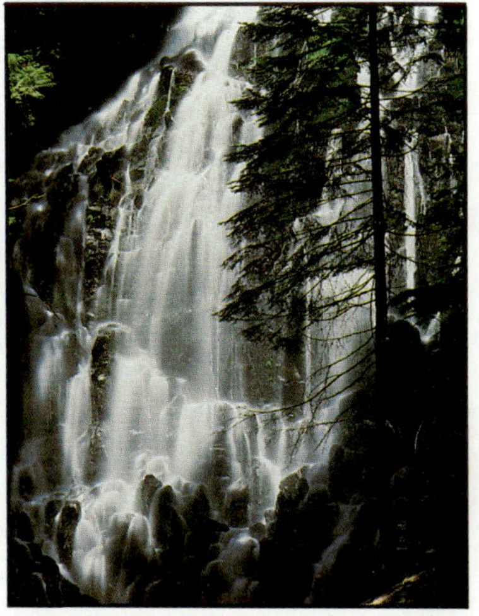

Oregonians can enjoy such beautiful sights as Ramona Falls in the Mt. Hood National Forest.

People also have rights that are not given to them by law. These are called natural rights. You have the right to clean air and water. You have a right to enjoy the natural beauty of your state.

Rights do not take care of themselves. If you want to enjoy them, you must work to keep them. People have certain **responsibilities.** Responsibilities are things that are one's duty to do. We are very fortunate to be able to choose the people who govern us. It is your responsibility as a good citizen to read newspapers and listen to the news so that you know who these people are. Then you can make wise decisions.

responsibilities things that are one's duty to do

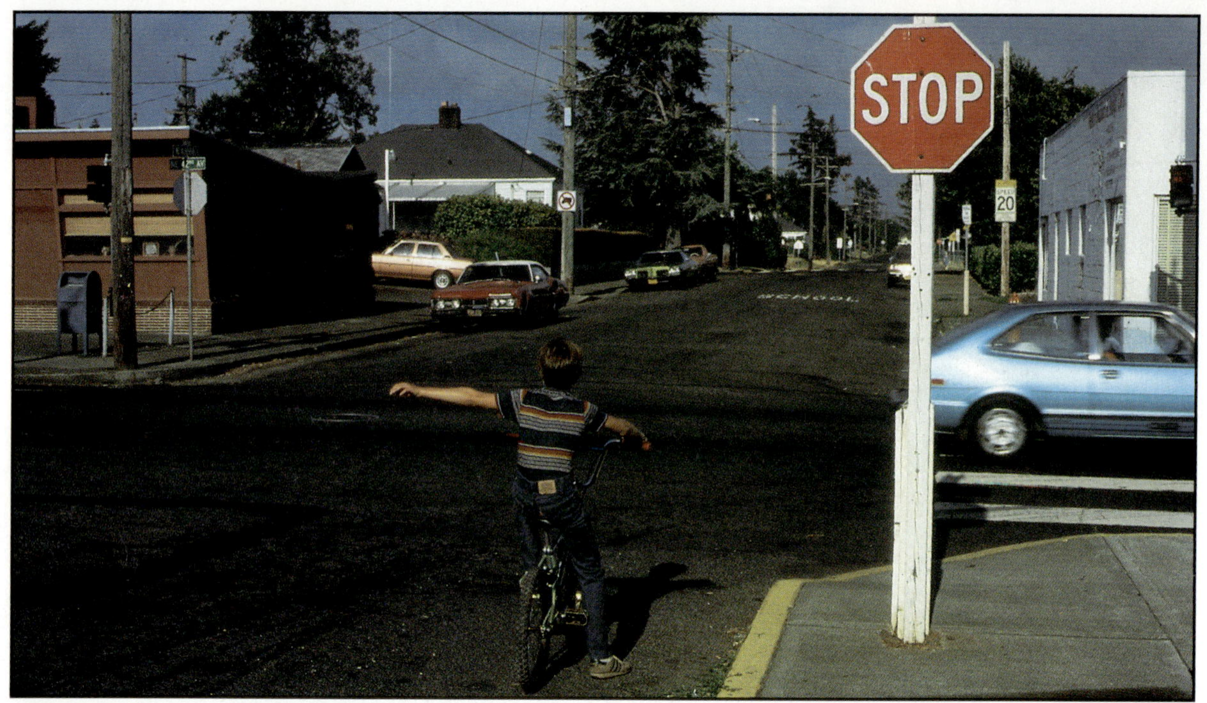

Obeying traffic laws and giving the proper hand signals are important to bicycle safety.

Government leaders like to know what the people think. You may have ideas about a certain issue. If so, you can write a letter to your **representatives.** A representative is a person who speaks or acts for others.

representative
a person who speaks or acts for others

Laws Protect Our Rights

Having rights does not mean you can do whatever you like. You may feel you have the right to ride your bicycle anywhere. But if you ride where people are walking, you might hurt someone. So laws are made to protect everyone's rights.

Laws Are Important

Some people think that laws are made just to keep them from doing something. Actually, most laws help people. For example, it is against the law for anyone to steal property. The law protects what a person owns. But everyone has the responsibility to obey that law. Every person's right to protection must be respected.

You have read about the migrant workers who came to Oregon. They did not always share the rights enjoyed by others. Japanese people and black people were also not always treated equally. Blacks were not guaranteed the right to vote in our country until 1870. They were not allowed to buy homes in some places. They could not work at certain jobs. Laws have been passed to help protect people's civil rights. But this happened only because people took the responsibility to correct these wrongs.

Good Citizenship

Education can help people understand many things. They can learn about each other. They can learn that it is the things a person does, not what he or she looks like, that matter. Education also teaches people about the world in which they live. There are many problems to solve. A good education helps in solving them. It will also help to make people good citizens. So it is your responsibility to be a good student and learn to think clearly.

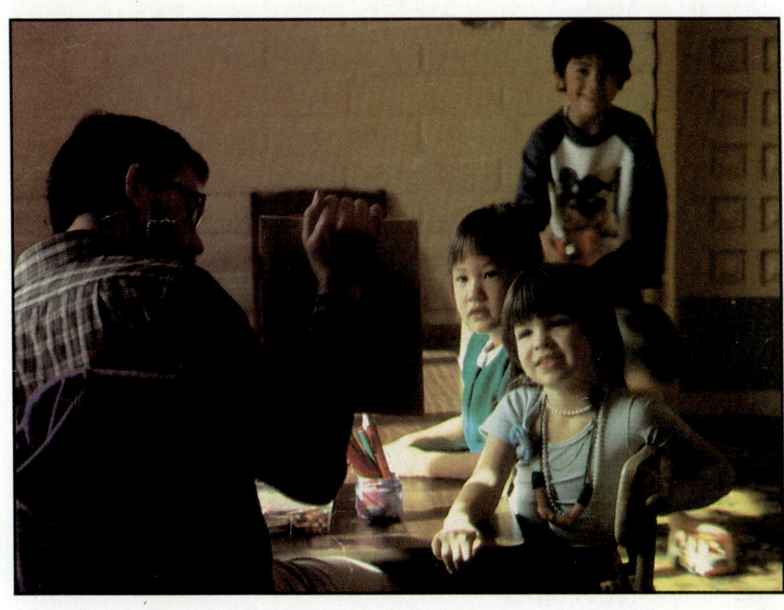

Young students in Oregon learn about the world.

This worker helps to keep Oregon's highways clean by picking up litter.

As a good citizen you must make sure that future people can enjoy the rights you have. You must make sure that leaders make fair laws. But you should do more than that. It is your responsibility to take care of your part of the planet. You want it to stay as beautiful as it is now.

The people of Oregon enjoy their state. They have passed laws to protect the environment. Laws have been passed to limit the number of fish that can be caught. Other laws keep people from dumping waste in Oregon's rivers. Such laws help to keep Oregon beautiful.

The future of Oregon's government depends on its citizens. This means that people should not litter the highways, cities, parks, or forests. They should not waste the state's resources. They should be careful about using water and electricity. They must use these things carefully so that there will be enough for everyone.

Good citizenship involves many things. Being a responsible citizen helps to preserve your rights. Rights and responsiblities go hand in hand.

Section Review

Write your answers on a sheet of paper.

1. Name some rights you have as a citizen.
2. Why are laws important?
3. How has Oregon tried to protect the environment?
4. What is one of the responsibilities of a good citizen?
5. How can you show good citizenship in your community?

2 Local Government

The governments of cities, towns, and **counties** make up **local government.** A county is the largest unit of local government in a state. Each unit of government has special duties. Sometimes the duties overlap. Local governments get their power from the state constitution.

county
the largest unit of local government in a state

local government
the government of cities, towns, and counties

County Government

Oregon and most other states are divided into counties. County governments make sure the law is obeyed in their part of the state. They also see that county roads are built and repaired. Counties operate a court system. They keep records of the taxes that have been collected. They also have lists of the people who may vote in county elections. Often, counties make sure that their citizens have enough schools and hospitals.

This courthouse in the town of Dallas, Oregon, is the headquarters for the government of Polk County.

elect
to choose by voting

department
a division, or part, of a government, school, or some other organization

Towns and Cities

Towns are smaller than cities. Some of them have their own governments. Other towns operate under the county government.

The chief officer of a city or town is the mayor. This person is often responsible for carrying out city rules. The people of a city may also vote for, or **elect,** a council. The council makes city rules. It also chooses people to help run the many parts, or **departments,** of local government.

Administration is often called the "housekeeping" department. It takes care of buying supplies, keeping records, and hiring city workers. Some departments take care of housing and transportation. Police and fire departments deal with the general safety of the people. Local governments are also responsible for some parks and recreation areas.

Each part of local government works for the people. You are served by the government of the town, city, or county in which you live. If you live in a city, you are served by the city government. You are also served by the government of the county in which you live.

Section Review

Write your answers on a sheet of paper.

1. Name three units of local government.

2. What are some duties of county governments?

3. Suppose you wanted your local government to change a law or consider a new law. To whom would you write to make your request?

MARGARET STRACHAN

Margaret Strachan (**strawn**) was first elected to the city council of Portland, Oregon, in 1981. She is one of five city commissioners, including the mayor, who direct the government of Oregon's largest city.

Strachan moved to Portland in 1973. Two years later she became the coordinator of the Neighborhood Project in northwest Portland.

When Strachan ran for the position of city commissioner in 1981, she was not expected to win. She had never been elected to political office, and 17 other candidates were running for the same position. But Strachan ran a well-organized, grass-roots campaign. This means that Strachan relied on neighborhood groups to talk with voters about what she wanted for the people of Portland.

In her position as city commissioner, Strachan has worked hard to improve housing and social services for the people of the city. She is also concerned about the future of Portland. In 1984, she introduced a plan for the growth and development of the city's downtown area through the year 2000. Due to the hard work of leaders like Commissioner Strachan, the people of Portland can look forward to a bright future for their city.

3 State Government

Oregon became a state in 1859. Two years before that, the people had drawn up a state constitution. The powers of the Oregon state government are described in the constitution. **Amendments,** or changes, have been made in the constitution to give the people a greater voice in their government.

amendment
a change made in a constitution

The Parts of Government

Oregon's state government is divided into three parts, or branches. Each part is as important as the other. It is the duty of each branch of government to check on what the other two branches are doing.

The **legislative branch** of the government makes the laws of the state. This branch is made up of two parts—the House of Representatives and the Senate. The people who serve in the House of Representatives and the Senate are elected by the people. The House has 60 members. Each member serves two years. The Senate has 30 members. Each member serves four years.

legislative branch
the part of government that makes laws

The legislative branch makes many kinds of laws. Some laws have to do with roads and highways. Some are tax laws. Others provide money for schools. Still others try to protect the environment. The members of the legislature also talk about many other things that are important to Oregonians. This talk sometimes leads to the passing of laws.

The **executive branch** of the government carries out the laws. The **governor** heads this branch. He or she is also the chief officer of the state.

executive branch
the part of government that carries out the laws

governor
the chief officer of a state

Oregon's governor is elected to a four-year term. He (or she if a woman were to be elected) can serve only two terms in 12 years. One of the governor's duties is to head the State Land Board. The Land Board is in charge of all land owned by the state. The governor also suggests what laws should be made and plans how the state will spend its money. The legislative branch must agree to any plan. This is an example of how one branch of government checks on another.

The **judicial branch** of the government decides on the meaning of the law. It is made up of the Supreme Court, the Court of Appeals, the Oregon Tax Court, and other state courts. The Supreme Court is the state's highest court. It has the power to change what a lower state court decides. Seven judges called justices are elected to six-year terms on the Supreme Court. The lower courts also have judges elected by the people.

judicial branch
the part of government that decides on the meaning of the law

An Oregon court in action

How Laws Are Made

Written ideas for new laws are called bills. Before a bill becomes a law many steps have to be taken. After a bill is introduced, it is given to a special committee. The committee studies the bill. It then holds hearings. At the hearings people speak for or against the bill. Then the committee votes on the bill. If the bill is approved, it is sent to the legislature. If the House and Senate vote for the bill, it is sent to the governor. If the governor signs it, the bill becomes a law. The governor might refuse to sign, or **veto,** the bill. If so, the Senate and the House vote on the bill again. Two thirds of the members in the House and the Senate must vote for the bill. Only then will it become a law.

veto
when a govenor or person in authority refuses to sign a bill

This picture shows a meeting of the Oregon House of Representatives.

The People's Role in Government

Oregonians have a responsibility to their government. They have to pay income taxes. Oregon's state government depends on this tax money to run the state. But the people have a right to tell the government what they want.

As you have read, people can change the law directly through the initiative and referendum. They also have the power to recall, or remove, officials who are not doing their jobs.

The people can also change the way the government is run by voting. They vote for leaders who often belong to **political parties.** A political party is a group formed by people who have similar ideas about how the government should be run. The two main political parties in the United States are the Democrats and the Republicans. If Oregonians do not like the way one political party is running the government, they can vote for members of another party.

political party
a group formed by people who have similar ideas about how the government should be run

Section Review

Write your answers on a sheet of paper.

1. Name the three branches of state government. What does each branch do?
2. Who is the chief officer of the state government?
3. What happens to a bill when the governor signs it?
4. What can you do to make the state government help your community solve its problems?

4 Oregon and the Nation

State laws are made to meet the needs of the state. But Oregon is not just a state. It is an important part of our country. Laws are made in our country's capital in Washington, D.C. These laws are meant for all the states, including Oregon. By taking part in making these laws, Oregonians have helped to change our nation in many ways.

How the Country Helps Oregon

federal government the government of the United States

Our country's government, called the **federal government,** has helped Oregon in many ways. Oregon's dams would not have been built without federal aid. The federal government has helped pay for some of Oregon's roads, highways, and airports. Good transportation has helped Oregon's cities to grow. The federal government has also worked to protect Oregon's natural resources. State and federal groups work together to control forest fires. They also protect trees from disease.

This picture shows a part of Interstate Highway 5 near Roseburg, Oregon. This highway was built with federal money.

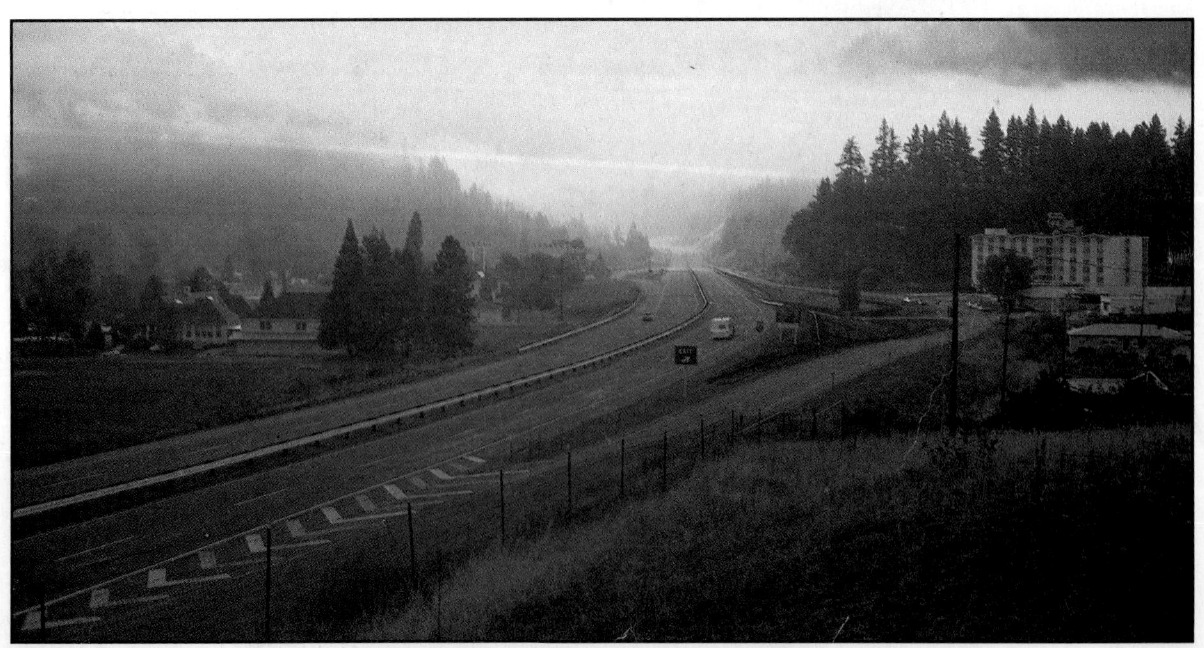

Oregon Chooses Government Leaders

Oregonians elect representatives to the Congress of the United States. Congress is the legislative branch of the federal government. It makes laws for everyone in the country. Congress is set up in the same way as Oregon's legislative branch. It is divided into two parts—the Senate and the House of Representatives. Each state elects two senators. The number of representatives each state sends to the House depends on its population. Oregon sends five representatives to the House.

Some Oregonians volunteer their time to work for a candidate they support.

Oregonians have elected good people to represent their state. These leaders help make the laws for Oregon and for the country. Senator Charles McNary worked to protect forests in Oregon and around the country. He was also partly responsible for the building of the Bonneville Dam. In the 1950's and 1960's, Senator Wayne Morse fought for workers' rights. He also kept a private company from building a low dam in Hells Canyon. Today Senators Mark Hatfield and Robert Packwood continue to work for laws that will help Oregonians and people around the country.

Oregon helps to elect the President of the United States. Oregonians vote in **primary elections.** In a primary election the people choose the person they want to represent their political party in the general election. The people choose **electors** in the general election. These electors cast the state's votes for the President. The number of electors for each state depends on the state's population. Oregonians vote for seven electors.

primary election
an election in which the people choose the person they want to represent their political party in the general election

electors
a certain number of people chosen in a general election to cast state votes for President

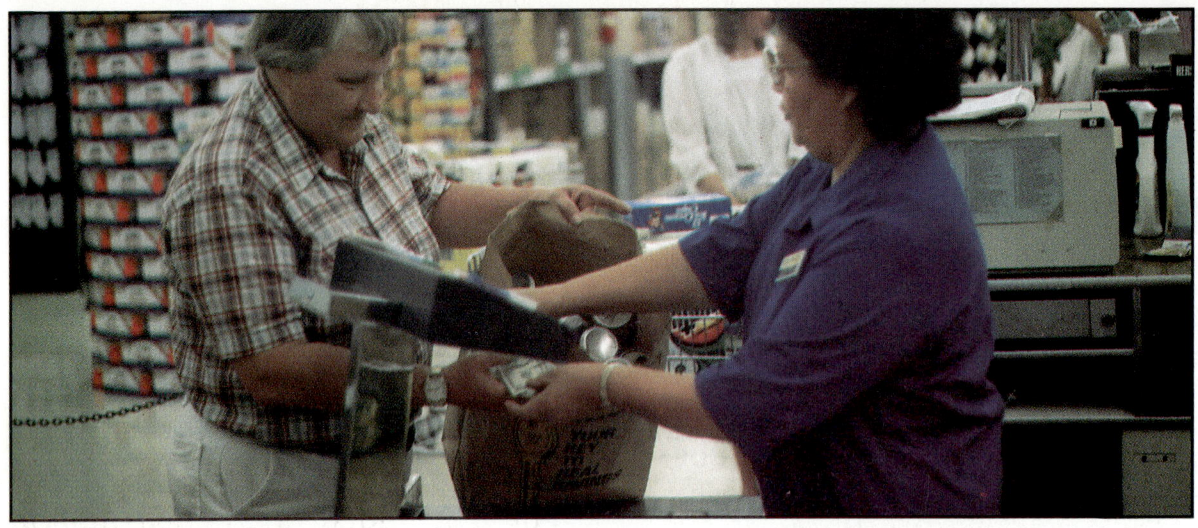

By returning bottles and cans for deposit, Oregonians help to protect natural resources and keep their state clean.

Oregon Helps the Country

Oregon has led our country in many important ways. Oregon was among the first states to give women the right to vote. It also passed laws to help workers without jobs and to help working mothers. In the early 1900's, Oregon made several **reforms** in its state government. A reform is a change for the better. Many states followed Oregon's lead in reforming their governments.

reform
a change for the better

Oregon is still working towards new ideas. Today it is a leader in the fight to save our natural environment.

Section Review

Write your answers on a sheet of paper.

1. How has the federal government helped Oregon?
2. What is the purpose of a primary election?
3. In what areas has Oregon led the country?
4. Five representatives from Oregon currently serve in the United States House of Representatives. How could this number change?

MARK HATFIELD

Mark O. Hatfield is a United States Senator in Washington D.C. He has represented Oregon voters in Congress for many years. Just before joining the Senate in 1966, Hatfield had been Oregon's governor for eight years. He served Oregon as a state representative and a state senator as well.

As Oregon's senator, Mark Hatfield has worked hard for the people of his state. He helped pass a law that added nearly 405 million hectares (1 million acres) of wilderness land to Oregon. He aided people who were out of work in Oregon's small timbering communities. Hatfield has tried to find ways to improve Oregon's trade. He also wants Congress to pass a national bottle bill.

But Mark Hatfield is not just interested in helping his state and his country. He wants to work toward world peace. When Hatfield was in the navy, he saw the damage nuclear weapons could do. Hatfield is working with others in Congress on a nuclear freeze bill. This would stop the development of nuclear weapons in the United States.

Senator Hatfield is often asked to speak at colleges and meetings about his ideas. Through his words, people are learning new ways to solve problems in the future.

SOCIAL STUDIES SKILLS

Understanding Time Zones

The earth turns on its axis once every 24 hours. As it turns, the side facing the sun has daylight. The side facing away from the sun has night. That is why all the clocks in the world do not show the same time. If they did, one side of the world would be dark at midnight, while the other side would be light at midnight.

time zone
one of 24 areas or zones of the earth in which the time is one hour earlier than the zone to its east

So instead of one world time, there are local **time zones** for each part of the earth. In the 48 United States with connecting borders, there are four time zones. In each zone, the local time is one hour earlier than the zone to the east.

Look at the map on page 255. Find the Eastern Time Zone. At about six o'clock in the morning, this part of the world is just beginning to face the sun. It will take almost three hours for the places in the Pacific Time Zone to face the sun.

Practice Your Skills

1. How many states are located in the Pacific Time Zone? in the Eastern Time Zone? in the Hawaii-Aleutian Time Zone?
2. What is the time difference between the Central Time Zone and the Pacific Time Zone? the Eastern Time Zone and the Central Time Zone?
3. When it is 4:00 P.M. in Utah, what time is it in Georgia? in California? in Arkansas? in Hawaii?

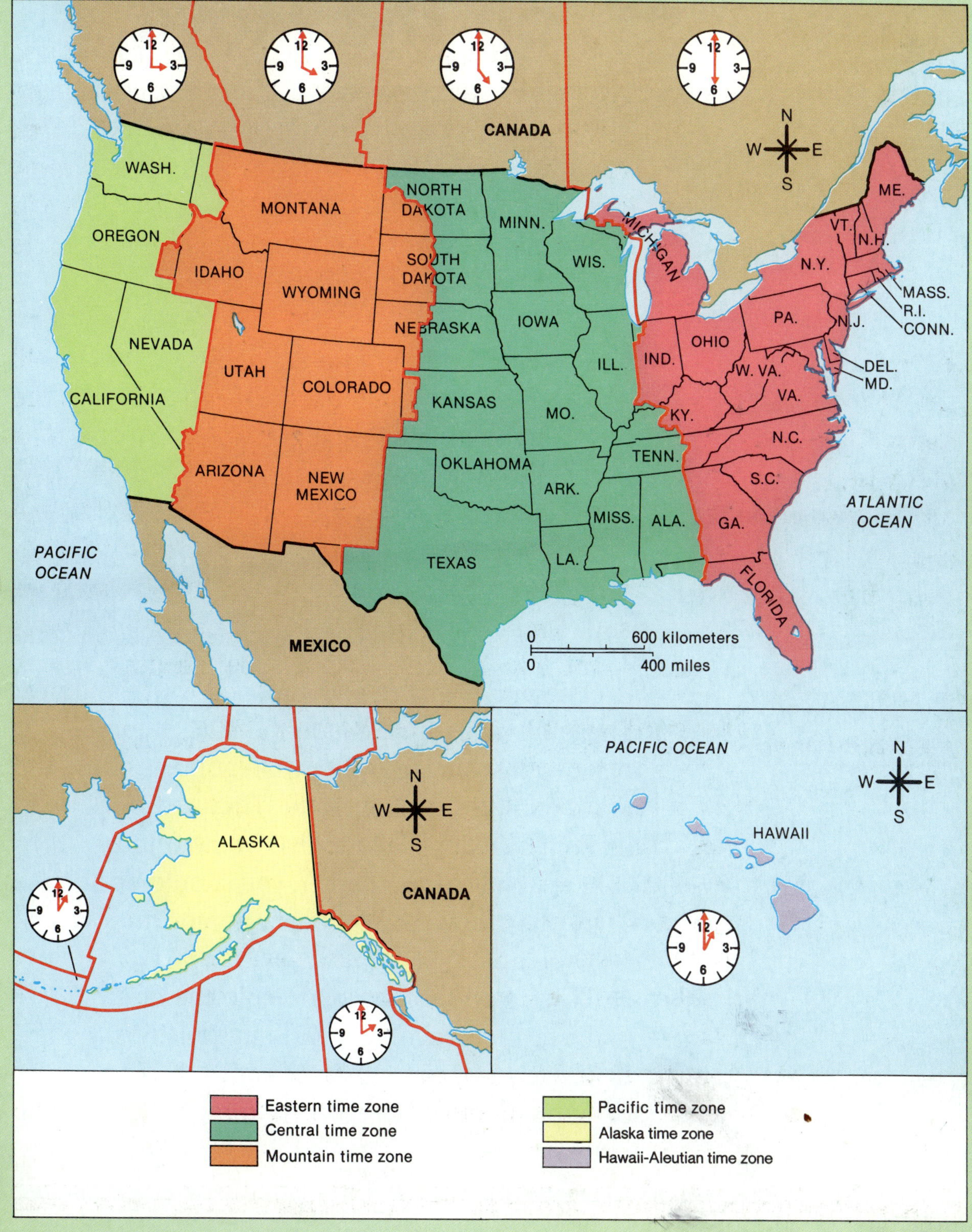
CANADA
WASH.
OREGON
CALIFORNIA
NEVADA
IDAHO
MONTANA
WYOMING
UTAH
COLORADO
ARIZONA
NEW MEXICO
NORTH DAKOTA
SOUTH DAKOTA
NEBRASKA
KANSAS
OKLAHOMA
TEXAS
MINN.
IOWA
MO.
ARK.
LA.
WIS.
ILL.
MISS.
TENN.
ALA.
MICHIGAN
IND.
OHIO
KY.
W. VA.
VA.
PA.
N.Y.
VT.
N.H.
ME.
MASS.
R.I.
CONN.
N.J.
DEL.
MD.
N.C.
S.C.
GA.
FLORIDA
ATLANTIC OCEAN
PACIFIC OCEAN
MEXICO
0 600 kilometers
0 400 miles
N
W
E
S
ALASKA
CANADA
PACIFIC OCEAN
HAWAII
Eastern time zone
Central time zone
Mountain time zone
Pacific time zone
Alaska time zone
Hawaii-Aleutian time zone

CHAPTER 12 Oregon on the Move

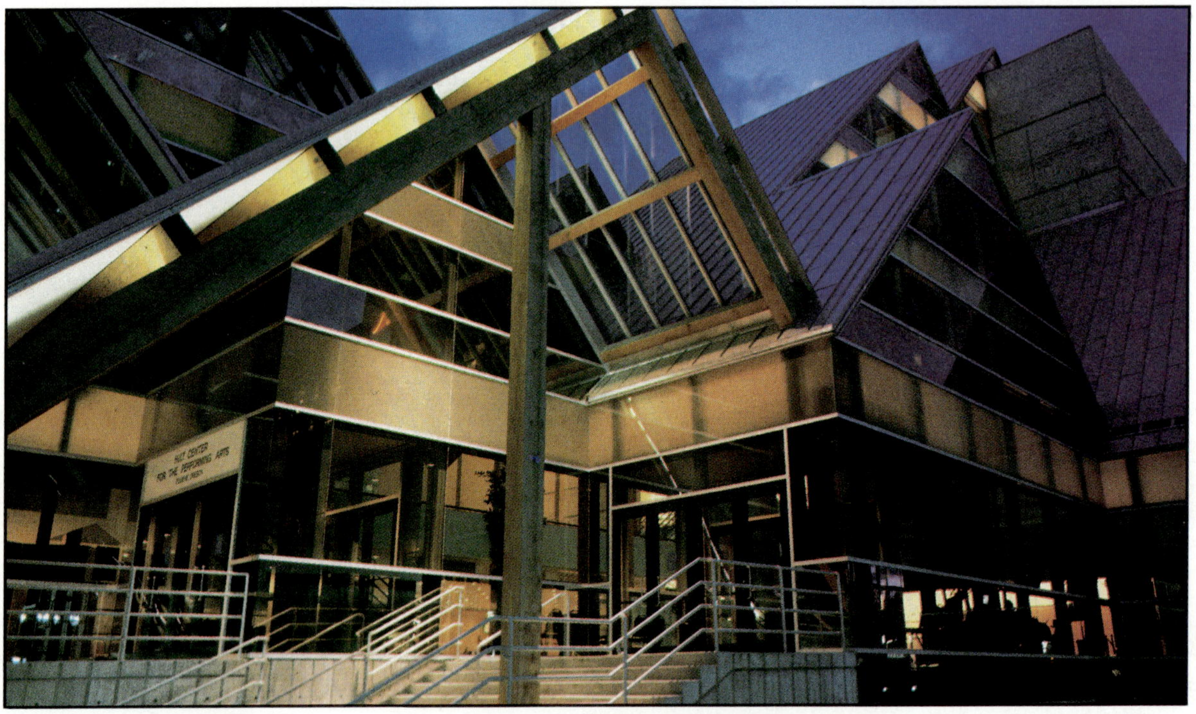

This modern building is the Hult Center for the Performing Arts in Eugene, Oregon.

Oregon has grown and changed with the times. These changes have made the state important to our country and the world. Oregonians value the good qualities of their state. They are working to make it a better place to live in the future.

At the end of this chapter, you should be able to:

- ○ Explain how education is being improved in Oregon.
- ○ List Oregon's contributions to the arts.
- ○ Describe Oregon's world relationships.
- ● Read an ocean currents map.
- ○ Explain how Oregon is preparing for the future.

1 Education, Culture, and Sports

As you have read, many of Oregon's early settlers dreamed of building a better life in Oregon. That dream has not died. Today Oregonians are still working on ways to improve their lives. They have built one of the best school systems in the country and are working to keep it that way. They have made contributions to the arts. And they have made sports an important part of their lives for both health and enjoyment.

Education

Over the years, Oregonians have worked hard to improve their school system. The legislative branch of Oregon's government is responsible for the public school system in the state. In 1951, it set up the State Board of Education. This board was given the responsibility for planning and checking on education in Oregon's elementary schools, high schools, and two-year community colleges.

In 1980, the State Board of Education made changes in the classes that high school students had to take. The changes were made to better prepare students for their future jobs or university studies.

Improving education takes a lot of money. It costs more today to hire good teachers and buy books than it did in the past. Oregon's constitution does not allow local governments to raise taxes for schools without the approval of the people.

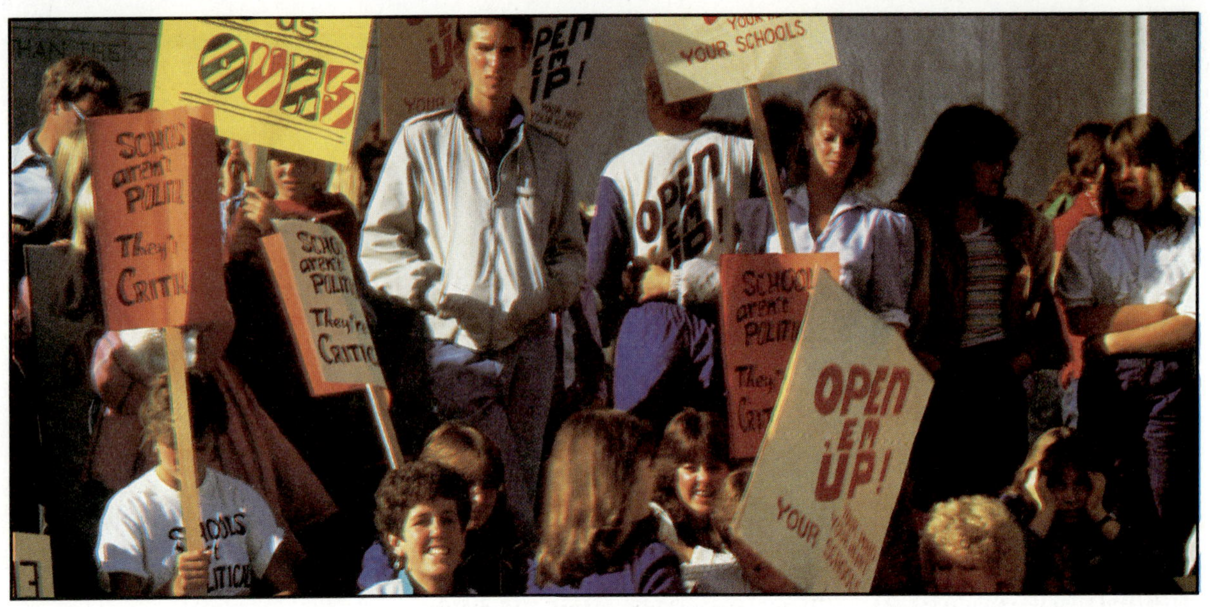

Students affected by school closings gather together to ask for support for their schools.

Each county in the state is divided into **school districts.** A school district is a part of a county that has a single school system. The people of each school district must decide if they want their taxes raised for the public schools in their district.

school district
a part of a county that has a single school system

In recent years, school districts all over Oregon have had trouble getting the people to agree to property tax increases. Property taxes support public schools. Some people feel that taxes are high enough already. Other people have lost their jobs because economic activity in the state has slowed down. These people cannot afford to pay higher taxes. Most Oregonians value good schools. But many do not want their taxes raised.

In the past, some school districts have run out of money. They have had to close schools until the people voted to give them more money. Closing schools hurts the students and the state as a whole. In the years ahead, Oregonians will have to work out ways to make sure that all schools have enough money to stay open and provide good education.

The Arts

Oregon's art museums have many paintings and pieces of sculpture. Much of this artwork represents the different cultures of Oregon's people. Northwest Indian art and Mexican art are found in some of Oregon's museums. The Warner Collection of Oriental art is an excellent one. It can be seen in the city of Eugene.

Oregon has given much to American **architecture** (**ahr**-kuh-tek-chure) too. Architecture is the art of designing buildings. One group of Oregon architects designed buildings to fit the natural environment. They used natural woods and open floor plans. The architects who started these ideas were part of the "Northwest School" of architecture.

architecture the art of designing buildings

Oregon has been the home of some well-known writers. In 1935, H. L. Davis wrote a book about the people of Oregon. The book is called *Honey in the Horn.* It won the Pulitzer Prize. The Pulitzer Prize is an award given to a person for outstanding writing.

Another well-known Oregon writer is Ursula Le Guin (**uhr**-suh-lah leh **ghihn**). Le Guin has written a number of science-fiction stories and books. Many are for young people.

Ursula Le Guin is a well-known Oregon author of science-fiction stories.

Thousands of runners race down Portland's Front Street as part of the annual Cascade Run-off.

Sports

Oregon's environment makes it a good place for sports lovers. Its mountains draw skiers in the winter and climbers in the summer. The state's many rivers and lakes are good for sport fishing. Many Oregonians have become runners. Races for runners are very popular in the state. Oregonians are interested in sports that keep their bodies in good shape.

The people of Oregon like to go to sports events. The Portland Trail Blazers are Oregon's professional basketball team. In 1977, the team won the National Basketball Association (NBA) championship.

Section Review

Write your answers on a sheet of paper.

1. What problems have schools in Oregon had in recent years?
2. What were some of the ideas of the "Northwest School" of architecture?
3. What do you think is the best thing Oregon has to offer its people? Why?

MARY DECKER
ALBERTO SALAZAR

Mary Decker and Alberto Salazar love to run. They have both set world records in running contests.

After his family fled Cuba in 1960, Salazar went to school in Massachusetts. After graduating from high school, he joined the outstanding college track program at the University of Oregon.

Salazar has won four marathons. A marathon is a run of over 42 kilometers (26 miles). In 1981, Salazar set a world record in the New York City Marathon. He ran the race in 2 hours, 8 minutes, and 12 seconds.

Mary Decker started running when she was 11 years old. At 14, she won her first national title in the 800-meter race. In 1982, Decker broke the world record in the 5,000-meter race.

Salazar and Decker both live and train in Eugene, Oregon. They were both members ot the 1984 United States Olympic Team. Although neither won a medal, they plan to run in future races around the world.

2 Oregon and the World

Have you ever heard it said that the world is getting smaller? This does not mean that the world is really shrinking in size. It means that better methods of transportation and communication are drawing people closer together. Satellites in space can bring news from around the world right into our homes. We can hear the news and see the pictures on television. Trips to and from other countries that once took many months now take less time. Ships can go faster. And airplanes can take people and goods from place to place in only a few hours. More than ever, Oregon's future has become tied to the future of the world.

import
product received by one country from another

World Trade

Goods from other countries pour into Oregon's ports each day. Products received by one country from another are called **imports.** Portland is one of the chief ports through which imported Japanese cars enter the United States.

These Japanese cars have just been unloaded from ships that docked at Portland.

Many of the imports that are shipped to Oregon are used by the state's industries. Spices for bakeries and food-processing plants are shipped to Oregon. Paper-manufacturing companies import tapioca (tap-ee-**o**-keh) starch. Bamboo and linen are imported to make curtains in the textile industry. Swedish steel is used by Oregon's lumber industry. Bauxite, a mineral used to make aluminum, is imported from South America.

But world trade is not all one way. Oregon also sends many goods to other countries. These goods are called **exports.** Oregon's grain and timber go mostly to Japan. Many other kinds of products are exported from Oregon's ports. Onions, dried prunes, and many kinds of fruit are shipped out. Wheat from Oregon feeds people all over the world.

export
product sent from one country to another

The Arabic writing on the boxes shows that these apples are probably being shipped to a country in the Middle East.

Students from many countries study in Oregon's colleges and universities.

Visiting Other Countries

Many Oregonians take trips every year to countries all over the world. Some of them go to meet with the people who plan to ship or receive goods to or from Oregon. Other Oregonians go just to visit other lands. They are interested in seeing how other people live and work. It is often easier to learn more about a group of people and their land by visiting their country.

Many people from other countries also visit Oregon. Oregonians have learned to accept differences in culture. This makes visitors feel welcome in the state.

Students from other countries have come to Oregon to go to school. Sometimes they are part of a cultural-exchange program. This kind of program gives young people the chance to live with a family and go to school in another country. Other foreign students attend classes at the state's universities. Portland State University has a large number of students from countries in the Middle East.

Oregonians and World Issues

The people of Oregon care about world problems. Many of them have worked hard to bring about change.

Protecting the world environment is a chief concern among Oregonians. They want to keep the oceans and air clean. They also want to protect fish and animal life. Some Oregonians have taken boats into ocean waters to stop Soviet and Japanese whale hunters. The whale population was getting dangerously small as more and more whales were killed. Many Oregonians feared the whales would die out if something was not done

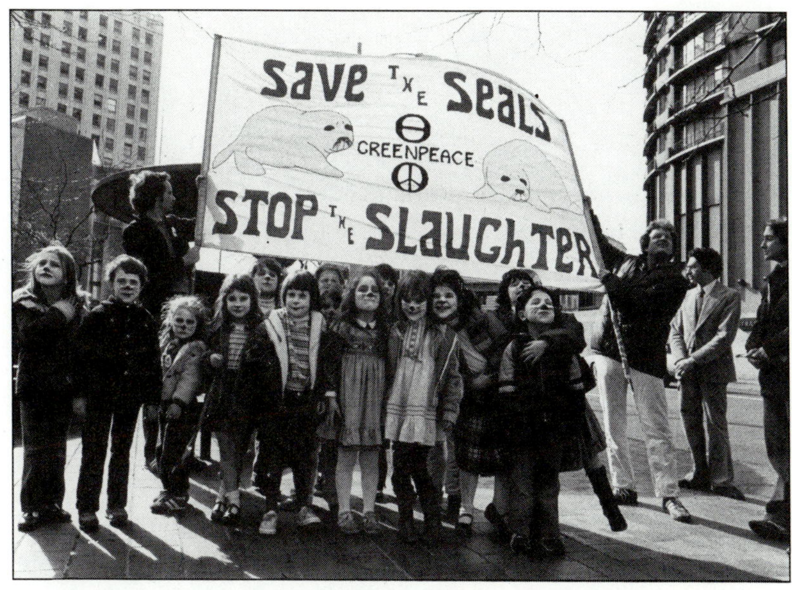

These Oregon children are showing their support for the Save the Seals campaign.

to stop the hunters. Oregonians have also worked to stop the killing of animals for their fur.

Like people everywhere, Oregonians care about world peace. They would like to see all people stop fighting. They would also like to see an end to the threat of nuclear war. These are very hard problems to solve. But Oregonians have not given up. They continue to work for a better world.

Section Review

Write your answers on a sheet of paper.

1. What is meant by the saying "the world is getting smaller"?
2. Name two imports that are used in Oregon's industries.
3. What country imports most of Oregon's grain and timber?
4. What world problems concern Oregonians?
5. What about Oregon would you share with a visitor from another country?

SOCIAL STUDIES SKILLS

Reading an Ocean Currents Map

current
a fast-moving stream of water in an ocean

Within our oceans are fast-moving streams of water called **currents.** The rotation of the earth and strong winds cause the ocean currents to move constantly. Some currents carry warm water from the equator north toward the cold waters near the North Pole. As cold currents flow back toward the warm waters near the equator, they become warm again.

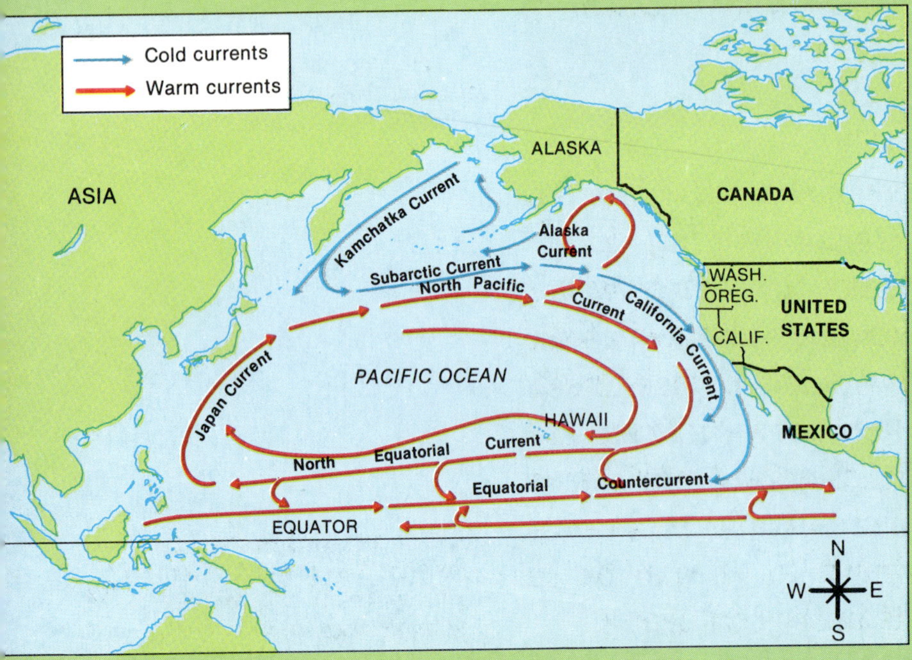

This map shows some cold and warm currents in the Pacific Ocean and the direction in which they flow. The arrows show the direction of currents.

Practice Your Skills

1. In which direction does the California current flow? Is it a warm or cold current?
2. Which current carries cold water directly into the California current? Why does that current cool the California current?
3. Which current splits in two as it flows west around Hawaii? Is it a warm or cold current?
4. Which current runs along the equator? Is it a warm or cold current?

3 Oregon and the Future

Oregon has become a state that is a good place in which to live. The people are proud of their history. They are proud of their state. Oregonians have a government that works for them. They have tried to take care of the environment. They have used their resources wisely. However, in the years to come, Oregonians will have to work hard to keep their state a good place in which to live.

Oregon's Population

Some Oregonians worry about how fast the population of the state is growing. They do not want schools and cities to become overcrowded. More people means that more housing will have to be built. More housing uses up more land. More cars make more air pollution and traffic.

One of the reasons for Oregon's population growth is that more and more people are moving to the state. Many are drawn to Oregon by its clean air and water and its unspoiled beauty.

Traffic lights feed cars onto Interstate 5 in Portland. The lights space the cars to help the traffic flow more smoothly.

Oregon's rate of growth is higher than that of most other states. By the year 2000, Oregon is expected to have over 1 million more people than it had in 1980. With more people moving in, Oregonians will have to work harder to keep their state clean and beautiful.

New and Different Industries

technology
the science of industry that involves the discovery of faster and better ways to do things

Early in Oregon's history, words such as canoe, cabin, and fur trading were commonly heard. Later, people talked about farming and the growth of industry. The words heard today are computer and high tech. High tech is the new **technology.** Technology is the science of industry. It is the discovery of faster and better ways to do things. The new technology has brought new industries and different kinds of jobs to Oregon.

During the 1970's, economic activity all over the United States slowed down. This hurt Oregon's lumber industry. Fewer trees were cut, and less lumber was made. Fewer workers were needed, and many logging and sawmill workers lost their jobs.

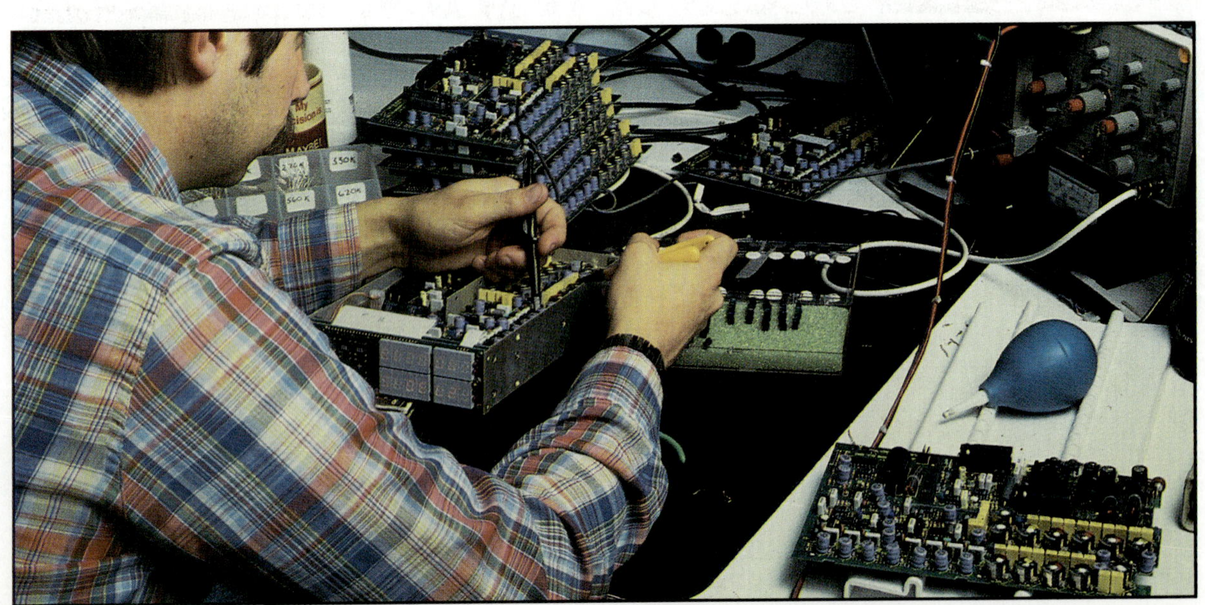

High-tech industries, such as electronics, have provided more and different kinds of jobs for Oregonians.

The slowdown in the lumber industry hurt many other industries in the state. Companies that sold equipment to workers in the lumber industry lost business. Truckers who carried the logs to the mills were without work. In time the slowdown in the lumber industry led to the loss of jobs for workers in many other industries.

In recent years, Oregon has tried to draw new and different industries to the state. This will help keep the economy of the state strong if another industry slows down. But Oregon does not want just any industry. It wants industries that will not pollute the air and water. It also wants industries that will not use up the state's natural resources. It would like to attract more high-tech industries, like electronics manufacturing.

These covered locomotives in Eugene, Oregon, were ordered by a railroad company. When the lumber industry slowed down, the locomotives were no longer needed.

The people of Oregon have been good to their state. They have always worked to improve life in Oregon. They have faced problems and worked out solutions. For this reason, Oregonians can look forward to a bright future.

Section Review

Write your answers on a sheet of paper.

1. What is expected to happen to Oregon's population in the next 20 years? How will this affect the state?

2. Why is Oregon trying to attract new and different industries to the state? What kinds of industries does it want?

3. What do you think is necessary to make a state or community a good place in which to live?

Close-up on

Oregon Shakespearean Festival
The Oregon Shakespearean Festival honors the plays of William Shakespeare. Shakespeare wrote in England in the late 1500's and early 1600's. But people still find his plays interesting. In fact about 260,000 people see his plays performed in Ashland, Oregon, every year.

The festival runs from February through October. Many of the plays are performed on an outdoor stage. Strolling musicians in costume sing and play before the start of each play. People picnic while dancers move on the park's lawn.

It all began with a teacher's dream. In 1935, Angus Bowmer decided to present two of Shakespeare's plays for a Fourth of July celebration. The Ashland bankers gave him $400. But Bowmer was asked to hold boxing matches on

OREGON

the stage during the day. The bankers thought the matches would make the money that the plays would lose. To the surprise of many, the plays were a hit. The boxing matches, however, were not.

In 1959, the present outdoor theater was opened. Over 1,100 people can watch plays by Shakespeare and others, under the stars. Visitors can take tours backstage to learn about the hard work that goes into putting on a play.

Because the festival is so popular, other theaters have been built in the town. In 1970, the Angus Bowmer Indoor Theater opened. It is thought to be the best of its kind in the country. Then in 1977, the 150-seat Black Swan Theater opened.

The people of Ashland who run the Shakespearean Festival are proud of what they do. The festival has received two major theater arts awards for outstanding work.

UNIT REVIEW

Word Work

Write the sentences below on a sheet of paper. Fill the blanks with the correct words from the list.

judicial branch	export	reform
import	architecture	technology
political party	legislative branch	county
representative		

1. The science of industry that involves the discovery of faster and better ways of doing things is called ____.
2. A ____ is a group formed by people who share similar ideas about how the government should be run.
3. The ____ is the part of government that makes laws.
4. The art of designing buildings is called ____.
5. An ____ is a product received by one country from another.
6. A ____ is a change for the better.
7. The largest unit of local government in a state is a ____.
8. The ____ is the part of government that decides on the meaning of the law.
9. An ____ is a product sent from one country to another.
10. A person who speaks and acts for others is called a ____.

Knowing the Facts

Write your answers on a sheet of paper.

1. Why are laws needed?
2. What branch of the state government carries out the law?
3. What happens to a state bill after the committee votes on it?
4. How many representatives does Oregon send to both parts of Congress?
5. Who has the responsibility of planning and checking on education in Oregon?
6. Name two imports and two exports that pass through Oregon's ports.
7. How is Oregon preparing for the future?

Using What You Know

Choose one of the following activities to do. Follow the instructions given here.

1. Make a chart of the departments in your local government.
2. Make a model or draw a picture of the Oregon state capitol in Salem.
3. Write a letter to one of your government representatives. Tell him or her what you think about a particular issue.
4. Watch or listen to the local and national news every day for a week. Write a report on what you learn about current events.
5. Write and perform a play about Oregon.
6. Research and write a report on someone you consider to be a "Famous Oregonian" who was not featured in this book.

Skills Practice

Use the following time zone map to answer the questions below. Write your answers on a sheet of paper.

1. Which city in Oregon does not have the same time as Portland?
2. Which cities in Idaho are in the Pacific time zone? Which are not?
3. If it is six o'clock in Spokane, Washington, what time is it in Boise, Idaho? in Bend, Oregon?

Use the following ocean currents map to answer the questions below.

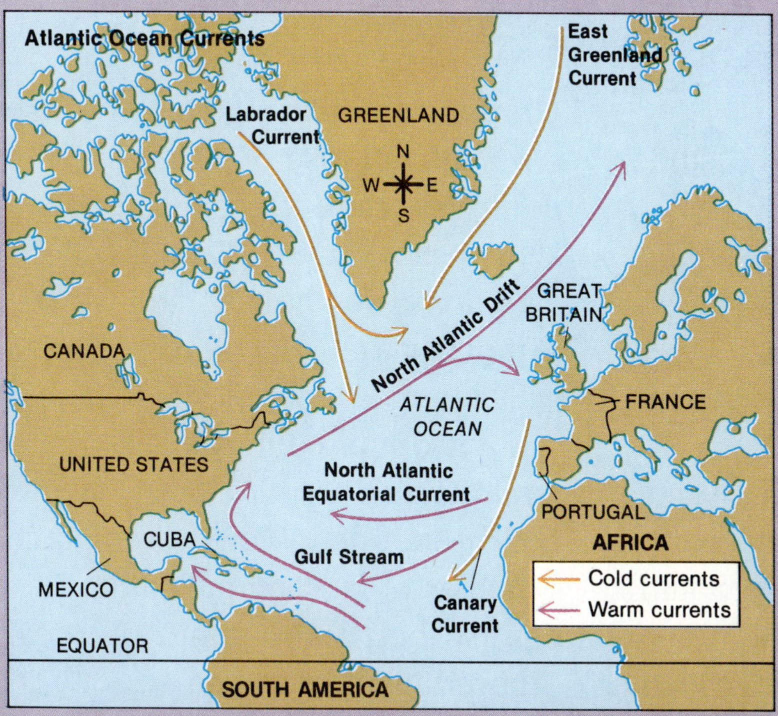

1. In which direction does the North Atlantic Drift flow? Is it a warm or cold current?
2. Which current flows along the western coast of Greenland?
3. Which current flows along the east coast of the United States? Is it a warm or cold current?
4. In which direction does the North Atlantic Equatorial Current flow?
5. Which current flows near Great Britain?
6. Which current flows along the eastern coast of Greenland? Towards which other current does it flow?
7. Which current flows along the northwest coast of Africa? In which direction does it flow.

GLOSSARY

altitude the height of land above the level of the sea

amendment a change made in a constitution

archeologist a scientist who studies artifacts

architecture the art of designing buildings

artifact a weapon, tool, or other article made and used by people who lived long ago

axis an imaginary line that runs through the center of the earth from the North Pole to the South Pole

ballot a voting sheet from which voters make a selection

bar graph a diagram using bars to stand for numbers

barge a large, flat-bottomed boat

basin an area of land that is surrounded by higher land

bay a body of water almost surrounded by land

bilingual in two languages

boundary a line on a map that separates one state or country from another

canyon a deep valley with steep sides

cedar a kind of evergreen tree found in the western regions of Oregon

civil rights rights given to each person by the Constitution

climate the kind of weather a region has over a long period of time

commercial fishing catching fish for the purpose of selling them

compass rose the drawing on a map showing the main directions of north, south, east, and west

Congress the part of the United States government that makes many of our country's laws

constitution a set of laws

continent one of the seven large bodies of land on the earth

county the largest unit of local government in a state

culture a way of life shared by a group of people who have the same customs, beliefs, past, and often language

current a moving stream of water in an ocean

department a division, or part, of a government, school, or some other organization

deposit large area deep in the earth where a mineral is found

desegregate to do away with the separation of people on the basis of race

distance scale a measuring line on a map that helps in figuring the distance in kilometers or miles from one place to another

double bar graph a graph that compares two sets of the same kind of information

dredge a machine that removes mud and sand from the bottom of a river

dry dock a place where a boat can be kept dry during repairs

economic activity a way that people use their resources to make money

elect to choose by voting

electors a certain number of people chosen in a general election to cast state votes for President

environment the land, climate, and living things surrounding a group of people

equator the imaginary line that circles the middle of the earth, halfway between the North Pole and the South Pole

erosion the wearing away of land by wind and water

executive branch the part of government that carries out the laws

expedition a journey for a special purpose

explorer a person who goes to faraway places in search of something

export a product sent from one country to another

fault a break in the earth's surface with a shift in the level of the land

federal government the government of the United States

fertile good for growing plants and crops

fish hatchery a protected place where fish eggs are hatched

fish ladder a series of small waterfalls built to allow fish to get around a dam

fold a buckle, or bend, in the earth's surface

food processing changing farm products into food products

forester a scientist trained in growing crops of trees

frontier land that is mostly unsettled

globe a round model of the earth

gorge a deep, narrow pass between mountains

government a group of people who are chosen to make laws and lead a community, state, or country

governor the chief officer of a state

grid a series of squares made by evenly-spaced lines used to locate places on a map

growing season the period of time during which the weather is warm enough for crops to grow

hemisphere half of a sphere; on a

globe, one half of the earth

humid moist or damp

hydroelectric power energy produced by waterpower

immigrant a person who comes from another country to live in a new land

import a product received by one country from another

industry a big business

initiative a way for the people to start, or initiate, a law on their own

irrigation supplying water to dry land through pipes, ditches, or canals

journal a written record of daily activities, like a diary

judicial branch the part of government that decides on the meaning of the law

labor union a group of workers that tries to improve its members' wages and working conditions

landforms map a map that uses colors to show the height and shape of the land, such as mountains, highlands, plateaus, and plains

land grant free land given by the government to a railroad, school, or other organization

latitude line east–west line drawn parallel to the equator on a globe

lava hot liquid rock that flows out of volcanoes

legislative branch the part of government that makes laws

line graph a graph that uses lines to show information and how that information changes

local government the governments of cities, towns, and counties

lock a box-like structure within a river used to move boats from one water level to another

logger a person whose work is cutting down trees, cutting them into logs, and sending them to the sawmill

longitude line line drawn from north to south from pole to pole on the globe

lowland a low area with small, rolling hills

Manifest Destiny the belief that the United States was meant to rule all the land between the Atlantic and Pacific oceans

manufacturing making finished goods from raw materials

map a drawing of part or all of the earth's surface that shows where things are located

map key the section that explains the symbols used on a map

merchant a person who buys and sells goods

migrant worker a person who goes from one region to another to earn a living

mineral a material dug from the earth

mining the process of taking mineral deposits from the earth

mission a community set up by a religious order

missionary a person who teaches his or her religion to others

moisture water in the air or on the ground; wetness

mountain range a group of mountains

mouth the place where a river empties into a larger body of water

mural a large picture painted directly on a wall or ceiling

museum a room or building where art, historical, or scientific objects are preserved and put on display

natural resource something from nature that people need or want, such as water, coal, soil, and forests

North Pole the point located at the most northern place on a globe

Northwest Passage an imaginary water passage that early explorers believed would lead through North America to Asia

ocean a large body of salt water that covers much of the earth's surface

pacifist a person who believes that all problems between countries should be settled by peaceful means rather than by war

petition a sheet of paper signed by people who support a specific course of action

pie graph a drawing of a circle divided into parts

pioneer a person who tries something first and opens the way for others to follow

plateau an area of flat land higher than the land around it

plywood thin sheets of wood that have been glued together

political party a group formed by people who have similar ideas about how the government should be run

population all of the people who live in a particular place

population density the number of people living in each square kilometer or mile of an area

port a place where ships can load and unload goods

primary election an election in which the people choose the person they want to represent their political party in the general election

prime meridian special longitude

line that is the starting point for measuring all other lines of longitude

provisional government a kind of government that is set up until a permanent government can be formed

ranching the raising of large herds of animals, such as cattle, sheep, or horses

ration to limit the amount of food or other goods that are in short supply

raw material a material in its natural state used in making finished goods

recall a process that gives the people a chance to vote a leader out of office in a special election

referendum a process that gives the people a chance to accept or reject a law

reform a change for the better

region an area of land

regulate to control, or set limits

relocation centers camps set up by the United States government to which many Japanese Americans were sent during World War II

representative a person who speaks or acts for others

reservation land set aside as a homeland for American Indians

responsibilities things that are one's duty to do

restocking building up the supply of something

rural away from cities and close to farms

salmon an important fish found in Pacific Northwest waters

school district a part of a county that has a single school system

segregate to separate people of one race from those of another

settler a person who comes to a place to make a home

South Pole the point located at the most southern place on a globe

steamboat a boat powered by steam

streetcar a large car or coach that runs on rails

suffrage the right to vote

symbol something that stands for a real thing

table a list of facts displayed in columns with titles

tax money that people must give to the government to pay for community needs

technology the science of industry that involves the discovery of faster and better ways to do things

temperature the measure of how hot or cold a place is

Territory a part of the country that is under the protection of the

United States, but does not have the standing of a state

textile cloth made from cotton, flax, or other materials

timber wood from trees that can be made into something useful

time line a way of listing important dates or events in the order in which they happened

time zone one of 24 areas, or zones, of the earth in which the time is one hour earlier than the zone to its east

tourist a person who visits an area for pleasure

transcontinental railroad a railroad that crosses a continent from one end to another

transportation ways of moving people and things from place to place

treaty a formal agreement made between countries and signed by each

tributary a river or stream that flows into a larger river or stream

university a school that offers the highest level of education

veto when a governor or person in authority refuses to sign a bill

volcano an opening in the earth's surface through which hot liquid rock and other materials are forced out

wage the amount of money a worker is paid for his or her labor

weather the condition of the air at a certain time or place

wood processing changing wood into useful wood products

wood pulp ground up wood fibers from logs

INDEX

I

J

K

L

M

R

S

T

U

V

W

Z

ART CREDITS

Felipe Galindo p. 136

MAPS

Network Graphics

PHOTO CREDITS

The photos on the following pages are from the Oregon Historical Society: 61, 66, 85–89, 93–94, 102, 104, 110, 124–125, 132, 135, 139, 142, 162–163, 168, 173,184–191, 194–199, 202–203, 208–210, 214–215, 220–224, 227

UNIT 1:
pp.18–19 Gary Braasch; p.20 John Marshall; p.22 Gildemeister/EKM/Nepenthe; p.24 Steve Terrill; p.26 Gary Braasch; p.28 Gildemeister/EKM/Nepenthe; p.29 Robert Ginn/EKM/Nepenthe; p.30 Jay Lurie; p.31 Steve Terrill; p.35l Devon Jacklin; p.35r Jill Cannefax; p.38 John Maher/EKM/Nepenthe; p.39t Pat O'Hara; p.39m R.L. Potts/EKM/Nepenthe; p.39b Jen & Des Bartlett/Bruce Coleman; p.40t Joel Rogers/Earth Images; p.40b Bryan Peterson; p.41 Bill Ross/West Light; p.42t Steve Terrill; p.42b Joy Spruce/Bruce Coleman; p.43 Steve Terrill; p.44 Kristin Finnegan; p.45 Ancil Nance; p.48 John Marshall; p.49 John Maher/EKM/Nepenthe; p.50t Steve Terrill; p.50b John Maher; p.51 John Marshall; p.52 Chuck O'Rear/West Light; p.53 David Hiser/Photographers Aspen; p.54t Ralph Perry; p.54b Gildemeister/EKM/Nepenthe; p.55 Bryan Peterson; p.57 © Tillamook Cheese Factory; p.58t Ralph Perry; p.58b Jantzen; p.60 Gary Braasch; p.63 Terry Domico/Earth Images; p.64 Jill Cannefax/EKM/Nepenthe; p.65 Steve Terrill; p.67 Bechere Arnoff/EKM/Nepenthe; p. 68 Len Ramp/Oregon Dept. of Geology & Mineral Industries, Grants Pass 338; p.69 Ancil Nance; p.70 Harold Sund/Image Bank; p.72 Tom Ballard/EKM/Nepenthe; p.73t Terry Domico/Earth Images; p.73b Ralph Perry; p.74 Jill Cannefax/EKM/Nepenthe; p.75 John Maher/EKM/Nepenthe; p.76 Bob Eckert, Sr./EKM/Nepenthe; p.77t Jill Cannefax/EKM/Nepenthe; p.76b Wilken Photographs.

UNIT 2:
pp.82–83 Granger Coll.; p.84 Museum of the American Indian; p.90 Royal Ontario Museum; p.91 Museum of the American Indian; p.92 Richard Harrington/Hudson Bay Co.; p.93 Museum of the American Indian; p.95 J.H. Sharper painting/Thomas Gilcrease Institute; p.96 Charles M. Russell painting/Amon Carter Museum; p.98 National Maritime Museum, Greenwich, England; p.103 John Maher/EKM/Nepenthe; p.107 Montana Historical Society; p.109 National Portrait Gallery; p.111 Bill Line/Still Images; p.112 Alma Parson drawing from *Red Heroines of the North West* by Defenbach, Courtesy Caxton Pub. Co.; p.113 Hudson Bay Company; p.114 McLoughlin House; p.115 A. Hemian painting/Hudson Bay Company Trading Post; p.116 Brown Bros.; p.118 Butler Institute of Art; p.119 Buffalo Bill Historical Society; p.121 Culver; p.122 Brown Bros.; p.123 Bettman Archive; p.125 Oregon State Highway Division; p.126 Coll. of Cull White; p.128 Paul Kane painting/Whitman House; p.129 Denver Public Library; p.130 Brown Bros.; p.133 Steve Terrill; p.137 California State Library; p.138 Southern Oregon Historical Society; p.140 Flag Research Center; p.143 Brown Bros.; p.145 John Maher/EKM/Nepenthe; p.150 Bettman Archive; p.155 John Maher/EKM/Nepenthe; pp. 156–157 Gildemeister/EKM/Nepenthe.

UNIT 3:
p.162 Peter Peterson/Tofft; p.164 Bill Lind/Clatsop County Historical Society; p.166 Columbia River Maritime Museum; p.170 Culver; p.171 Columbia River Maritime Museum; p.172 Brown Bros.; p.176 Robert Potter, Courtesy of Binford Mort Publishing Co.; p.179 Bettman Archive; p.180 Columbia River Maritime Museum; p.182 John Mix Hanley painting/Amon Carter Museum; p.183 Bettman Archive; p.192 Harry Wentz painting/Portland Art Museum; p.201 San Francisco Lightworks/Northstar Tahoe Louisiana-Pacific Corp.; p.204 HRW Photo by Russel Dian/Courtesy of the New School for Social Research; p.207 Frank Woodfield/Columbia River Maritime Museum; pp. 212–213 Columbia River Maritime Museum; p.216 Culver; p.225 Jill Cannefax; p.226 Gary Braasch; p.228 Southern Oregon Historical Society; p.229 Ancil Nance; pp. 230–231 Kristin Finnegan.

UNIT 4:
p.236 Harold Sund/Image Bank; pp. 238–240 Steve Terrill; p.241 Robert V. Eckert, Jr./EKM/Nepenthe; p.242 Corky Rohrbaugh; p.244 John Maher; p.245 Office of Margaret Strachan; p.247l Kristin Finnegan; p.247r John Maher/EKM/Nepenthe; p.248 John Maher; p.250 Jack Fields/Photo Researchers; pp. 251–252 Corky Rohrbaugh; p.253 Cathy Cheney/EKM/Nepenthe; p.256 Hugh G. Barton/Hult Center; p.258 David Pogel; p.259l HRW Photo by Richard Haynes; p.259r Lisa Kroeber, Courtesy of Harper & Row; p.260 Ancil Nance; p.261l Heinz Kluetmeier/*Sports Illustrated;* p.261r Mitchell Reibel/*Sports Illustrated*; p.262 John Maher/EKM/Nepenthe; p.263 Port of Portland Oregon; p.264 Corky Rohrbaugh; p.265 Greenpeace; p.267 Steve Terrill; p.268 Ron Cooper/EKM/Nepenthe; p.269 Marty Katz; pp. 270–271 Robert Eckart Jr./EKM/Nepenthe.